World Politics and the Jewish Condition

Essays prepared
for a Task Force on
the World of the 1970s
of The American Jewish Committee

CONTRIBUTORS:
Chaim Adler
Haim Avni
Saul Friedlander
Zvi Gitelman
Louis Henkin
Sidney Liskofsky
Edward Luttwak
Henry L. Roberts
Eugene V. Rostow
Zachariah Shuster

World Politics and

Project Coordinator
Morris Fine

Editorial Assistant
Phyllis Sherman

Published in Collaboration with the
Institute of Human Relations Press

the Jewish Condition

Edited, with an Introduction,
by LOUIS HENKIN

QUADRANGLE BOOKS, INC.

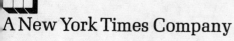

A New York Times Company

The publication of this volume was made possible
by a grant from The Jacob Blaustein Institute
for the Advancement of Human Rights.

Library of Congress Card Number: 70–190130

ISBN 0–8129–0265–3

Preface

The essays in this volume were written for the Task Force on the World of the 1970s, convened by the American Jewish Committee to guide it in preparing future foreign affairs programs. The look ahead at the world of the 1970s is not an exercise in prophecy but a quest for understanding as a basis for planning. The authors do not pretend to foretell particular events; they seek to identify forces and project trends.

The genesis and sponsorship of this volume should not lead the reader to expect a parochial book. Publication of this volume implies a judgment that these essays are of substantial interest to all who are concerned with world events and human welfare. Jew and non-Jew alike may read with interest and profit—if not necessarily with full agreement—expert evaluations of the major forces shaping our world.

The creation of the State of Israel has given many Jews around the world a special interest in peace in the Middle East and in the international politics on which that peace depends. All Americans will be concerned with what is happening and what is likely to happen in this area where vital United States interests are at stake. Essays on the prospects for Jewish well-being in Europe and Latin America are essentially essays about the condition of life and of liberty for all who live there. If Jews have been particularly involved in international efforts to promote and protect human rights, they have hardly been alone in that concern; the rights in question are the human rights of all, everywhere. The implications for the American Jewish community are pertinent also for other Americans concerned with international peace and individual welfare.

Since the papers in this volume were prepared by different authors on themes selected out of a complex whole, Louis Henkin, consultant to the Task Force, was asked to introduce them and tie them together. His introduction draws on the Task Force Report, which he prepared; * the final chapter, "Implications for the American Jewish Community," also derives from that report.

> *Bertram H. Gold*
> Executive Vice-President
> The American Jewish Committee

---

* *The World of the 1970s: A Jewish Perspective.* A Task Force Report, The American Jewish Committee, 1972.

Contents

CHAIM ADLER, Ph.D.—Senior Lecturer on the sociology of education, School of Education, Hebrew University of Jerusalem; formerly Research Associate at the Center for International Affairs, Harvard University; Co-Editor of *Integration and Development in Israel*.

HAIM AVNI, Ph.D.—Director of the Latin American Division of the Institute of Contemporary Jewry and Deputy Head of the Institute; Lecturer on Latin American Jewish History and Institutions, Hebrew University of Jerusalem; Department Editor on Latin American Jewry in the *Encyclopedia Judaica*; recent books include *Argentine Jewry* and *Argentina: "The Promised Land."*

SAUL FRIEDLANDER, Ph.D.—Chairman of the Department of International Relations of the Hebrew University of Jerusalem, and Professor of International Relations at the Graduate Institute of International Studies in Geneva; author of many books on diplomatic history and problems of the Middle East including *Prelude to Downfall: Hitler and the U.S., 1939–1941*.

ZVI Y. GITELMAN, Ph.D.—Assistant Professor of Political Science, University of Michigan; visiting Senior Lecturer at Tel Aviv University; author of *Jewish Nationality and Soviet Poli*[...] articles on East European and Soviet politics in sc[...]

LOUIS HENKIN, LHD—Ha[...] national Law and Diploma[...] tute, Columbia Univers[...] Rights; Member, Boa[...] *tional Law*; formerl[...] U.S. Member Perm[...] *tions Behave*, and [...]

SIDNEY LIS[...] tional Organiz[...]

ber, Board of Directors, International League for the Rights of Man and the American Immigration and Citizenship Conference; formerly Chairman of NGO Committee on Human Rights Research; has written extensively on U.S. immigration policy and international human rights.

EDWARD LUTTWAK—Associated with the World (Tevel) Institute of Jerusalem in the field of Strategic Studies; author of *Coup d'Etat: Dictionary of Modern War*, and co-author of a forthcoming study on Israel's defense policy and military organization.

HENRY L. ROBERTS, Ph.D.—Class of 1925 Professor of History, Dartmouth College; formerly Director of the Russian Institute and Professor of History at Columbia University; author of many books and articles on Eastern Europe and world politics; his most recent publication is *Eastern Europe: Politics, Revolution and Diplomacy*.

EUGENE V. ROSTOW, LLD—Sterling Professor of Law, Yale University; formerly Under-Secretary of State for Political Affairs, and previously, Dean of the Yale Law School; author of *Law, Power and the Pursuit of Peace, Is Law Dead?*, and *Peace in the Balance*.

CHARIAH SHUSTER—Consultant on Foreign Affairs to rican Jewish Committee; prior to his retirement, Director an Office; frequent contributor to English, Hebrew, lications.

May 1972

Introduction

Introduction

The 1970s have already begun, bringing both continuity and change in world politics, in the affairs of nations, in the lives of groups and individuals. The roots of both continuity and change in the years ahead lie, of course, in how things have been and are today.

Prospects in World Politics

Since the last world war the world has suffered instability, tension, and rapid change. Despite ventures in international cooperation—in the United Nations system, in the European community, and elsewhere—international politics have been largely dominated by a more or less "cold" war between nuclear superpowers bearing ideological banners, with the United States and the Soviet Union in confrontation and competition and Communist China casting its large and growing shadow.

Some former big powers have been reduced to middle-size, and the near-end of white colonialism in Asia and Africa has proliferated new nations which are behind the older ones in wealth and development. The quality of international relations has reflected the transformed character of weapons and war and the possibility of instant crisis and instant annihilation. It has been shaped by transnational ideologies seeping into perceptions of national interests, and by explosions and fissures in national societies drawing inspiration and inviting intervention from without. International relations have been affected, too, by the chasm between the few developed and the many less-developed nations, which has prompted some of the latter to favor radical institutions and policies which they believe are conducive to rapid modernization and industrial development.

Still, there has been no world war, not even a big war between big powers, and confidence is growing that there will be none—only limited, "proxy" wars and competing interventions in internal struggles. Ideological ties among nations have attenuated, and even "bloc leaders" have often subordinated ideology to pragmatism in the pursuit of national interests. The superpowers have learned the limitations of military prowess and of wealth, while smaller states have achieved some influence through other forms of power and authority. New nations have turned international institutions, where the force of numbers can dominate, to matters that concern them most: they have pressed for aid and trade to speed their development and have driven against the remnants of colonialism and white rule in southern Africa.

The Tangle of International Relations

In the early years of the new decade, relations among nations are in a confused and threatening tangle. The United States is still deeply involved in Korea, Taiwan, and Indochina; the situation in the Middle East remains tense; India and Pakistan have fought and may yet fight again. Elsewhere, nations are at peace, or a least not at war, but deep divisions between East and West and between North and South persist. Old sources of conflict and old threats to peace are only quiescent. The Berlin issue is eased but remains basically unsolved. Sino-Soviet tensions grow and recede. Sino-American relations have thawed to an undetermined extent, but China continues to claim Taiwan and the United States is committed to prevent its seizure by force. Southern Africa remains a source of international trouble. In Latin America, Asia, and Africa, nations ridden by internal conflict and disorder invite Soviet, Chinese, or other intervention, engendering international complications.

The United Nations is more than twenty-five years old; but some are asking whether it will survive, some whether it has survived. Transnational forces which have generally favored order, such as the churches, have lost some authority and influence; other forces, like the New Left, scale national boundaries with doctrines of disorder. International economic relations, which are also political, are equally unsettled. The world is very far from monetary order. The United States threatens protectionism, and others threaten retaliation. The want of a new order in North-South trade and the decline in foreign aid by the United States and other nations only confirm that hopes of giant leaps in development for most countries are illusory.

Relations between the United States and the Soviet Union are ambiguous. There has been agreement on nuclear non-proliferation and sea-bed disarmament, and the Strategic Arms Limitation Talks (SALT) continue. There have been an accommodation over Berlin, discussions of a European security conference, some increase in reciprocal trade, and other small steps and larger, more relaxed attitudes. (At times other nations have even come to fear that the two giants are "ganging up" on the rest of the world.) But the United States has been deeply troubled by the Soviet invasion of Czechoslovakia and its threatening implications for other countries in Eastern Europe and perhaps elsewhere. The Soviet Union supported India's invasion of East Pakistan, which the United States condemned.

In the Middle East, unresolved Arab-Israeli hostility and various inter-Arab conflicts made it possible for the Soviet Union to extend its military and political presence in the area and to gain dominant influence in a growing number of "socialist" Arab states. Some observers believe that this success has engendered grandiose Soviet hopes, if not plans, to help topple the remaining pro-Western governments in the Middle East, achieve domination of the area, and be master of the Mediterranean, the Persian Gulf, and access routes to the Indian Ocean. The USSR would then control much of the oil on which Western Europe and Japan live, drive the United States out of Europe and the Mediterranean, and suppress Chinese political infiltration. NATO would be outflanked and would disintegrate as Western Europe turned inward, responding to Soviet blandishments of détente and cooperation. The United States would withdraw into isolation, and the Soviet Union could turn its full attention to its long-standing and deep differences with China. Although other observers regard this scenario as a nightmare, few Westerners are sanguine about Soviet intentions in the Middle East or beyond; few are confident that a grave Soviet-American confrontation with worldwide consequences can be avoided.

Unresolved doubts about Soviet intentions and policies have also affected Western attitudes toward the North Atlantic Treaty Organization, for more than twenty years the cornerstone of American foreign policy and, many believe, of general peace. Many in Europe and some in the United States perceive the Soviet Union as a "satisfied" power, no longer interested in expansion, and indeed an influence for restraint in the conflicts of Europe, the Middle East, and Asia. Such attitudes, prevalent in public opinion, of course engender resistance to the financial and other burdens of the NATO alliance. In the United States important voices have also urged a sharp reduction in the American military presence in Europe. But in 1967–68, when the NATO allies reviewed the need for the alliance and its future tasks, they concluded unanimously that while NATO should devote a major political effort toward reaching an understanding with the Soviet Union about the security of Europe, such security had not been achieved; the Treaty, the NATO military deterrent, including conventional forces with a strong American component to give credibility to the American nuclear umbrella, remained indispensable. (Although de Gaulle withdrew from the NATO integrated command structure, French forces in Germany and the Mediterranean continue to cooperate with the NATO command, in continuous liaison.)

Many Europeans resent their continued dependence on the United States and the inevitable reflection on them of the interests and commitments of their American ally outside Europe. In one mood, Europe yearns for a more independent role in world politics, equal to that of the Soviet Union and the United States. But thus far it has been unwilling to take the steps necessary to achieve that position, and, if only because of the nuclear problem, there is doubt whether it would be possible to establish a political "Western Europe" even if the will existed. During this decade, then, Western Europe will remain in its present relationship to the United States, the prevailing mood continuing to accept the deepening integration of the Atlantic community, which is proceeding at an accelerating pace in economics, science, education, and social relations.

Regional and National Uncertainties

Uncertainty and flux in various regions of the world have international implications. Europe's mood is European; Great Britain has agreed to join the Common Market; de Gaulle is dead but Gaullism survives, though with some changes; West Germany pursues its *Ostpolitik*. Despite shock and sobriety following the Soviet invasion of Czechoslovakia, Western Europe looks for a détente; there is hope that the USSR will not repeat that "mistake," that West Germany's diplomacy will bring an improvement in intra-European relations, that SALT will bear fruit, and that the European security conference will produce some agreement to confirm a détente, perhaps even a mutual, balanced reduction in the size of conventional armies and in arms.

Eastern Europe is concerned with itself, as it assimilates the rape of Czechoslovakia, adapts to Rumania's aspiration to autonomy, watches the effects of turbulence and political succession in Poland, waits for readjustments in a post-Ulbricht East Germany, anticipates potentially explosive nationality conflicts in Yugoslavia associated with succession to Tito, and feels out new attitudes toward, and relations with, West Germany.

In Latin America populations continue to swell and go hungry. Nationalism is growing, but in many countries institutions and leadership are bankrupt; violence is not uncommon. The region has few leaders and no common political ideology, and its historic love-hate relationship with the United States has been exacerbated by China, the Soviet Union, Cuba, and "third world" elements.

In Asia, China is moving out of isolation and Japan is beginning to shed its postwar military innocence. Taiwan faces increasing diplomatic abandonment and the passing of Chiang Kai-shek. Vietnam's neighbors struggle with civil war or terrorism. Korea maintains its hostile division. Other Asian and African nations are beset by ever-rising population, increasing poverty, and the snail's pace of development. While many African countries pursue pragmatic economic policies, Africa as a whole broods over abiding white rule in the south.

Internal developments in particular countries, too, cast their shadows. Political changes in China, dissidence in the Soviet Union, riots and political succession in Poland, military rule in Greece, hunger in India, natural as well as man-made devastation in Pakistan and the loss of East Pakistan, troubles in Northern Ireland—all have international consequences. And if divisions in the United States are sometimes exaggerated, Vietnam, economic difficulties, and racial and urban tensions dampen enthusiasm and harden attitudes toward the outside world.

A Simmering Decade [1]

The years ahead promise no reprieve from turbulence and drama. The United States and the Soviet Union will bestride the world, as they do now, their military power making itself felt everywhere, if only by its very existence. China has joined the United Nations and the Security Council, and will move into other big-power councils. It will seek to lead and speak for the "third world." World politics during the decade will be dominated by that irregular triangle— China, the USSR, and the United States—modified as Japan, and perhaps Western Europe, assume responsibilities commensurate with their power. It can be hoped that the United States will use the triangle to bring increased respect for public order, since its co-operation will be indispensable to both China and the Soviet Union if the triangle is not to become an alliance of two against one. It remains to be seen whether the tensions of this complex relationship can be managed so as to produce stalemate and restraint in the international use of force.

The counters of power and influence will not change. There is reason for hope—but not for optimism—that agreement in SALT or tacit, parallel self-restraints may stabilize the balance of terror. China will continue to develop its strategic power but will not achieve superpower status.

Happily, it is reasonable to expect that there will be no world war and no major war between the big powers in the 1970s. Surely, deliberate nuclear war between the United States and the Soviet Union is most unlikely, for by no rational calculation can either hope to obtain any advantage that would warrant the cost in nuclear destruction. And increasingly sophisticated and improved safeguards make nuclear war by mistake or accident highly unlikely. The United States, the Soviet Union, and China also realize that war between any of them could very well become nuclear war. There is little likelihood, then, that one of them would attack either of the others or a country which either can be expected to defend. Neither would one of the three resort to overt intervention which another is likely to resist in full force. But war by miscalculation cannot be

---

[1] The prognostications ventured here are highly tentative, but qualifying terms such as "probably," "likely," "might be," are frequently omitted for readability.

ruled out, especially if there were a radical change in the nuclear balance in favor of the USSR.

Alliances and alignments will change, but the major powers will not easily be drawn into the smaller wars of others; each will be particularly cautious not to intervene where another major power is already engaged or is likely to become involved, although each may try to deter the other by threatening to fight. (The Soviet Union was able to support India in its attack on East Pakistan, confident that neither China nor the United States could effectively intervene.) In the Middle East the Soviets will go into an Arab war against Israel only if they can do so without risking American intervention. Sanctions against the remnants of colonialism and white rule in southern Africa will continue, but the major powers will not join any efforts to end them by force of arms.

The danger of major war during this decade lies where the interests and intentions of the major powers are ambiguous, and one power might act in the mistaken expectation that another will not, or that it could terminate or limit its intervention short of full-scale war. The most dangerous "unknown" will be the intention of the Soviet Union; the critical factor will be the ability of the United States and its allies to convince the Soviets of their determination and capability to continue to contain any Soviet expansionism. For if the USSR (and perhaps China) should come to believe that the Vietnam war and domestic preoccupations will force the United States to withdraw into defensive positions, it will dare much. The Soviet Union's commitments—and perhaps ambitions—in the Middle East might tempt it into substantial military participation which the United States would feel compelled to resist. The passing of Chiang Kai-shek or some other political change in Taiwan, might encourage China to reach for the island by force. And would the West sit by if the Soviet Union moved into Yugoslavia, or even Rumania, and the victim fought back?

No End to Instability

Even if big wars are avoided, there is little reason to expect a stable, placid world. Small wars will doubtless be fought and, though localized, will be terrible for those directly affected, and will inevitably concern others. Some "small" wars, moreover—like that between India and Pakistan—can be big enough. Clashes on India's frontiers with China also may occur again, posing difficult choices for both the Soviet Union and the United States.

Though actual fighting between major powers is not to be expected, big-power competition in ideological garb will continue by political means, including the political uses of military power. Genuine peace in the Middle East is unlikely, and U.S.-Soviet (or NATO-Soviet) confrontation in that area will surely continue for some time. Berlin cannot be defused permanently. Nor will racial tensions and the remnants of colonialism disappear; and though some African states will wish to accommodate to them, others will seek to intensify economic war and insurgent sniping against them. The gap between rich and poor will widen, and relations between nations grossly unequal in wealth and development will inevitably be roiled, as the "have-nots" seek more aid and better trade than the "haves" will grant.

Few parts of the world will escape instability, regional or national upheavals, uncertain political successions; but they will agitate particularly the Middle and Near East, Latin America, Southeast Asia, and parts of black Africa. Lacking established, accepted institutions and strong leadership, and under pressures of poverty aggravated by relentless population growth, disturbed nations will remain unstable and the instability of others will become apparent. Turmoil and abrupt change will spill over national borders and attract support and intervention, sometimes competing support and interventions from the great powers. Even without foreign intervention, ripples will be felt in other countries. Political upheaval and some external involvement will also continue to trouble the Persian Gulf states and perhaps North Africa. In some Arab countries the future of rulers and leaders is uncertain. Ethiopia may not have a calm succession to Haile Selassie. The Sudan will not hold together without difficulties. China may remain stable after Mao, but Yugoslavia might not after Tito, and there may be grave international repercussions, especially if the Soviet Union should decide to meddle.

In Latin America economic difficulties have tarnished Castro's revolution and might yet push him (or his successor) toward some accommodation with the United States. Yet he will remain an example for dissidents in other countries, and the "leftist" regime in Chile and the very different "revolutionary" regime in Peru will improve on the example, since they have escaped the stigma of subservience to the USSR. Wherever "revolutions" occur, they will be followed by long periods of economic and social instability. Elsewhere, conservative forces will be frightened into resorting to repression. Even if no change in regime or in its political hue occurs, new alignments and new moves toward greater independence of the United States will breed domestic instability, aggravate hemispheric tensions, and tempt the Soviet Union and China to become involved.

Directions of United States Policy

For the United States the 1970s will be a decade of dilemma and reappraisal. It will extricate itself from Vietnam, but that national tragedy will continue to influence attitudes and policies for some time. Inevitably, policy makers will tend to avoid direct action abroad, surely military action. They will be disposed to seek collective action, whether in the UN, the Organization of American States, or with particular allies, not because of a deeper commitment to collective action on principle, but because of a reluctance to act alone; and the pursuit of collective action will in fact often be tantamount to, or result in, inaction.

The major change in American policy will be in regard to China. The United States will accept Communist China in big-power councils and, if China does not insist on seizing Taiwan by force, will recognize the Peking government and establish diplomatic relations with it. As a result, relations with other Asian states, particularly with Japan, will be affected. For the rest, American foreign policy will undergo no major change of commitment, direction, or method. The United States will seek stability and friendly relations, contribute modestly to economic development, and cooperate in nonradical arrangements to bring more order into trade and finance, with some special benefits to the developing countries. It will also support traditional activities of the UN and other international organizations, as well as more venturesome methods to protect the environment and exploit the riches of the seas.

Washington will cautiously explore the possibilities of coexistence with the USSR and China, will pursue SALT, and will join its allies in the European security conference in the quest for détente in Europe, including the limitation of arms and military forces there. The United States will distinguish between international Communism and national "socialisms," and improve relations with willing socialist states.

But since neither Mao and post-Mao China nor the collective leadership of the Soviet Union will be ideologically or politically restrained, the United States will continue its policy of "containment," under a different name. American leaders will continue to act on the assumption that the balance of power, the integrity of our post-World War II national policy, the fate of our allies, and the complexion of world society depend on our power and determination to meet Soviet or Chinese pressure and on our skill to match their blandishments by tried means, including aid and arms to bolster friendly regimes. The United States will have to stand firm in the Middle East, perhaps even without the active support of principal allies. It will have to maintain the resolution and strength of NATO and the balance of power in Europe at a time when Soviet "softness" in Europe and aggressiveness in other areas—where the United States and its allies do not see things identically—will strain NATO, test our commitment, and challenge our diplomacy. The United States will also seek to continue its present close collaborative relationship with Japan.

Latin America's geographic propinquity and economic dependence, and our historic commitments there, will continue to give the United States a major voice in the affairs of this continent. But explosive internal forces, variously supported by Cuba, the Soviet Union, and China, promise changes not to our liking that will test the contemporary significance of the Monroe Doctrine and our commitment to nonintervention. Despite the "lesson" of Vietnam, despite unhappy memories of the Bay of Pigs debacle and adverse reactions to American intervention in the Dominican Republic, the United States will go to lengths to resist the establishment of new Communist regimes. Washington will not intervene to frustrate regularly elected "leftist" regimes, like the Allende government in Chile, but the inevitable polarizations, "radicalizations," and near civil wars will be a temptation to support, as covertly as possible, more acceptable aspirants to power.

In the Far East—despite the lessons of Vietnam—the United States will feel responsible for maintaining stability. We will salvage what we can in Indochina; bolster Thailand and other allies; and encourage Indonesia and the Philippines, and especially Japan, to assume substantial responsibility, both political and military, for balance and stability.

Even in black Africa, which has generally resisted penetration by superpowers, the United States will not be irrelevant. We will be a supplier of aid and arms (and our allies will surely continue such aid) and will compete with the Soviet Union and China in various forms of influence. We will continue to support limited economic sanctions aimed at the policies of our trading partner the Republic of South Africa and of Great Britain's "rebel" offspring, Rhodesia.

Lesser Powers and Other Forces

The less-than-superpowers will not be unimportant in the 1970s, and some will modify their relations with major powers. Great Britain and France, moving slowly toward some larger unity in Western Europe, may later take small steps even toward political and nuclear integration. They will maintain their presence on other continents with which they have historic ties, supported by diplomacy and economic and cultural cooperation. West Germany, still in the shadow of the past and constrained by Soviet opposition, will not build nuclear weapons. It will regularize its relations and expand trade in all directions, and move with greater confidence into middle-power political activity. In Asia Japan has achieved economic growth without precedent in world history, and by 1980 its GNP will approximate that of the Soviet Union. It will assume some responsibility for security and balance in Asia, and though the Japanese will not soon move to join the "nuclear club," they will assert some independence of the United States and improve relations with China, establishing a new and developing triangle. (They will also improve their relations with the Soviet Union.) India, too, will move closer to the Soviet Union and act with new confidence after its victory in East Pakistan.

Other states and groups of states will continue to influence events beyond their boundaries, principally by banding together in the United Nations and in regional or ideological groups. Some or all of the divided countries will achieve recognition and gain independent admittance to the United Nations. Nuclear proliferation will be resisted, but many nations will continue to spend beyond their means on armaments—from fear for their security, in competition with neighbors, for domestic reasons, or out of pride or the quest for prestige.

The UN will have no dramatic part in world affairs but will remain politically available and useful, and will seek increasing justification in new, important forms of economic and social cooperation. Transnational forces will remain important: the Catholic Church and other, less integrated religious groups will have impact, but in smaller measure, mobilizing as well as responding to domestic religious forces. International Communism will continue to be a small instrument of Soviet or Chinese power, but a big bone of Sino-Soviet contention. The New Left, though declining, will remain influential beyond its numbers, principally by infecting the young and the disaffected and confusing their attachment to established ways, institutions, and policies.

In Chapter 1, Professor Henry Roberts dwells on three major themes in the world politics of the 1970s. Will the prospect of ever more advanced strategic arms and the proliferation of nuclear weapons to additional nations inspire some agreement to bring a measure of security against the possibility of instant annihilation? He sees the once bipolar world—if it ever was—further transformed into more complex political configurations. And world politics will reflect new domestic forces in many countries that are changing national attitudes and priorities as regards foreign affairs.

The Middle East

All was not calm in the Middle East before the State of Israel was created, and much of its present turbulence is unrelated to the Arab-Israeli conflict; but the drama of that conflict has overshadowed all other disorders. Long the scene of intermittent war and unremitting tension, the Middle East remains a principal locus of international trouble. War could break out again at any time, but now it might include some active participation by the Soviet Union, with possible United States involvement. The years ahead are critical, and no one can predict with confidence what will happen. Will there be peace, or at least agreed "non-war"? And if so, on what basis, and will it last? If there is no peace agreement, will the present stalemate continue? For how long, and what will break it? If there is another war, how and to what extent will the Soviet Union and the United States participate, and how will it end?

These are major concerns not only for the State of Israel and its Arab neighbors, but also for the United States and the Soviet Union, and therefore for the world. Much will depend on the policies and interactions of the principals and their supporters; not even they can predict what those policies and reactions will be.

Interests of Principal Parties

Fundamentally, uncertainty as to what will happen in the Middle East is due to an extraordinary lack of agreement on the essential interests and true aims of the protagonists and their champions or supporters. Israel and Egypt, the Soviet Union and the United States, have all proclaimed their desire for peace, but there are reasons to doubt the protestations of the Soviet Union and some of the Arab leaders. There is also serious doubt whether the minimum peace requirements of the Israelis and of the Arabs can be reconciled or accommodated.

Since November 1967 the political situation has had a fixed pattern. The Security Council has called on the parties, with the help of Ambassador Gunnar Jarring, to reach an agreement, a "package deal," that would establish conditions of peace in the area, based on the withdrawal of Israeli forces to secure and recognized boundaries established by agreement of the parties. Egypt, backed by the Soviet Union, has refused to participate in any kind of negotiations to reach such agreement. Until 1971, indeed, it was unwilling to say publicly that it was prepared to reach a peace settlement with Israel. Instead, it has insisted on advance assurance that the whole of the Sinai Peninsula would be returned to Egyptian sovereignty and control, even before security arrangements and guarantees of maritime rights were seriously discussed. In 1970 Ambassador Jarring obtained the consent of the parties that they would participate in any procedure he would designate for reaching an agreement under the Security Council resolution, but so far he has not sought to convene a conference of the parties in his presence—the procedure used effectively at Rhodes in 1949.

Israel certainly wants peace with security, but it is not clear whether what it considers to be the essential geographic, political, and military conditions acceptable to both the Arabs and the Soviet Union. Many Israelis, convinced that the Arabs and the Soviet Union do not intend genuine peace but seek Israel's eventual destruction, are opposed to making any irreversible concessions for what they feel would be a scrap of international paper to be discarded at will. Some Israelis consider the borders achieved by the 1967 war essential to Israel's security and not to be sacrificed. Very few are prepared to give up East Jerusalem; most insist on retaining other territory important to security; some will resist sacrificing areas of major historic and religious significance to Jews, such as Hebron.

The Arab states went to war in 1948 to destroy Israel. The commitment to eliminate Israel was infused into the Arab mind and spirit. They were dedicated to this sole aim they held in common, one that often overrode deep differences. This common aim intensified authentic Arab nationalism and served the cause of Pan-Arabism, as well as Nasser's dream of leading the Arab world. It helped rally popular sympathy for the Palestinian "liberation" movements.

The Security Council resolution of November 22, 1967, affirmed that the UN Charter required "a just and lasting peace" on the basis of two principles: Arab acceptance of Israel, and withdrawal of "Israel armed forces from territories occupied" in the 1967 war. Repeated efforts to have the resolution amended to read "from *the* territories occupied," that is, all the territories, were defeated. By accepting that resolution, Egypt and Jordan in effect agreed to abandon their commitment to the destruction of Israel and to accept its existence provided the Israelis met the terms of the resolution. (Other Arab states and the Palestinian guerrilla leaders rejected the resolution.) Since then, Egypt has insisted, despite the clear intent of the resolution, that Israel must withdraw from *all* the territories occupied in 1967.

Some observers believe that Egypt and Jordan do not really seek peace on the basis of the Security Council resolution; that, rather, they hope Israel will take actions and political positions that will cast the onus for the failure of peace on itself, that the United States will then reduce, if not abandon, its support of Israel and the Soviet Union will actively support an Arab war to destroy Israel. There is some doubt, too, whether the Arab states would make peace with Israel, or keep it for long, even if Israel met all present Arab conditions.

At bottom, then, peace may depend on whether Egypt in particular wants it or prefers to maintain hostility in the hope of ultimately defeating Israel in war and achieving political preeminence in the Middle East and beyond.

Big Power Stakes

Ideally, the United States would like to reduce the presence and influence of the Soviet Union in the Middle East, safeguard American and Western interests there, maintain the integrity and security of Israel, and keep the Arabs happy and friendly to the United States. But no terms can fully achieve all those aims, and it is not clear which the United States would sacrifice or compromise. Effectively, the United States would like to see peace between Israel and its neighbors achieved on the basis of the November 1967 resolution, which it believes would be fair and dignified for both Israel and the Arab states.

The choices for the United States are neither easy nor without cost and danger. We must contain the Soviet Union, but do not want war with it. We are committed to the survival and security of Israel, but there are differing views as to what is essential to that security. And we are reluctant to take on further commitments to guarantee Israel's security. We are aware that the Soviet Union is the Arabs' champion, but we do not wish to appear to be Israel's champion, preferring the role of intermediary. (Our principal NATO allies, Great Britain and France, tend to favor the Arabs.)

The United States is on record against an imposed peace, in part because of the history of the "peace" imposed in 1957. Will we insist on terms acceptable to Israel, stand firm against Soviet pressures on Israel, and effectively deter Soviet military participation? Or will we press Israel to accept an "unacceptable" peace in the hope that this might eliminate the danger of confrontation with the Soviet Union, bolster the pro-Western Arab governments, regain wider Arab sympathy for the West, and shore up American and allied interests in Arab lands? And what will we do if Israel refuses?

The crucial question is what the Soviet Union is really up to. Officially, it still is for the survival of the State of Israel, whose creation it supported; but it is now wholly committed to the Egyptian cause, has hardened that commitment in a fifteen-year treaty, and has supported terms for "peace" in the Middle East which would make Israel's survival highly questionable. No doubt the Soviet Union is eager to eradicate the stain of the Arab defeat in 1967, which tarnished its credibility in "socialist" countries and had unhappy repercussions even within the Soviet bloc. Helping the Arabs regain territory would also encourage other governments around the world to seek Soviet friendship. The USSR would like to reopen the Suez Canal for easy access to the Persian Gulf and the Indian Ocean. It also would like to eliminate, or reduce, Western power and influence in the Middle East, without going to war with the United States.

According to some observers, the Soviet Union would like to see the destruction of Israel for several reasons: traditional Russian anti-Semitism; historic Communist hostility to Zionism; the desire to eliminate a Western bastion in the Middle East which is also a source of inspiration and agitation for Soviet Jews. Others believe that neither the destruction of Israel nor a true Arab-Israeli peace would serve the Soviet interest, for either might reduce Arab dependence on the USSR, remove an obstacle to Arab friendship with the West, and unleash forces that eventually could militate against Soviet presence and influence. A military victory that restored lands lost in 1967, but stopped short of destroying Israel, might bring the USSR most of what it wants; but that might well require its major participation in war and draw in the United States. An arrangement that gives to the Arabs practically all, but not all, of their territories and brought some peace, but not too much, might be best for the Soviet Union, though it would leave the Arabs less than happy. Of greatest advantage to the USSR, no doubt, would be any major development that appeared to the "third world" as a retreat by the United States under Soviet threat.

Israel's Negotiating Posture

In peace negotiations Israel's position is no less difficult than that of the Arab states in important respects. Israel has the geographic advantage and military superiority, but it needs peace. It bears the political, economic, and social costs of confrontation, guerrilla activity, a hostile environment, a worsening world political climate, and the constant threat of another war, which the Soviet Union might not allow the Arabs to lose. In peace negotiations, as in war, Israel's stakes are survival and security; the Arabs' stakes are chiefly honor and prestige (which, however, are not necessarily more amenable to rational consideration and compromise). For Israel, the price of peace is the surrender of territory which is important to its security and which, once returned, is irretrievably lost. The concessions required of the Arabs are intangible, political, and reversible, for they can make peace tomorrow and revoke it the day after.

Politically, too, there are asymmetries in the two sides. The Soviet Union apparently believes its interest lies in supporting the Arab states completely. Even though the fifteen-year treaty may not make Egypt fully a satellite of the Soviet Union, the two countries seem to have no substantial differences regarding conditions for peace. On the other hand, the United States, though Israel's friend, is not necessarily Israel's champion and committed ally; its interests are not always identical with Israel's; neither are its views on both policy and tactics. Perhaps most important, the United States does not always see Israel's needs as Israel sees them.

The United States is eager to restore Western influence and to protect Western interests in Arab lands. It is reluctant to become militarily involved and has been far more willing than Israel to accommodate Arab demands to achieve a settlement. Whereas Israel has insisted on a formal peace agreement—for its legal and political significance and as evidence that the Arabs are abandoning their commitment to the elimination of Israel—not everyone in Washington shares that concern. Israel sees its security primarily in its military strength and in secure, defensible frontiers; there is a tendency in the United States to believe that Israel can find security and peace only by buying them from the Arabs, even at the price of restoring virtually all the territory won in 1967.

These basic differences make Israel's relations with the United States delicate and sometimes strained. Israel will be pressed to make distasteful and risky concessions and compromises. Refusal to concede will also be risky, for the relationship with the United States, and especially continued American military aid, is very important for Israel.

Israel will be under pressure to accept less than favorable conditions for its security. The United States may press the Israelis not to insist on retaining some territory they value if that would cause negotiations to break down. Despite past disappointments, Israel will be urged to rely on others—perhaps on American assurances, or on other deterrents. But Israel should be able to convince the United States that it is entitled to assure its security against threatened aggression, which initiated the 1967 war.

Possibilities for Agreement

In sum, Israel and the United States are seeking peace in conformity with the 1967 Security Council resolution, which reflects their deep and parallel national interests. Whether such a peace can be achieved depends on whether the Arabs (principally Egypt) and the Soviet Union desire it. Of course, the wishes and policies of all are subject to modification. Even if the Soviets do not want peace, they may prefer it to war, or to protracted dangerous confrontation with the United States. If they seek peace, they could exert strong pressure on the Arabs to pursue it. At least marginal influence will be exerted by France and Great Britain, by other members of NATO, and by other nations, both directly as well as through the UN. (Israel, too, works within the UN and in its context, even though it feels the UN has denied it due process and the equal protection of the law of the charter.)

But there are limits to how far outside pressure can move either side, and domestic forces restrict how far the sides can move in response to such pressure. Though they have lost power and prestige, guerrilla extremists will surely attempt to obstruct peace, if peace becomes likely. A rapprochement between China and the United States, however, based on the overriding national interests of both countries, should obtain some modification of Chinese policies in this as in other areas of conflict.

Given the will to peace, most issues, and perhaps all, might be negotiable. Israel has at least temporarily dropped its insistence on direct negotiations; it seems willing to return a large portion of the occupied areas. While the Arab states continue to insist on the unconditional return of all the territories, there might be some possibility of compromise as to one or more of the territories basically in issue, for example, agreement on a combination of devices like demilitarization, United Nations presence, and a contractual Israeli presence that would not deny Arab sovereignty. The issue of the Arab refugees involves difficult questions of principle, prestige, and politics, besides its practical consequences, but in the context of an agreed peace the international community could contribute importantly to its permanent resolution.

If there should be peace, it will be fragile. Extremist groups, perhaps with Chinese support, will make every effort to break it. Arab-Israeli relations will remain tense, and the Soviet Union will not become Israel's good friend overnight. The United States will have a special interest in, and responsibility for, maintaining a peace achieved principally through its efforts.

If There Is No Peace

Whether a peace is agreed upon will depend chiefly on what the parties believe will happen if there is none. The status quo, difficult as it is for Israel, the United States, and perhaps even for the Soviet Union, is even more difficult for Israel's Arab neighbors.

In the absence of agreement, the Arabs will prepare for war and will urge the Soviet Union to help them. They will press the United States to stop aid to Israel; they will make threats against American and other Western interests and may lash out at them in frustration or anger. For Israel, it will be essential that the flow of arms and money from the United States continue; it will be critical that substantial Soviet participation in Arab military activities be deterred by fear of the United States. Resistance to the Soviet Union and support for Israel have been the firm policy of both the Johnson and Nixon administrations and overwhelmingly supported by Congress. But there will be pressures and temptations for the United States to veer from its firm support of Israel, and Israel's standing with American public opinion will be of considerable importance to the President in withstanding them. The American public will continue to support Israel, especially if the onus for the continued absence of peace cannot plausibly be placed upon Israel.

No one—in all likelihood not even the Soviet leaders—would venture to predict how far the Soviet Union would go to help the Arabs defeat Israel. Much, perhaps all, would depend on what Soviet leaders believed the United States could and would do. The United States is committed to prevent Soviet predominance in the Mediterranean and the Middle East, a predominance that could be achieved by a decisive Egyptian military or political victory over Israel. The United States does not want war with the Soviet Union, but is committed to help Israel defend itself and does not think Israel should return occupied territory without a peace agreement giving it security, at least as the United States sees Israel's security.

Commitment to Israel reflects the conviction of the United States that Soviet expansionism in the Middle East is a threat to its own security and that of its allies, to its other interests, and to its fundamental post-World War II policy. In this, as in other Soviet-American crises since 1945, the success of American policy will depend on the skill with which the United States deploys its political and military capabilities so as to deter Soviet action. If the United States impresses upon the USSR that it will not tolerate the destruction of Israel and Soviet expansion, war against Israel will be less attractive to the Soviet Union and the Arab states and the prospects for an agreed peace will be brighter. Even if peace is long in coming, there will be no war, and there will be opportunity for peace some later day.

If Egypt can be persuaded that it cannot afford to resort to war, a special agreement, e.g., to reopen the Suez Canal, might be in the interest of all, not least to the Soviet Union. It might make nonpeace less difficult and more durable, and might even lead to further agreement or agreements. An accommodation between Jordan and Israel—which is not out of the question—also may point the way for others.

Professor Eugene Rostow sees American foreign policy in the years ahead as essentially, and inevitably, what it has been since World War II—to maintain balance in world power. That means balance not only in Europe but also in the "third world," and certainly in the Middle East, which flanks NATO nations. The issues of the Middle East have been and are big-power issues. The national interests of the United States coincide with Israel's need for peace with security and demand unambiguous deployment of military and political forces to deter Soviet expansion.

Dr. Saul Friedlander and Dr. Edward Luttwak provide an Israeli perspective on the Arab-Israeli conflict today and its prospects.[2] They describe Israeli perceptions of Arab attitudes, policies, and politics, and of the interests and policies of the United States and the Soviet Union. They project the military balance between Israel and the Arab states, with and without varying degrees of military intervention by the superpowers, with and without nuclear weapons;

---

[2] Their paper was written in 1970 but it is not essentially dated.

the choices before Israel in relation to the occupied territories and its Arab neighbors; Israel's military and diplomatic options; and the possible outcome in the next years.

Inside Israel

A world in turbulence and uncertainty is turbulent and uncertain for all, and Israel is in the eye of the storm. The state of non-war, non-peace, the continuing Soviet-Arab threat, the pressing diplomatic maneuvers, the burdens of occupation, and occasional sabotage—these dominate Israeli life. But life goes on and bears other concerns. Whether or not the 1970s bring peace for Israel, it will continue to have grave economic and social problems. Indeed, some will become more acute as peace relaxes the ties that, in crisis, have united the nation and sublimated or postponed divisive issues.

Israel's major social problem continues to be the sharp difference in development between the nation's European and Oriental Jews. The Oriental Jew's impressive performance in the 1967 war gave him new and warm acceptance, and common army experience elevates and equalizes the young of all origins. Nevertheless, important differences remain—in income, in level of education, in economic and political achievement, and, consequently, in social status.

Special treatment of recent immigrants from the Soviet Union and the United States has led to resentment. Taking pages from the different story of the underprivileged in other countries, some elements have taken to the streets. Intellectual dissidents have taken up their cry, raising their voices against the passing of Israel's pioneering socialism and the rise of materialistic pragmatism.

Obstacles to further social and economic development are formidable, and the inevitable cost of defense limits the resources available for it. There is tension between demands for war on poverty and insistence on Western living standards; there is tension between the demand for mass education for the better integration of the Oriental Jews and the need for elitist, quality education in a modern developed state. Israel will have to struggle to resolve these differences and to increase social mobility and participation. And they must be resolved, not only because of Israel's basic egalitarian commitments, but because its continued political and social stability depend on national unity and on the successful development and use of all its human resources, of which Oriental Jews constitute a large and growing part.

The place of religion in Israel continues to be a major social problem which resists solution, although its impact may well be softened by changes in the electoral system modifying the political influence of the religious parties. There can be only continuing accommodation, in recognition of the special role of religion in the past and present life of Israel. On this issue, too, the willingness to compromise will fluctuate with the ebb and flow of tension between Israel and its neighbors; in any event, one must expect legal and institutional changes that will offend, if not estrange, some religious elements in Israel and abroad.

The future of Israel's Arab population—another difficult problem—also depends heavily on the issue of war or peace in the Middle East. The Arab citizens of Israel live better than Arabs in other lands and benefit from improvements affecting the country as a whole. A genuine peace settlement would make it easier to remove remaining security restrictions on them, but if non-war continues they will remain open to suspicion of sympathy with Israel's enemies.

Professor Chaim Adler provides a sociologist's perspective on a "revolutionary" society in tension between its pioneering origins and the aspirations of a relatively affluent society; between cosmopolitanism, reflecting its enlightened beginnings and its network of transnational relations, and a growing isolationism and parochialism; between unusual physical growth and lagging innovation; between military preoccupations and the needs of a liberal society. He focuses in particular on the problems of social integration for a society of variegated origins; on consequent problems of education and youth and of the changing family; on the inevitable transformations of the place of religion in Israeli society; on the troubling status of minorities, particularly the Arab minority; on the consequences of continuing military preoccupation for a civilian society; on continuity and realignment in the political system.

Israel has other problems as well. Despite the remarkable imagination and success of Israel's economic planning, it will remain difficult to satisfy all the demands pressed upon the economy. From the beginning, Israel's economy has been strained by efforts to give the people a European standard of living and has depended heavily on aid from abroad, particularly from American Jews. Increasingly, demands of defense and security have added to the burden: since the 1967 war, defense spending has more than doubled, from 12 to 25 percent of the gross national product. Some of it, however, has gone to build up Israel's military industry to make the nation less dependent on arms from abroad; this will spill over to develop civilian industry and eventually reduce both military and civilian imports. For this and other reasons, experts are optimistic about the future of Israel's economy.

Much will depend, however, on what the defense needs will be, as well as on any further drain on the economy by a substantial new *aliyah* (immigration) from Eastern Europe. Much will depend, too, on maintaining and improving trade relations with the European Economic Community and others; on American economic and military assistance and favorable terms of trade with the United States; and, as always, on the continued support of the American Jewish community. Israel will, of course, continue to strive to reduce its dependence on such generosity by developing its trade and investment.

Israel has to look also to its foreign relations. Some waning in world sympathy for Israel's cause is due to Communist, New Left, and more sophisticated Arab and Palestinian propaganda, some to the change in Israel's circumstances. Israel is no longer viewed as the underdog; in some quarters it is described as arrogant, militaristic, expansionist and neo-Prussian. There is also some disagreement, often reflecting error or misunderstanding, with Israel's position on peace in the Middle East and its occupation policies. Loss of sympathy has occurred not only in "leftist" countries: in the United Nations, for example, "nonaligned nations" have continued to support even extremist Arab condemnation of Israel, although this does not necessarily reflect their bilateral relations with Israel. Influenced by the New Left, some church and youth organizations and other groups and individuals have become confused and defensive, and avoid pro-Israel identification.

A Middle East settlement would no doubt radically improve Israel's foreign and public relations. Without it, Israel will almost inevitably continue to get a "bad press" in some quarters as an occupying power, one closely identified with the United States.

Of special concern to Israel must be its relations with the American Jewish community. The accommodations and arrangements developed over the past twenty years require constant and sensitive care. Israel will have to give special attention to American Jewish youth, many of whom, disturbed though not necessarily persuaded by New Left propaganda, are confused and defensive about Israel. Some of them, caught in the general malaise over Vietnam, have found it difficult to recognize the difference between American involvement in Vietnam and in the defense of Israel. Others, responding to internal urban and race problems, hesitate to identify as Jews because of Jewish-black tensions.

Jewish Welfare in Other Lands

International instability in the 1970s will both reflect and engender internal instability in many countries having substantial Jewish populations. There is some reason for concern also for the welfare of Jews living in more stable countries, especially for their communal life.

Inevitably, the welfare of Jews and Jewish communities will be affected by developments in the Middle East. A genuine settlement between Israel and the Arab states would improve the fearful plight of the Jewish remnants in Arab lands and relax tensions under which they live in other Moslem countries. Peace, war, or continued tension in the Middle East may make the difference between less or more intense anti-Semitism, between ease and uneasiness for West European Jews; between relaxation and acute tension for East European Jews; between less and more instability for Jews in Latin America. But what happens in the Middle East is hardly the only or the principal determinant of Jewish welfare in other regions; anticipated developments in Europe and Latin America will be of import for the substantial Jewish populations there.

Three chapters in this volume deal, respectively, with the prospects for Jewish welfare in Western Europe, Eastern Europe, and Latin America. Like Jews in many times and many places, they have in common a concern for their relations with their neighbors and varying fears of anti-Semitism; the struggle to maintain Jewish identification and vital communal institutions; and the quest for contemporary meaning to Jewishness for themselves and for transmission to their youth. But the differences in status and prospect for Jews in the three areas are greater than the similarities, and even their common problems and concerns are essentially different.

Western Europe

Western Europe has been hospitable to human rights; its citizens, including more than a million Jews, have enjoyed individual liberty, personal security, political and social integration, and economic well-being. Although developments in the years ahead may complicate their lives, nothing warrants fear that their personal condition will seriously deteriorate.

Jewish welfare in Western Europe depends, of course, on the general welfare. Although the national societies are in flux, there is no reason to fear retreat from liberal democratic government and substantial personal freedom, even in countries with large Communist parties, like Italy or France, or in those where rightist sentiment has been widespread, as in Germany, Austria, and Italy.

In Great Britain and France the dominant political parties lean toward the Arab side as consistent with their national interest, and in both countries active support of Israel by the Jews could be misrepresented as "disloyalty." In West Germany radical right-wing parties will not be alone in questioning whether continued support for Israel is in the German interest and becoming hospitable to "anti-Zionism."

Unless there is a Middle East settlement, the 1970s will see ever stronger "anti-Zionist," "anti-imperialist," and "anti-capitalist" campaigns, nourished by anti-Americanism, which will trouble Jews generally. (The recent "rumor of Orléans" was an incredible recurrence of a medieval "blood libel" against Jews.)

Although the New Left has lost momentum, some of its views and much of its propaganda will be particularly troubling to many Jews. Many in the New Left see Israel as an ally and outpost of "U.S. imperialism." Though anti-Semitism is not a policy, and perhaps not an aim, of the New Left, it sometimes results from New Left teachings, especially among those who cannot or will not distinguish between anti-Zionism and anti-Semitism, between the State of Israel and Jewry, between Israelis and Jews; or, between disagreement with views and sentiments, on the one hand and hostility toward those who hold them, on the other. Israel apart, many characteristics of Western Jews are objects of New Left antagonism: most belong to the middle class, having risen from underdog to "establishment" status, from beneficiaries of radical sympathy to targets of radical hostility.

The New Left responds to a contemporary mood of romantic antirationalism, of violent protest against the prosaic character of life in modern welfare states. It will continue to have special appeal to young people who are impatient with, and alienated from, established institutions and policies.

There is also reason, Zachariah Shuster tells us, to be concerned over the future of Jewish communal life in Western Europe. Jewish communities have been supporting Jewish identity and culture and continue to represent their members in official and other relations. They have conducted dialogue and cooperated with Christian leaders in many different causes, including the struggle against anti-Semitism, and have helped shape the largely pro-Israel attitudes of the peoples among whom they live and of those Christian denominations whose headquarters are in Europe. West European Jewry has been a bridge between the large communities in the United States and Canada and the Jews in Eastern Europe, and it has ties as well with the Jewish communities in North Africa and Latin America.

Increasingly, however, combating anti-Semitism will be a task beyond the powers and means of these communities, and they will have neither the resources nor the skills to carry on their communal tasks, meet the needs of the East European communities, and maintain contact with North African and Latin American Jewry. They will need counsel and cooperation in their individual and collective quest for the meaning of Jewish identity in the contemporary world.

Eastern Europe

Whatever their dissimilarities in geography, history, political culture, style of leadership, and level of development, all East European states will remain in a more or less uneasy condition during this decade, their politics unstable, their political institutions maturing slowly. The fate of the East European Jews will depend primarily and directly on governmental policy in particular countries; witness, for example, the gap between Poland's official anti-Semitism and Hungary's relatively liberal attitude. The condition of the Jews in each country will depend also on the size and "quality" of their total population, relations with the non-Jewish people, the history of local anti-Semitism, and in some countries, as in Poland, on the importance of the Catholic Church and the kind of influence it wields. But Soviet policies and politics, and developments in East-West relations and in the Middle East in particular, will affect Jews in all Eastern European countries.

The situation of the East European Jews has been, and will remain, precarious. They will, of course, suffer any unhappy fate that might befall the general population. In addition, however, "anti-Zionism" will remain official policy and an active propaganda theme almost everywhere, and varying degrees of official and semiofficial anti-Semitic repression will continue. East European Jewry is only a shadow of what it once was, and communal life in the Soviet Union is virtually nonexistent. In general, outside the Soviet Union, the few Jews who survived in their countries or returned after World War II concealed their Jewishness; but reemerging anti-Semitism has compelled or impelled them to identify as Jews and, if possible, to emigrate. Many have also identified with Israel, and official anti-Israel policy and anti-Semitism in the guise of anti-Zionism have only strengthened their loyalties.

The revival of Jewish feeling among Soviet Jews is one of the remarkable phenomena of our times. Since religious, cultural, and communal life, however, is discouraged and almost nonexistent, the "identity crisis" among Soviet Jews is growing.

As for decades past, the Soviet government has been preoccupied, even obsessed, with the "Jewish question"; in recent years it has also become an element in Soviet relations with the Arabs and its non-relations with Israel. The Jews are considered by the authorities as somewhat of an "internal security" problem and a source of domestic tension, especially as the Soviet government pursues a virulent anti-Israel policy. Scrutiny and clamor abroad have made the condition of the Jews a sensitive political issue. The treatment of Jews has implications for other non-Russian nationalities in the USSR and for the internal struggle between liberalism and conservatism.

Professor Zvi Gitelman delineates the less than happy prospects for Jews in the different countries of Eastern Europe, the options open to them, and the tasks for those who would help them.

Latin America

In Latin America, too, the position of the Jews differs from country to country, according to the history and geography, the size and
quality of the Jewish population and Jewish institutions, the attitudes of the general population, and the influence of the Catholic
Church and other transnational forces. Here, too, the welfare of the
Jews will depend on political, economic, and social developments in
their countries, which, in turn, will be affected by regional and
world forces and events.

Most of Latin America is underdeveloped. The prevailing mood,
until recently, was "rightist" and conservative. Liberal democracy
exists in only a few countries; most countries are ruled by military
dictatorships, but these too differ in constitutional legitimacy, in efficiency, in degree and form of repression or toleration. Economically and socially, most of the countries have been backward and
oligarchical. There has been some land reform, but large holdings of
land in private hands persist in many countries. Industrialization
has been slow, and what industry has developed is concentrated in
a few hands. The Catholic Church has been ubiquitous, powerful,
and with exceptions generally reactionary. The dominant fact of
Latin America's international life has been overwhelming dependence on the United States. Latin American governments have
generally supported the United States in world politics; they have
been pro-Israel.

The Jews have fared well. Most of them belong to the prosperous
middle class. Despite widespread ignorance, misconception, church-
inspired prejudice, class and racial distinctions (especially in Mexico), and cultural anti-Semitism, there has been little official, overt
anti-Semitism. Jews have flourished, maintained Jewish identity, and
established communities and communal institutions. They strongly
support the State of Israel and in the major countries the Israeli
ambassador frequently serves the Jews as a kind of "papal nuncio."
Jewish efforts to establish dialogue and cooperation with Christian
groups and to persuade the local Church to abandon anti-Semitic
teachings in keeping with Vatican directives have begun to meet
with some small success.

Lately, Latin America has undergone political change. The Cuban revolution is established. Peru's revolution is leftist in charac-

ter, and Chile has elected a Marxist president. In these countries, as well as in Venezuela, the Church is losing influence. Elsewhere, as in Bolivia and Brazil, left-wing subversion and terrorism alternate with official repression. A mood of disorder exists among students and workers, on the right and the left, and has reached even into the armed forces. Within the Catholic Church, especially in Brazil, there are known radical and revolutionary groups. There has been increased land reform and expropriation of private industry, much of it directed against American holdings.

Movement to the left has brought a certain amount of pro-Arab sentiment, and even non-leftist Latin American governments have relaxed their support for Israel. Increasingly, left-wing groups have propagated anti-Zionism and even some anti-Semitism: the Jews, they maintain, support "U.S. imperialism," their sympathy for Israel is "imperialistic," and they have divided loyalty. The leftward trend has made many Jews apprehensive for their economic welfare, but fear of anti-Semitism is not far below the surface. Pro-Israel Jews are also concerned about waning support for Israel in non-leftist countries.

The Jewish communities are also troubled by internal problems —by intermarriage and assimilation and concern for Jewish continuity, by a sense of alienation in their own countries. Young Jews, attracted or confused by the New Left, are undergoing a crisis in identity and identification. The Jewish communities are suffering from a lack of leadership and professional communal workers, as well as from financial difficulties, uncertainty of direction and purpose, and division of counsel.

The prospects for stability in many countries of Latin America are dim and the fate of Jews and Jewry uncertain. Their future will be affected by relations between their countries and the United States and by continuing American influence. But even countries friendly to the United States are turning to Latin American interests, and Brazil, for example, may yet lead other Latin American nations into greater independence of the United States. As long as governments and societies remain pro-American and anti-left, they will be pro-Israel and more friendly to Jewish interests. Further movement to the left will erode American influence and support for Israel and will bring apprehension to the Jews.

Dr. Haim Avni paints a picture of a vast and diverse region crying for development and rumbling with political change; its Jews, mostly middle class, apprehensive; their institutions weak and in disarray.

International Human Rights and Jewish Welfare

Jewish rights are human rights and, in principle, international society is increasingly committed to protect them. Since World War II there have been continuous and intensive endeavors to promote respect for human rights by international declaration, exhortation, scrutiny, criticism, and intercession. There is also a growing body of international law on human rights. There has been less success in establishing machinery to enforce the law or promoting voluntary respect for human rights.

Regional protection of human rights has fared better. Intercession by individual governments is a delicate matter, but it is not unknown and it has brought some results. International nongovernmental organizations and media have performed impressively, especially where governments and intergovernmental organizations cannot, or will not, help. An international outcry impelled the Iraqis to stop the hanging of Jews and the Soviet Union to commute the death sentences of Jews convicted of attempting to hijack a plane to flee the country.

Only a few would estimate with confidence how much these international efforts have contributed to respect for human rights. They are political efforts and subject to political limitations. Governments do not care to have their own actions scrutinized and are therefore reluctant to bring charges against others with whom they enjoy friendly relations. And, of course, international protection of human rights is least welcome where it is most needed: in closed societies; in places and times of intense international hostility; before, during, and after revolutions; in countries bent on promoting other values, such as rapid modernization. Differing concepts of and priorities in human rights, ideological or political conflict, and other national and international preoccupations also often override national efforts. Moreover, they cannot be mobilized as effectively against daily, routine discrimination and repression as against discrete, dramatic violations.

Human rights, however, have been placed permanently on the international agenda, and it is not entirely an act of faith to insist that nations are sensitive to international attention and scrutiny, that no government can indulge in repression without some thought to international consequences. Institutions and machinery are now available for emergency rescue or aid and for the undramatic but vital task of promoting human rights in general and every day.

International protection of human rights will be of some, unmeasurable help to endangered Jews, but it also has another connotation for Jews. In recent years the Soviet Union and the Arab states have launched violent propaganda attacks against Israel in UN human rights bodies for alleged violations of human rights in the occupied territories. Some Jews also became discouraged about UN human rights activities when the Soviet Union and the Arab states vilified Jewish organizations devoted to the protection of human rights and maligned and hindered their activities in the UN.

Israel's human rights record has been remarkably good despite provocation; for example, there has not been a single execution for terrorist activities. But as long as there is no peace in the Middle East, Israel will continue to be a target of accusations that it is violating Arab human rights. And organized support for Jewish rights in the Soviet Union and the Arab states will bring recurrent confrontations between the governments of those countries and Jewish organizations.

Sidney Liskofsky gives us a brief history of international efforts to protect human rights since World War II, as foundation for his projections of trends into the future and for the pessimistic as well as hopeful perspectives upon them. More nations will adhere to the general and special covenants that have been prepared, and new international law will be made. International machinery to implement human rights will be improved; the glare of international publicity and the activities of nongovernmental organizations in particular will retain the power to undo, to remedy, to deter. Rights of particular interest to Jews in certain countries—cultural freedom and opportunity, the right of peaceful association, the right to leave one's country and return, the right to emigrate—will be more widely promoted.

On the other hand, there is little hope of effective new machinery to help vindicate rights of Jews in Communist and Arab countries. The optional protocol to the UN Covenant on Civil and Political Rights, which provides for private petition, will not gain many adherents, and none among nations where human rights are most vulnerable. Nor will a universally relevant institution like a High

Commissioner for Human Rights be accepted by countries where
intercession in behalf of Jews is most needed.

The picture painted in this volume is uneven. If its projections
are generally accurate, there will be some causes for satisfaction in
the world of the 1970s and many for concern, for human interests
generally, and for Jewish interests in particular. Satisfaction or concern will have special implications for American Jews; a few of
these are suggested in the final chapter, reprinted from the Task
Force Report for which the papers in this volume were originally
prepared. But the implications, whether of satisfaction or concern,
suggest continuing engagement, commitment, planning, and action in the unending struggle to make the world a place which decent men can contemplate with equanimity rather than in tears.

Part I

The Larger Context

Chapter 1

World Politics in the 1970's

Henry L. Roberts

This chapter is intended to be neither prediction nor prophecy, though a little of each may slip in here and there. Prediction responding to a reasonably well defined question concerning a restricted span of time can be a legitimate undertaking, and at times the need for present action obliges us to make the best possible guesses about an uncertain future. But panoramic crystal gazing for a whole decade of international politics is surely an exercise in futility. It is impossible to construct a logically persuasive or operationally useful scenario of all the potentialities and contingencies that may determine the course of events. Any effort to do so would invite hedging, devising Delphic formulations that will be irrefutable no matter how things actually turn out.

Prophecy is a more serious matter. In contrast to the presumably value-free extrapolations of a prediction, prophecy passes normative judgments on individual and societal behavior and indicates the consequences to be revealed in future drama or catastrophe. Human affairs, including world politics, is the appropriate sphere for prophecy. The sweep of history may appear like a tidal wave; the individual may be shattered by impersonal forces utterly beyond his control. But for all that, history is not a tidal wave; it is what men do. If at times men behave like sheep or jackals or lemmings, it is human decisions that determine that behavior. True prophecy is great, not because it foretells, but because it attempts to speak to men and in so doing becomes itself a part of the movement of human events. The aim of this chapter is more modest.

As an introductory essay this chapter will provide a setting for the more precisely directed studies that follow. It attempts to indicate

37

some salient features of constancy and novelty in the world scene, to suggest their impact and interplay in the coming decade, and to highlight those problems which promise to be major items on the international agenda in the 1970s.

At the risk of simplification we may say that world politics in the 1970s will be most powerfully influenced by developments in three sectors of human activity: (1) the challenge of technological innovation and application, (2) the evolution in international relations, and (3) the movement of domestic politics throughout the world. The dynamics of these three sectors and some of the ways in which they might interact will be the theme of the discussion that follows.

Technology: The Shadow of the Mushroom Cloud

In the 1950s the late German philosopher Karl Jaspers began a book with the statement: "An altogether novel situation has been created by the atom bomb. Either all mankind will physically perish or there will be a change in the moral-political condition of man. This book is an attempt to clarify what strikes us as a choice between two fantasies." [1] Instant apocalypses have now become so prevalent (though most of them are symptomatic rather than explanatory) that it is tempting to brush aside the seriousness of Jaspers' proposition.

Simply put, Jaspers' argument was that for the first time in his history man now had the means at his disposal for the quick obliteration of mankind. Given that unprecedented potentiality, the continuation of human "business as usual"—i.e., people and societies acting and reacting much as they had in the past—seemed to point to the likelihood of total destruction in the not distant future. He found neither the "balance of terror" nor the restraints of prudence to be more than temporary and uncertain answers. Without resorting to fantasy, one had but to juxtapose the power of the bomb and a mind like Hitler's to envisage a final catastrophe.

Curiously, while Jaspers' argument still strikes one as logically sound, the international mood about the bomb, especially the sense of desperate urgency, seems to have changed over the past decade. Why should this be so?

---

[1] Karl Jaspers, *The Future of Mankind*, trans. by E. B. Ashton (University of Chicago Press, 1961), p. vii.

It may be that we simply have become accustomed to the thermonuclear presence. (During World War II a reporter told of seeing sailors unconcernedly flipping cigarettes over the deck of an old and leaky oil tanker: the ancient craft had been around a long time and hadn't blown up yet. So it may be with us all.) Or the answer may lie in certain major events of the 1960s. The Cuban missile crisis brought the two principal nuclear powers eyeball to eyeball, yet it passed without holocaust. Limited wars, notably in Vietnam, have been fought with great violence over an extended period without escalating "even" to the level of tactical nuclear weapons. Perhaps, the conclusion might be, the world was discovering through experience that life, and even wars, could go on indefinitely even with the bomb at hand.

The absence of the mushroom cloud in consequence of the test ban treaty has removed from TV screens one overwhelming visual reminder of the power we are living with. Other items, moreover, have been filling the screens and the front pages to divert our attention. The gas-killed sheep of Utah, the darkening skies of our cities, the sludge-filled rivers and lakes indicate that our technology can produce many threats besides the atom bomb, some fast, some slow, some immediate, some lingering, but all potentially fatal. And we have seen the popularization of destructive technology, the do-it-yourself weapon, ranging from the gasoline-filled bottle (nonreturnable ones are preferable) to quite sophisticated means of mayhem. Faced constantly with these sharply focused threats, it is perhaps not surprising that the thermonuclear danger occupies a less commanding place in our awareness.

Nevertheless, nothing in the last decade has really invalidated Jaspers' conclusion; in a way it has been broadened and reinforced. Infernal powers of destruction are at the ready, and itchy fingers willing to unleash them. Despite the technical, institutional, and political safeguards, one need not be wildly imaginative to fear that sooner or later that awesome power will be accessible to a malignant or frantic human being.

Hence, one may propose that in the 1970s the world will be concerned with a threefold set of problems connected with thermonuclear power. First, how to conduct international disputes in such a way as not to set off a nuclear exchange. Second, how to check the increasing destructiveness (increase in arsenals, means of delivery, proliferation) of the nuclear potential. Third, how to seek ways of reducing and controlling the nuclear arsenals that already exist. Although they overlap, each of these problems deserves separate comment.

(1) Since the implications of thermonuclear war were first recognized two decades ago much thought and energy have been devoted to considering *how* to carry on power politics below this fearful level of violence. Various efforts can be traced. One sought to avoid the shattering consequences of a "central nuclear war" by exploring the possibilities of a limited use of "tactical" nuclear weapons. The aim was to utilize the technology now available but to maintain limits on the range and intensity of the power employed. There seems to be much less public advocacy of this today than in the late 1950s, partly because of a general repugnance against any discussion of nuclear warfare, partly because the prospects for limitation have come to appear very tenuous, and partly because tactical weapons threaten unacceptable retaliatory destruction to those who use them and to their allies. Still, tactical nuclear weapons have their advocates, and the possibility cannot be excluded that in the course of the next decade some state finding itself particularly pressed in an area considered vital to its interests may venture down that most dangerous road. It is not difficult to envisage such a development in Europe or the Middle East.

Another field of active exploration, both in theory and practice, has been guerrilla warfare and counterinsurgency. In the 1950s and 1960s so-called brushfire conflicts seemed to constitute the most likely type of encounter. Along with the direct experience gained in such places as Algeria and Vietnam there sprang up a considerable body of literature on how to conduct a guerrilla war with limited resources and how to put down such a war by appropriate countermeasures. It is difficult to forecast the future of this form of conflict. There has been some disillusionment on both sides. The high expectations of the Maoist and Cuban proponents of hit-and-run tactics have hardly been fulfilled except in the areas of their original success, and counterinsurgency has been a bitter experience for Americans in Vietnam. Still, it would be reasonable to anticipate further experiments with this form of conflict, chiefly in the third world.

A special form of low-level conflict, which shows every promise of increasing in the 1970s, is terrorist activity: political kidnappings, airplane hijackings, seizure of hostages, bomb throwing, and occasional assassination. Guerrilla fighting has thus moved from the village to the city and, in a highly individual way, the terrorists use the instruments of technological society (e.g., the jet plane) against that society itself. It illustrates too in virulent fashion the implosive effects of our technological achievements when the upper reaches of power are rendered impotent by the thermonuclear danger.

From the above we may conclude that the decade of the 1970s will see little protracted formal warfare but a good deal of paramilitary skirmishing together with individual and small-group violence. If conventional conflict does break out in any intensity it will carry the growing risk of escalating, via missile and small-yield nuclear weapons, to an unholy encounter. The cops-and-robbers violence, while less likely to feed into such an escalation, can have extremely detrimental effects on both domestic and international relations. (Some of these will be considered below.)

(2) Two major problems that will urgently require solution in the 1970s are the increasing destructive potential of the existing nuclear arsenals and the proliferation of the number of nations possessing nuclear weapons and the means of delivery. Both subjects are highly technical, involving much classified information, but the nonspecialist may offer a few observations.

With respect to the competition between the two major nuclear powers, the Soviet Union and the United States, it seems unlikely that either will be able to achieve (or, rather, be fully confident that it *has* achieved) an assured first-strike capability, that is, the ability to knock out the other side without suffering utterly devastating retaliation. Even were one to obtain first-strike capability on the drawing board, the risks involved (technical or human errors on one's own side, faulty intelligence about the other side's capabilities, etc.) make it very doubtful that either party could enjoy the confidence to launch an attack. Moreover, we must assume that unless it were hopelessly paralyzed domestically, each nation would respond to narrow any glaring gap in nuclear capabilities.

Despite this probable stalemate with respect to gaining a decisive margin, pressures for continued escalation will remain. Even if both sides wish to achieve only "parity," their respective definitions of the term may well not be the same. If there is a zone of uncertainty in one nation's estimate of the other's capabilities, simple prudence would dictate that it amass a nuclear force corresponding to the upper limits of that zone. Such reasoning on both sides obiously provides a built-in escalator.

But while this would appear to provide a classic model for an arms race even in the absence of aggressive intentions, we have not in fact witnessed quite such an inexorable build-up in recent years. By now both the United States and the Soviet Union are fully aware of the endless implications of a purely competitive stance. Each, in different ways, has other strong demands on the allocation of resources. The future picture with respect to avoiding multiple-reentry and antiballistic missiles is not very encouraging, but there do seem to be these significant retarding factors.

This uneasy balance between the two powers—one can hardly call it an equilibrium—can be rendered much more complex by the advent of new nuclear powers. So long as the USSR and the United States have only their own relative capabilities to wrestle with, the problem can at least be dealt with directly. The addition of a third, or a fourth, or a fifth power greatly increases the difficulty the major powers will have in achieving any agreement about their respective armaments. Inviting these additional powers to the negotiating table will bring into play the usual complexity of multilateral negotiations as well as a likely opposition between the major and the minor nuclear powers. This promises to be a sensitive item for world diplomacy in the coming years.

Quite apart from its impact on the two major nuclear powers, the danger of proliferation is a matter of deep concern because the multiplication of states capable of using nuclear weapons—if only as a demonstration weapon or a *force de frappe*—enhances the possibility of triggering a chain reaction of nuclear responses. There has long been the fear that a small state might use a modest nuclear arsenal, either of its own making (increasingly a feasible task) or a gift from a well-wisher among the great powers, to resolve a vital issue with one of its neighbors, without the sense of responsibility that the possession of a mighty arsenal is supposed to give. This possibility cannot be disregarded, and yet we have not witnessed the pell-mell rush into nuclear production that we might have anticipated a decade ago. Moreover, although small powers at times engage in rash actions, they are acutely aware that they live in a world of dangerous giants and are disinclined to take any forward action without a reassuring nod from one of these giants.

In this connection the Arab-Israeli conflict, explored in detail in a later chapter, promises to be the most dangerous, because of the intensity of the dispute, because of the marked qualitative difference in the type of capabilities each side can muster, and because each has one of the nuclear giants in its camp. Of all the sensitive areas of the world the Middle East appears to be the one where the pressure for nuclear proliferation is the greatest and could most seriously involve the great powers.

(3) We have been concerned with the need to prevent exacerbation of the nuclear menace. But it is bad enough right now, without further sophistication in the hardware or new entrants in the competition. So long as the present missiles are in existence the human race lives under a constant threat.

Is that an exaggeration? Perhaps. Some have drawn comfort from the nonuse of poison gas in World War II, when both sides had plentiful supplies and were tempted to throw everything they had into a total war. Indeed, there do seem to be similar hopeful signs with respect to chemical and biological weapons, which, for all their deadliness, have not (at least publicly) occupied center stage in the post-1945 arms race. One reason these hideous agents have been withheld is that they cannot be confined to a sharp military focus, which gives even megaton bombs a justification of sorts. Moreover, the threat of retaliation in kind, along with their evident ecological shortcomings, has been a powerful deterrent. Still, one cannot find much comfort in the absence of chemical and biological weapons when thermonuclear missiles stand poised in their launching sites.

Getting rid of this threat, however, confronts two major difficulties beyond those which face efforts to prevent the expansion of nuclear arsenals. Man cannot unlearn what he has learned; he cannot eradicate the possibility of nuclear power in the world without eradicating scientific knowledge. Although an antitechnological, antiintellectual mood is at large these days, there seems to be little prospect of an effective, world-wide Luddism. If the nuclear jinni cannot be returned to the bottle, then it must be put under control, either by agreement between nations or by an agency transcending them. Some of the problems connected with this essentially political task will be discussed in the next section. They are obviously very difficult, with few or no relevant precedents from the past.

Apart from the inherent difficulty of achieving a significant reduction of nuclear power, there is the ironic possibility that success would not be all blessing: it is not an unreasonable fear that in the absence of the nuclear terror, hostile nations might revert to conventional weapons, which are deadly enough. It has been argued that the world would have witnessed direct military encounters between the major powers in the last twenty-five years had they not been inhibited by the nuclear danger. This could be. In any case, the effort to bring about a reduction of nuclear weaponry must consider the risks of increasing the likelihood of other forms of international conflict.

It is impossible to say just how much progress in nuclear limitations may be anticipated for the 1970s; so much depends on the innumerable variables making up the international climate and on surmounting the political and technical obstacles to confidence that the parties would live up to any agreement. It is not unlikely that the superpowers will enter the next decade, too, taking the threat of nuclear destruction as given, inescapable, but not overwhelming. Still, if no headway is made in the 1970s, the question will remain on the agenda for the next decade. The threat will not go away by itself or dissolve through the mere passage of time.

From Bipolar to Multilateral Relations

The picture of a bipolar world as it emerged after World War II was never an exact description of reality. Perhaps at war's end there was actually only one power, the United States, but Stalin's remarkable genius in concealing Russia's weakness after Hitler's dreadful mauling contributed to the generally accepted thesis in the late 1940s and the 1950s that only the two superpowers, locked in the cold war, counted; all other states were seen to cluster around these two magnetic poles. To be sure, even in the accepted view, even in those years things were not that simple. For example, the third world with its anticolonial, national liberation movements was a largely independent factor from the outset. Moreover, the polarity was never perfect; the so-called satellites or client states frequently went, or attempted to go, their own way. Neither camp was the monolith it sought or seemed to be. Still, the bipolar concept did contain a substantial measure of truth.

In the 1960s this pattern began to break down. The most dramatic evidence was the Sino-Soviet rift, involving two of the world's largest powers, but there were significant divergences in the Western camp, especially in the independent course followed by de Gaulle's France.

It seems highly likely that this trend will continue in the 1970s, that in place of a predominant bipolarity in world affairs we will see triangles, quadrangles, and a variety of intertwined polygons. But one should not write off the bipolarity completely so long as the USSR and the United States continue to have marked superiority in military strength. Habits are hard to break, and the relative postures assumed by the two countries—and accepted by others—have been so conditioned by twenty-five years of apparent global confrontation that bipolarity is almost a reflex with them.

Nevertheless, the 1970s must cope with elements of novelty that will probably stem from the multilateral nature of the states-system, to use the nineteenth-century phrase. The obvious feature of this system is the fact that stability or instability is not determined by the frontal encounters of a bipolar relation but by elaborate patterns of checks and balances, ententes, and fancy footwork. For that reason it is fruitless to try to guess just how this pattern may develop and articulate itself. Many arrangements are possible. We may consider some of these possibilities, more as illustration than as forecast.

From the American perspective, with its long preoccupation with the "Soviet bloc" and "international Communism," the most tempting way to define the movement away from bipolarity is to posit a Washington-Moscow-Peking triangle. If, as seems likely, no full, mutually agreed upon restoration of a united Communist bloc is in the cards, even after the death of Mao Tse-tung, such a triangle has its attractions for the United States. Rather than being confronted by a Sino-Soviet coalition threatening to dominate the Eurasian land mass, the United States may be able to deal independently, and to its advantage, with these two great powers, which appear increasingly to regard one another as the principal enemy, both for ideological and traditional power-politics reasons. Given the evident movement of United States policy toward China in 1971, it is probable that this triangle will constitute a major area of maneuver in the near future.

But this is a very tricky framework for political behavior. "In a triangular relationship, it is advantageous to have better relations with the other two parties than they have with each other." [2] Thus each party will be driven to exploit all possible approaches to the others and, if it sees signs of collusion between the other two, must seek to disrupt that collusion or to mend fences with one or the other.

Even in the most simplified model the triangular relationship is productive of complex diplomacy. It will be even more complex in this case because there are such disparities in power and in the nature of the mutual antagonisms. For the next decade at least the Soviet Union and the United States will remain far stronger economically and militarily than China. China and the Soviet Union have the longest common frontier in the world and compete for influence in areas very close to the vital interests of both. The Soviet Union and America have had few direct disputes, but in their search for dominant power in the decades of the cold war they have supported opposing nations and groups in a whole range of foreign conflicts. China and America differ on several highly charged issues (the status of Taiwan probably being uppermost), complicated by the peculiar passion with which each has regarded the other since 1949. The triangle is not equilateral.

Of even greater importance is the fact that this triangle does not exist in isolation and does not encompass all the major powers. Some analysts have spoken of a quadrangular relationship, adding Western Europe. Certainly if Western Europe, with its population, wealth, and skills, were to function as an entity, it would be a very major power indeed. One must speculate, then, about the movement toward European unity. After two world wars Europe ceased to be the locus of the international system of power; it would be in the interest of all the European states to pull together to become a major weight in a new configuration of states. Such an impulse has existed for a number of years; steps have been taken to increase economic integration and political cooperation. But the impulse does not seem to have gathered great momentum and appears to have faltered at the point of transition between the limits of bureaucratic-technical cooperation and the beginnings of real political integration. The task of achieving a supranational organization by means other than conquest or hegemony is monumentally difficult, con-

---

[2] Zbigniew Brzezinski, "The New Triangle," *Newsweek*, June 28, 1971.

tending as it must against a host of traditional and particularist sentiments and interests (not all of them negative by any means). It remains to be seen how far and how quickly Europe can proceed in this direction.

In this connection Great Britain's role could be very important. For a number of years Britain was inhibited from closer connections with the continent because of two presumed assets, its ties with the Commonwealth nations and its rather special relationship with the United States; both of these seem to be of diminished value. But it is by no means clear just where domestic British party politics will lead. Moreover, the impact of Britain's entry into the Common Market may be ambiguous. Some argue that the addition of Britain is what is needed to bring Europe to the level of political integration.[3] Others argue that Britain's presence will always be that of a foreign body, obstructing any further achievement of European unity.

What of Eastern Europe? It is always perilous to make predictions about this singularly neuralgic area, in which two world wars and the cold war had their start. Yet it is possible that Eastern Europe may be off the main track of international concerns in the coming decade, partly because of events there in the 1950s and 1960s. Put simply, by its invasions of Hungary in 1956 and Czechoslovakia in 1968, the Soviet Union demonstrated that it could move in to suppress what it regarded as excessive deviations and that no other great power was going to do anything about it.

There are, of course, some marginal situations, of which the Yugoslav case is the most significant and could be the most explosive. One expects that Yugoslavia would vigorously resist any effort to bring it back under the Soviet aegis, unless it were helplessly paralyzed by a post-Tito crisis among its own national units. Open fighting here could create a most dangerous situation, since it would have implications not only for Eastern Europe but also for the Mediterranean area.

One must anticipate that the division of Europe, which has persisted for twenty-five years, will continue through the next decade. In that connection the recent diplomatic activity relating to both East and West Germany would appear to be part of the process of

---

[3] For example, Andrew Shonfield, "On Finding a Role," *Encounter*, September 1971, pp. 26–28.

stabilizing this division. Soviet policy will remain at once tough with respect to areas it defines as within its own sphere of influence and accommodating in seeking a stabilized frontier.

This expectation of European stability is, however, like a railway timetable, subject to change without notice. Soviet concern over it's eastern-flank relations with China may well be conducive to this western-flank policy of combined toughness and accommodation (especially as there are currently no very promising opportunities for expansion in Western Europe). But a Sino-Soviet détente could completely alter the picture. Conversely, a heightening of Sino-Soviet tension could lead to greater Soviet pressure in the West: were the Soviet Union to conclude that it faced an inevitable showdown with China it might move to eliminate any possible future danger on its European flank.

Factors in other areas could also complicate our triangular model. Japan has the third-largest and the fastest-growing economy in the world, with a productive capacity nearly three times that of China. Because of its defeat in World War II and its subsequent dependence upon the United States, Americans have until recently been inclined to regard Japan as something of a client state. But clearly, a nation of such obvious dynamism is bound to make itself felt, and not merely economically. Moreover, if a Moscow-Peking-Washington game of triangular tug-of-war should occur, a Washington-Peking-Tokyo triangle will also emerge. The United States may make its moves toward China with an eye to the Soviet Union; Japan will make its own reading of these moves. Here again, by the nature of the game, the situation becomes indeterminate: there would be obvious grounds for mutual Chinese-Japanese approaches; there would also be obvious grounds for interesting Soviet-Japanese maneuverings. Neither can be posited, and neither excluded.

Another complicating factor involving great powers (great in numbers if not in present economic or military strength) is the tension between India and Pakistan, which recently erupted into open conflict. This vexed situation, which has persisted since the partitioning of the subcontinent and was heightened by the civil strife in East Pakistan (Bangladesh), cannot be indefinitely relegated to "third world" issues that do not vitally affect the structure of world politics. One can envisage the further development of a China-Pakistan and a Soviet-India axis, each reinforced by continued Sino-Soviet and Indian-Pakistan hostility. But where does the United

States fit in, and what might be the implications for the Washington-Moscow-Peking triangle? It seems unlikely that the United States, in a contest of such tremendous magnitude, would enjoy the privilege of playing *tertius gaudens* on the sidelines.

From these few intimations it should be evident that the 1970s, in continuing the trends that emerged in the 1960s, will witness a pattern of international relationships far more complex and indeterminate than that obtaining in the two decades after World War II. While there will surely be a persisting element of bipolarity, the picture can no longer be described as two camps engaging in mutual encounters and controlling deviations among underling nations.

This situation of increasing fluidity, full both of promise—of releasing the world from the deadlock of the cold war—and of danger —of promoting new and perhaps uncontrollable forces—will undoubtedly also have its impact on Latin America, Africa, Southeast Asia, and the Middle East. We will comment only briefly on each of these regions.

The long tradition of unchallenged American predominance in the affairs of the Western Hemisphere was jolted by the advent of the Castro regime in Cuba. The tradition will probably be further eroded in the coming decade, more by the independent actions of the Latin American states themselves than by the intrusion of another foreign power. The orientation of the area, or of significant portions thereof, toward an alignment hostile to the United States would still induce American countermeasures. The vigor and effectiveness of these, however, could hinge on the climate of American domestic opinion and the intensity of unpleasant recollections— both at home and in Latin America—of American interventions in the 1960s. Although American influence seems likely to wane, there is little to suggest that the Latin American states in the next few years will progress markedly either toward internal political and social stability or toward very effective cooperation among themselves. Nor does Castroism appear to be quite the export commodity it was thought to be in the early 1960s.

In the next decade black Africa will be faced with the pressing tasks of establishing national and cultural identities, assimilating (or rejecting) the complex inheritance of the colonial past, and creating viable economies. There may be efforts to ignore or bypass these formidable tasks, but the impression is that national and economic survival will largely absorb the energies of the continent. Attacks on the remnants of colonialism will persist. South Africa will remain a brutally intractable problem: a fearful human tragedy seems hardly escapable there, but the 1970s may not witness it. It is unlikely that in a decade's time a pan-Africa movement will have developed sufficient strength to become an independent force in world politics. On the other hand, it appears less likely than it did some years ago that Africa will fall under the influence of the "Communist bloc," partly because the bloc is in disarray, partly because of African distrust of alien influences from abroad, whether of left or right, which bring echoes of past subjugation.

Southeast Asia has already felt the impact of the Moscow-Peking-Washington triangle, although the American perception of this has been blurred because our involvement in Vietnam was for so long defined in bipolar terms. The probable disengagement of the United States from its extended support of South Vietnam seems likely to lead to a complex scenario over the next several years, with strong indigenous impulses, Sino-Soviet rivalry, American Pacific concerns, plus the interests of Japan, India, and Australia at the fringes, creating an extraordinary cacaphony. In a word, one may anticipate a very confused situation, probably not carrying the seeds of general war or leading to any domino-theory type of domination by a great power, but surely not conducive to any stable self-determination among the peoples of the region. The very confusion of Southeast Asia bids fair to invite the active, though limited, intervention of the great powers. Prospects for stability are not bright.

The Middle East, and in particular the question of Arab-Israeli relations, is considered in much greater detail in later chapters. Here we will provide only the most general setting.

For a variety of geographic, economic, and historical reasons the Middle East has been one of the most fought-over regions in the world, and for centuries great-power conflicts have had a way of finding expression there. Russia, tsarist or Soviet, has been especially concerned with the Middle East. The zone from the Bosphorus to the Persian Gulf and extending southward has variously appeared as one where Russia was threatened with being outflanked or as one with tempting opportunities for expanded influence and control. The presence of oil in the area (including North Africa) has of course given the Middle East a very important economic significance. For these reasons it seems probable that the bipolar pattern is likely to prevail in the next decade and give a special edge to

Arab-Israeli disputes. The cold war may well linger on in the Middle East while being blurred or superseded elsewhere.

When one contemplates the prospect of a disconcerting complex pattern of power politics in the coming years, with the possible resurrection of a multiple states-system and all the quandaries which that has produced in times past, one is led to ask whether either above or below international politics—i.e., at the supranational or domestic level—there are elements which may check this troubling multiplicity of contending nations. We will look at the prospects for a supranational agency in the remaining portion of this section, and at the domestic possibilities in the final section.

For the past half-century, ever since people began pulling themselves from the wreckage of World War I, it has been recognized in principle that sooner or later a supranational political entity must come into existence if the world is not to lie under the shadow of total disaster. It is doubtful that such an entity can be called into being by an appeal to tradition, and it certainly won't bloom spontaneously. The ecumenical movement in the world today is beneficial in working against prejudice and parochialism, but one cannot escape the thought that this may be a twilight phenomenon: one becomes ecumenical when one's doubts and skepticism are stronger than one's will to be combative for the truth as one sees it. At the most, in our secular age, the ecumenical spirit can assist in checking hatreds. It seems doubtful that the Vatican, or pan-Islam, or Judeo-Christian fraternity can be of more than marginal influence.

Nor can we expect that the "hidden hand," some automatic agency, will be effective. Proletarian internationalism at this point seems as dated and unpromising as free trade and the international division of labor. Relying on the hope that a functional solution can replace some desperately difficult decisions is only an evasion of the issue.

The act, ultimately, must be a political one. Governments must make decisions about powers to retain and powers to place in the common pool. The recent historical record is not very encouraging. The last fifty years have seen many schemes, some of them highly intelligent and perceptive,[4] for arriving at international control over the chaos of nations, but they have had little impact. It is true that

---

[4] For example, Grenville Clark and Louis B. Sohn, *World Peace Through World Law*, 2d rev. ed. (Harvard University Press, 1960).

in the immediate wake of major disasters—the Napoleonic wars, and the two world wars of our century—nations have created international agencies, only to have them dissolve in the particularist interests of the states. The world can ill afford another such shattering stimulus.

What of the prospects for the United Nations? Partly because of limitations present at its creation, the UN has not suffered the kind of discrediting that befell the League of Nations in the 1930s. It has periodically served a valuable peacekeeping function. Still, it may have been permanently crippled by the decades of the cold war, and there is little reason to believe that seating of the People's Republic of China will provide any great infusion of energy or unity of purpose.

The likelihood of increased multilateralism in world politics promises ambiguous consequences for the United Nations. On the one hand, it may at last remove the dead weight of cold war politics, where one side's *yes* was the other's inevitable *nyet*. But insofar as this multilateralism is an expression of new or rediscovered national wills, it is doubtful that the climate will be conducive to the strengthening of a supranational body. In the next decade it seems probable that while the UN will come to reflect world realities more adequately, it will not be in a position to surmount them.

What are the prospects for more limited or regional organizations, such as the North Atlantic Treaty Organization? Although at the height of the cold war NATO may have appeared more effectual than the deadlocked UN in representing and advancing the interests of a particular group of states, and even raised hopes of being the initial step toward a true North Atlantic community, it has been unable to transcend the specific challenge—the military defense of Europe—which led to its creation. One must anticipate that NATO will prove to be, not the nucleus of an enduring community encompassing both the United States and Western Europe, but rather a useful negotiating agent vis-à-vis the Soviet-dominated Warsaw Treaty powers for reducing tensions within Europe. One should not underestimate the utility of this function.

At least for this decade, then, we see slight chance of any existing supranational organization being in a position to resolve the new problems created by a multilateral pattern of world politics. We are still faced by the old squaring-the-circle quandary of finding means to induce nations, without catastrophe, to give up elements of sovereignty which are central to their very definition as a nation. This leads us in turn to the question whether in the domestic complexion of the nations themselves there are forces at work which may significantly impinge upon their international relations.

Domestic Influences

The relation of domestic to foreign politics has long been a subject of heated and often dogmatic debate. That there is at least an intermittent connection is undisputed, but which is the prime mover, which the dependent variable? In the Marxist view the mainspring is domestic, the class struggle, which ultimately finds expression, via imperialism, in foreign politics. The tradition of diplomatic historiography, on the other hand, has tended to stress the primacy of foreign politics.

Doubtless there is merit in the classical view that the need for a state to survive in a universe of actual or potential enemies gives to foreign policy a special urgency, a priority which can profoundly affect the domestic social and political order as well as the allocation of resources and energy. The United States, as a continental power and in times past relatively removed from the deadly grind of power politics, has been less accustomed to think in this manner than more hard-pressed nations. Even so, we have heard the cry that politics must stop at the water's edge, intimating that somehow the international "national interest" is an identifiable entity transcending domestic issues and disputes.

In a revolutionary and ideologically imbued age, such as much of the twentieth century has been, the distinction between foreign and domestic affairs tends to weaken. Such issues as Communism versus imperialism or colonialism versus national liberation go well beyond national concerns and have important implications for the domestic organization of a society. A few years ago there was a growing expectation that the future would witness less of this revolutionary or transnational impulse, that there would be an "end of ideology" and an increasingly pragmatic spirit in world politics. Some of the traditional ideological cleavages do seem to be disappearing. Ideology alone is evidently unable to determine the relations between states, and it may be anticipated that growing multilateralism in world politics will carry with it a predisposition toward pragmatism, such as occurred at the end of the wars of religion when the classical European states-system began to take shape.

From our current perspective, however, it appears that a new set of domestic developments may have a profound and unprecedented impact on world politics, an impact deriving in good part from the unresolved quandaries outlined above. Perhaps the best way of suggesting this is to look at the year 1968, which in retrospect may turn out to have been a watershed in contemporary history. Even now it is surprising how frequently one can tell, from a glance at a few pages, whether a book on virtually any social or political issue was written before or after 1968. That cataclysmic year witnessed among other things two political assassinations in the United States, with angry demonstrations in the wake of Martin Luther King's death; President Johnson's decision not to seek reelection; riots at the Democratic national convention in Chicago; waves of student protest in the United States, France, and Germany; massive strikes in France; and a remarkable surge of liberalization in Czechoslovakia, followed by the Soviet invasion. Unlike 1914 or 1939, the year did not reach a climax, and yet things have been different since then: certain trends moved from the edges of our awareness to the center, and promise to remain there for years to come.

What happened? A central theme was an extraordinarily widespread, international expression of revolt—temperate and intemperate, creative and destructive—against political systems that had dominated lives for a generation. It was a time of passionate iconoclasm, by the young, by the New Left, by disadvantaged groups, by subjugated nationalities—an effort to prove that the emperor had no clothes, that he had feet of clay. The long-standing American posture of defending freedom in the remotest reaches was savagely challenged in the anti-Vietnam war movement. The mounting reforms in Prague represented a similar challenge to the Soviet Union: its labors of a quarter-century threatened to become undone.

For those in revolt it was a frustrating year. The idols did not topple, the emperor obtained a new suit of clothes, and the very chaos of the attacks brought about counter-responses. Still, in many parts of the world a new set of questions had been posed. The search for answers will continue to occupy the 1970s.

If we try to identify the strands that fed into this critical year and that seem likely to continue into the next decade, what do we find?

First, in many nations there seems to be a marked turning inward, a preoccupation with domestic deficiencies, a weariness with internationalism, whether Wilsonian or proletarian. This tendency is by no means complete and may be of uncertain duration, but it does promise to be a significant feature of the future, expressing itself in different ways in different countries. In the Communist world it may be reflected in tensions between efforts to maintain cohesion within the bloc and efforts to allow greater latitude to nations seeking a separate road to socialism. In Western Europe it may militate against the progress of political integration. In the United States it may link up with traditional isolationist sentiments, though it would be a mistake to describe neo-isolationism as a simple atavism: it is an active rejection of preceding policies.

This turning inward can have both positive and negative effects. It may reduce international tensions simply because the thrust of energy will be less externally directed. But it also carries the dangers of self-centeredness in an interlocking world which could produce beggar-my-neighbor attitudes in times of economic stress or political crisis.

A second strand, intimately linked with the first, has been the emergence of a profound mistrust of authority. Assaults on the establishment are very popular where they are tolerated, and dreamed of where they are not. One may expect that in the coming decade leaders of governments, even of one-party governments, will not enjoy an automatic rallying to the foreign policies they elect. This impediment might instigate either of two possible responses: (1) a trimming down of policies to what the traffic will bear; or (2) an attempt to manipulate opinion or resort to outright coercion. In world politics this could produce a striking asymmetry between those states constrained to follow the first course and those able and willing to follow the second. Such an asymmetry was not lacking in the past; it often provided a point of comparison for the foreign policies of democracies and dictatorships.

In the next decade, domestic opposition may lead to some ponderous questions. Can leaders in democratic states count at all upon consensus? If not, how are they to achieve the backing for any but the most minimal foreign policy strategy? Will the leaders of authoritarian countries feel obliged to rely on neo-Stalinism or fascism, with all the dismal deadends they have produced?

A third strand is the reaction to the incessantly increasing impact of technological innovation. A few years ago the principal problem in this regard was seen as escorting backward nations over the hurdles of industrialization up to the level of "mature" societies. This problem still exists and will remain an important challenge for the third world. But the notion of a "mature" society has become highly questionable. In the last few years a significant body of writing, in its references to post-industrial societies, the oncoming technetronic age, and the like, points to the fact that the notion of "maturity" as a kind of stable equilibrium is utterly fallacious. The most advanced societies are undergoing changes as fantastic as those confronted by tribal communities.

The growing sense of the perils of rapid transformation has contributed to the widely expressed concerns about pollution and ecological imbalance and to the remarkable unpopularity of new power installations (thermal, hydroelectric, or nuclear) and new oil explorations, not to speak of subsoil atomic tests. Growth for growth's sake is no longer a self-evident virtue, whether it be of population, gross national product, or technical prowess.

It is difficult to judge how much of this concern is a matter of sober criticism and how much a scream of panic, but the implications for world politics are apparent. The capacity of nations to compete in power politics has not, regrettably, been measured by the quality of life they can promote, but by such indices as manpower, industrial output, and technological sophistication. We now have the prospect in the next decade of statesmen trying to play international politics with a sizable, and highly articulate, part of the population arguing violently against the promotion of those factors that traditionally defined the strength of nations. An interesting asymmetry could emerge if one nation or group of nations is influenced by considerations of zero population growth, ecological stability, and qualitative rather than quantitative economic advance and another nation or group of nations continues to be dominated by the "metal eaters" (to use the Soviet term).

A fourth strand can be discerned in a decided antihistorical turn of mind, especially among the young. This seems to have several sources, may continue to affect perceptions in coming years, and could have a role in international affairs. Part of the reaction is against history and toward the more systematic social sciences as a discipline, presumably in the hope of finding formulas which can bring about a rapid correction of social ills. Deeper than this is a tendency to find history itself unbearable: the sense that if the past, with all its accumulated inertias and its deeply imbedded, impossibly refractory problems, is taken seriously, the individual must become helpless and paralyzed.

Insofar as this mood is a revolt against the historicist fallacy or against a passive fatalism, it can be constructive. But insofar as it disregards the continuing relevance of past events it can be singularly dangerous. It is not a matter of learning the "lessons" of history (these can too easily lead to seeing Munichs in every international crisis) but rather of recognizing that things as they are at the present got that way through an intricate historical process which it is unwise to overlook. Not infrequently a new generation has moved into positions of power, found the inheritance from the past inconvenient or distasteful, and briskly moved in to rearrange the furniture without being fully aware of the implications of their actions.

In world politics such disregard of history can have two different but equally perilous results. The world today is full of political booby traps potentially explosive situations that are quiescent only because people in the past have let sleeping dogs lie because no real solution was visible; stirring things up might turn untidy situations into dangerously insoluble ones.[5] A different peril lies where an uneasy balance of power has been maintained through a combination of numerous elements: the unthinking removal of one of these may lead to a serious imbalance (the domino theory is not *always* wrong). There is danger, then, that this antihistorical temper could activate issues that were better left fallow or could let fall some element of security that will produce a serious vulnerability.

A fifth strand is the communications explosion, which will surely continue into the next decade, amplifying the jolting effects it has already had. Increasingly, all parts of the world will know, instantly and vividly, what is going on in all other parts. The world will be ever more intimately linked. Brzezinski is probably correct in doubting that Marshall McLuhan's "global village" is an appropriate term for the outcome. Brzezinski's image of the "global city" seems more to the mark: "a nervous, agitated, tense, and fragmented web of in-

---

[5] A classic example of the disregard of this fact was the action taken by Russia and Austria to bring the Balkan question to life in 1908 after it had been on ice for a couple of decades; the consequences were a chain of events that led directly to World War I.

terdependent relations." [6] The communications net will, of course, not be absolutely effective, for there will be areas of jamming and blackout; but on the whole there will be fewer overlooked deeds, fewer dark corners remaining in ignorance.

Basically, this trend would seem to be all to the good; let the winds of knowledge circulate freely. But the burden of adjustment promises to be formidable. The impact upon the individual who becomes eyewitness to all the horrors and tragedies which the world spawns daily will be heavy and could lead to either frantic overreaction or callous apathy. Let the reader reflect on his reactions to scenes from Vietnam or East Pakistan and imagine these multiplied many times over.

Moreover, it is possible that at times our wicked world has maintained its equilibrium simply because many crimes and tragedies were not known, they did not send out endless waves of repercussion. Obviously there is a certain inhumanity in leaving serious misdeeds unreported, as there is in reducing human suffering to statistics. But we have yet to face the full consequences of the massive assault of instant communications upon our nerve ends. Of all the implications of the communications explosion, this may be the most significant and difficult to predict. And if we know so little about the effects on our own, highly conditioned society, what will be the impact in those parts of the world where literacy, the press, and satellite TV will suddenly be impinging all at once?

At the very least, we can say that it will have a multiple effect on world affairs: on the intensity of international disputes, on the way local issues become disseminated at an early date, and on the timing and techniques for handling them.

A sixth strand, related to the communications explosion, is the vastly increased amount of knowledge generally available: the new discoveries of science, the instant replay of history, the encapsulation of information as symbolized by the TV-cassette. This is all to the good in principle, but again, the problem of assimilation will not be easy as societies try to extract what they need from a staggering array of possibilities and individuals try to define themselves in the face of endless models past and present.

A seventh strand is the appearance of new life styles, of "counter-cultures." It is hard to gauge the profundity or permanence of all

---

[6] Zbigniew Brzezinski, *Between Two Ages: America's Role in the Technetronic Era* (New York, Viking Press, 1970), p. 19.

these novel modes of feeling and behavior; some of the manifestations are faddish and of no great significance. But surely the expansion of the drug culture, the changes in sexual mores, the new directions in music and the visual arts, the rapid erosion of ancient taboos, the far-reaching demands of liberation movements represent
more than surface phenomena. In both their positive and their
negative effects, whether in bringing fresh insights or in undermining indispensable institutions, in pointing to an age of Aquarian
bliss or to the stupefaction of lotus eaters, they intimate that the
last third of the twentieth century may be the scene, especially in
the more affluent lands, of one of mankind's most staggering cultural transformations.

Admittedly, these strands extend far beyond our present subject
and well beyond the 1970s, but the domestic and international influences they represent, by the universality of their impact upon human life everywhere, will surely affect the way nations relate to one
another. The intensity of the impact will vary from country to
country, as will the nature of the response. But it would surely be
unwise to disregard the potential enormity of these factors in attempting to chart the course of world politics in the 1970s.

To summarize: world politics in the 1970s will represent an in-
credibly complex mélange created by the interplay of such components as the technological-military threat, the apparent shift to a
multilateral world pattern, and the growing influence of domestic
factors, plus all the precipitating and crystallizing agencies of the
contingent and the unforeseeable. We cannot say what the world
will look like in 1980. But ultimately that is not the question: 1980
is not a peak hidden by the clouds. It does not yet exist. It is for the
world's communities to create.

Part II

The Middle East

Chapter 2

American Foreign Policy and the Middle East

Eugene V. Rostow

I

The only assumption about American foreign policy during this decade that I can accept as realistic is that its major premise will not change. The experience of being dragged into the whirlpool of two great wars has, I believe, convinced a stable majority of the American people that it is more dangerous to stay out of world politics than to take part in them. This conviction has not been shaken, or shaken much, even by the traumatic experience of Korea and Vietnam and the other costly troubles of the last twenty-five years. Despite the intermittent revolt of opinion against the burden of foreign relations, this sense of the national interest in world politics has governed the general course of American policy since 1947 and will, I conclude, continue to guide that policy, though not without further setbacks, missed opportunities, and failures to act in time, like those which have characterized American policy during the last generation.

I do not dismiss the outcry about foreign policy, which has been a recurrent phenomenon of American life since the turn of the century and has been notably audible during the recent past. Nor do I minimize the political effect, either at home or abroad, of the current round of debate, especially with regard to American policy in Asia and the Middle East, and the third world more generally. The

---

[1] I have elaborated some of these views in *Peace in the Balance: The Future of American Foreign Policy*, Simon & Schuster, Inc., 1972.

bitter and emotional battles of the last few years are bound to influence the positions taken by American politicians and bureaucrats, and the calculations and expectations of foreign governments, in the years ahead.

This constellation of doubt and tension about American policy is in itself a major influence in world affairs. The history of this tragic and brutal century is a chronicle of miscalculation about intent. In 1914 Germany thought Britain would not fight for Belgium, and would be a negligible, a "contemptible" military force if it did; Germany was confident, too, that America would never enter the war. Hitler fell into the same traps. Those who planned and initiated hostilities in Korea believed that the United States, which had just withdrawn its forces from South Korea, would not resist the takeover of that country by force. And it is reasonable to suppose that the men who made the comparable decisions in Vietnam gave far too much weight to the popular American slogan of the times, "No more Koreas."

That slogan dominated the electoral campaign of 1952. But a few years later President Eisenhower, with the full support of Congress, entered into a series of treaties and other commitments putting the military power of the United States behind the security of many countries and regions of the world threatened by Soviet or Chinese expansion (and later on, and on its own scale, by Cuban policies) or by policies of expansion supported by those countries. Neither President Eisenhower nor his successors hesitated to use or to threaten to use American force in a variety of situations deemed to endanger national interests.

The election of 1968 was dominated in turn by the slogan, "No more Vietnams." But in the spring of 1970 President Nixon attacked hostile bases in Cambodia and later in that year convincingly intervened in the Jordanian crisis by threatening the use of force.

In short, it is apparent that whatever recent American presidents have thought, and said, before they came to the White House, their responses to the world they perceived from that vantage point have been broadly uniform.

There have of course been differences among the postwar American presidents—differences of temperament, of ability, of style, and of luck. But for all their differences, the pattern of what they did is remarkably consistent. Policy was explained in a bewildering variety of ways. The spokesmen of American policy talked of protecting freedom and democracy; of demonstrating that aggression would not be tolerated; of promoting or assisting social progress. They spoke too of even less tangible goals—the "mission" of great power, for example.

But the code of what they did corresponds to no such formulae. The United States and its allies have not become the universal policemen of the United Nations Charter. There has been no anti-Communist crusade, no ideological opposition to "Communism" or "revolution" as such, no "globalism," whatever that may mean. Many acts of aggression were in fact ignored, like the attacks on Hungary, Czechoslovakia, and Pakistan. There have been nearly sixty wars since 1945. We have exhibited a serious interest in only five or six. Help was given to some states, i.e., Iran and Yugoslavia, which were not democracies, and some democracies, Czechoslovakia, for example, were abandoned to their fates. No serious attempt was made after 1945 to unseat Communist regimes in the Soviet Union, China, Eastern Europe, or even in Cuba (where the Bay of Pigs foray was half-hearted, to say the least), or otherwise to remake the world in the Western image. American policy did not bespeak hegemonic ambition. On the contrary, it was guided by a nonideological, far more limited concept of the national interest.

Since 1947 the United States has used or threatened to use military power mainly to prevent an extension of Soviet or Chinese control (or Cuban influence) through the international use of force. The threat of force has also been employed to deter international attacks on the territorial integrity and political independence of Middle Eastern states, in a sensitive area of great importance both in itself and in relation to the security of Europe and of Japan. When Communists have come into power through elections, as in Chile, or through what seem to be purely internal coups d'état, as in China or Cuba, the United States has taken no action.

In short, the United States and its allies have been following a line of policy as old as the history of international affairs—that of achieving and preserving a balance of power in world politics.

The present paper is written on the assumption that this will continue to be the case, i.e., that an awareness of the national interest in achieving and preserving a balance of power in world politics will

remain the compass of American foreign policy. It may be that the
nation will abandon this course for a time, as it did for two decades after 1920, but such an assumption is so irrational as to make
conjecture about the future altogether impossible, save to be certain that such a course would lead once more to disaster.

The outcry about American foreign policy, exacerbated by the
cost and anguish of Vietnam, is world-wide. Many Americans are
frustrated and resentful, convinced that there must be a magic formula, a program not yet tried, that would permit the United States
to bring the boys home and return to "normalcy." In Europe and
in some other parts of the world the words are different, but the music is the same. There is a general conviction that if only the United
States were not so stupid, so stubborn, so naïve about world affairs,
so much the prisoner of cold war illusions, peace would prevail—at
least in Europe; NATO and other expensive rituals could be abandoned; and Western man could concentrate on the arts of progress and of leisure.

My own review of the literature of protest persuades me that for
the most part the outcry is about the state of the world, and not
about the state of American foreign policy. A few of the critics offer
genuine alternatives to the approach which has been followed: the
pacifists, for example; the true isolationists; those who favor all-out
ideological war to extirpate the heresy of Communism; and those
who believe that the goal of the foreign policy of the United States
should be not peace but the sword of "revolution." These views apart,
however, the remaining critics fail to define an alternative major
premise for foreign policy. Their vocabulary is different from that of
Dean Rusk or Henry Kissinger. Their books ring with eloquent de-
nunciations of nearly all that has been done since 1945. But when
one reads the fine print and puts aside the rhetoric, the literature divides itself into two classes. Some writers never succeed in articulat-
ing a coherent policy at all. And the others, for all their anger, turn
out in fact to be advocating the same policies that have been pursued since World War II—the patient, costly effort to organize coalitions that could achieve a balance of power in world politics, and
a system of politics consonant with it.

Despite the scale, intensity, and confusion of the debate about
foreign policy now raging in the United States, I therefore conclude
—although here perhaps "hope" would be a more exact word—that
American opinion on foreign policy will continue to be dominated

by our instinct for self-preservation. By that I mean that in the end American policy, like that of every other major nation which has survived the stresses of human history, will rest on an awareness of the need to achieve and maintain a balance of power in world politics. On analysis, the literature about foreign policy offers no real alternative. American policy will rest as well on the realization that the United States must now take primary responsibility in the effort to reach that goal, since Britain and France do not have the capacity to do so as they did before 1914.

I do not mean to suggest that American policy since 1947 will be projected in a straight line during the 1970s, without ebbs and flows. The country is frustrated and angry about having had to have a foreign policy for the last twenty-five years, and there is a strong impulse to withdraw, to reexamine our commitments, to anguish over the nature of the world. That mood is dangerous. It can lead to a policy as flaccid as that we pursued in the age of stupidity between the wars, or to an outburst of rage that could carry the world much closer to Armageddon. At a minimum, it produces an atmosphere of hesitation and uncertainty which multiplies the risk of miscalculations on the one hand, and of "too little and too late" on the other.

This premise, however debatable, is no more than a point of beginning. It tells us nothing about how particular problems will be resolved nor where the United States and its chief allies, Western Europe and Japan, will decide to draw lines of resistance to the changing and turbulent tides of Soviet and Chinese expansion. After all, it is important to recall that the map of Europe, and of world politics, would be different today if President Truman had reacted to Soviet policy earlier than he did, and insisted that the Potsdam and Yalta agreements be carried out, or, later on, if he had prevented the takeover of Czechoslovakia in 1948, while we still had a nuclear monopoly. These accidents of history are no comfort to the Czechs, the Poles, and the other peoples of Eastern Europe, who live in slavery as a result.

Democracies are notoriously slow in perceiving danger. The moral of Churchill's career and of his books cannot be repeated too often: the tragedy of both world wars could have been prevented by alert and insightful Allied policy, willing to act on the available evidence in time.

All I mean, then, by my assumption of general continuity in

American foreign policy is that we should exclude the possibility of a suicidal attempt, like that of 1920–41, to escape down the rabbit hole into the nineteenth century. It does not follow that risks will be dealt with or tragedies averted any better during the next ten years than has been the case since 1945. Nor does it follow that citizen efforts at education in this field and vigilant public concern with the conduct of foreign relations can be relaxed on the assumption that all will be well automatically.

To the contrary, my view is that the danger to peace is greater now than in the late 1940s and that citizen programs of education and political action are more urgently needed than at any time since the 1930s.

II

What is implied by the hypothesis that American foreign policy will continue to be dominated by a concern for national interests, and that the balance of power is the principal national interest of the United States in world politics today?

In this perspective there can be no distinction between "conservatives" and "liberals," or between a "conservative" and a "liberal" foreign policy. These are important words, to which many are passionately attached. They suggest real differences of outlook and temperament about many problems—the perfectability of man, and the proper boundaries between order and liberty, for example—and the strength of one's response to the appeal of tradition and reform. But they have no application to foreign policy. Foreign policy can be wise or foolish; realistic or quixotic; too zealous or not zealous enough; measured or intemperate; too slow or too fast. But there is no meaning in the usage that describes some foreign policies as "liberal" or "idealistic" and others as "conservative" or "cynical."

In this realm the only appropriate standard, as Justice Holmes pointed out long ago in another connection, is what makes sense. Citizens who are genuinely liberal or genuinely conservative about many issues of domestic life can come together with equal conviction behind policies intended to protect the safety, prosperity, and freedom of the nation.

What is the national interest of the United States in world politics today?

President Washington warned the nation against foreign entanglements. But his admonition was not intended to be absolute. The United States should not commit itself, he urged, "in the ordinary vicissitudes of [world] politics, or the ordinary combinations and collisions of [its] friendships and enmities." But he and his contemporaries knew from vivid experience that the safety, and indeed the existence of the United States, necessarily depended upon the effective functioning of the balance of power, and that we had to be concerned with extraordinary events which threatened the vitality of that balance. It was not by accident that these astute men sought French help in their revolution against British rule and then turned to France's rivals when they (and the French) had won. They knew too that the Bourbon king of France had not supported the American revolutionaries because he was a secret republican at heart. Like Palmerston, they understood that nations have interests, not friends.

Washington's precepts measure our interest in world politics today as wisely as they did in the period when potential threats were calculated in terms of the speed of sailing vessels.

The goal of American foreign policy, I suggest, is a system of world politics assuring a state of general peace, a system within which the United States could continue to develop as a free and democratic society. American democracy can be safe at home, to recall a speech by Senator J. W. Fulbright, only in a world of wide horizons, organized under the charter of the United Nations—a world of balanced power, tolerant of different social systems, flexible in allowing and encouraging social progress, but free of the threat of change achieved by external force. There can be no safety, no national freedom, and little future for democracy in the United States if we are forced to live as a garrison in Fortress America, hemmed in by missiles, alone and armed to the teeth in a world of hostile or resigned states.

At a minimum, therefore, the most primitive and direct national interests of the United States require it to help restore and preserve a balance of power in the world and to establish a political process through which basic rules of public order would be respected and generally enforced.

No such system of law and politics now exists. And no system meeting this standard can conceivably be developed without powerful, sustained, and difficult efforts by the United States. The struggle to achieve a system of this kind is not an act of benevolence on the part of the United States, but one of self-preservation in the most fundamental sense—self-preservation as a nation, and as a free society.

The present array of power and ambition in the world and the prevalence of ideas glorifying the international use of force as an instrument of national and ideological aggrandizement make the task of peace more difficult, and more problematical, than at any time since the first decade of this century.

Why isn't immunity from invasion a sufficient measure of national safety? Why can't America be safe at home behind a shield of ICBMs and Polaris submarines? Because it is extremely doubtful whether nuclear weapons can be used. The nuclear deterrent has to be preserved, in a condition of nuclear stalemate at least, as a safeguard against nuclear blackmail. But after Hiroshima no American president could bring himself to use nuclear weapons unless hideously pressed, and even then the issue would be in doubt. Uncertainty about the use of nuclear weapons can be a deterrent in situations of ultimate tension, like the Cuban missile crisis. But the Soviets cannot believe that the United States would risk using nuclear weapons to prevent one more slice being taken off the salami. During the years between 1945 and the middle 1950s the American nuclear monopoly did not prevent Soviet takeover in Eastern Europe or the Soviet threats to Iran, Greece, Turkey, and Korea. Nor has nuclear stalemate, more recently, prevented progressive Soviet or Chinese penetration in the Middle East, Southeast Asia, and elsewhere. And if we were to arrive at the final nuclear redoubt, surrounded by an overpowering array of passive, neutral, or hostile nations and divided at home by plausible appeals for "cooperation" and "compromise," would we then opt for *Götterdämmerung* and use nuclear weapons, knowing that we should be bombed in return? Or would we bitterly accept the wave of the future?

The answer, I think, is obvious. The vision of safety under siege in Fortress America is a terrible illusion.

Thus far the balance of nuclear forces has neutralized nuclear power as a credible diplomatic influence, save perhaps during crises where major passions are deeply engaged. The preservation of that balance, and of the nuclear stalemate which it brings about, must remain the first task of American foreign and defense policy. It is a task of far-reaching implications, since nuclear technology never stops changing and the stalemate must be monitored from more and more distant and sometimes exotic stations. But, as Hans Speier has written, if the Soviet Union accomplishes a technological break-through in the military field or surpasses the United States in nuclear power, "it might not be necessary for the Soviet Union to wage war in order to reach its political objective. It could 'win' by creating and exploiting the fear of nuclear war in a far more effective manner than it has done in the past . . . Recklessness may replace prudence at any time in high places. Nor have passion and error been eliminated from human affairs merely because man can afford less than ever not to be reasonable and prudent." [2]

The nuclear weapon, then, does not radically change the problem of maintaining peace. It complicates it with a new dimension. But it remains true, now as in the past, that to minimize the possibility of general war and to maximize the possibility of remaining a free and democratic nation at home, the United States has no choice but to function in world politics at two levels—one, that of conventional diplomacy and conventional weapons, seeking to gain general acceptance for a stable equilibrium based on understood limits for international conflict; the other, which affects the first but is distinct from it, the level of nuclear deterrence and nuclear control.

It is often said that the existence of nuclear weapons makes any form of warfare between the nuclear powers impossible. Thus far, indeed, no such warfare has broken out. But the assumption cannot be treated as an iron rule. The United States and the USSR were close to a clash with conventional weapons, *not* nuclear weapons, during the Cuban missile crisis. And comparable risks can readily be imagined elsewhere. The heart of the matter in Soviet-American crises since the war is that thus far neither country has fired the first shot at the forces of the other. The Soviet Union did not itself fire on American forces in Berlin, in Korea, in the waters off Cuba, or in Vietnam. Correspondingly, the United States did not use force against Soviet troops operating in Eastern Europe. This powerful restraint makes the chess of crisis management par-

---

[2] Hans Speier, *Force and Folly* (Cambridge, Mass.: M.I.T. Press, 1969), p. 4.

ticularly important, in putting a premium, perhaps a critical premium, on the effective and credible deployment of forces in advance.

The dynamics of this process are generally assumed to extend at least to the chief allies of each major country—to the Communist nations of Eastern Europe, in the case of the Soviet Union, and to Western Europe and Japan, at a minimum, in the case of the United States.

Here again, assumptions based upon the pattern of the past may be unreliable for the future.

A policy of deterring the first shot is the underlying reason why the nations of Western Europe, which often appear to believe that a modus vivendi with the Soviet Union has already been achieved, are so insistent on the continued presence of American conventional forces in Europe. The United States agrees, but for another reason: the presence of substantial American and allied conventional strength in Europe, Japan, and elsewhere is indispensable, not only as a symbol which might continue to inhibit the first shot, but to make it possible to respond to crises through non-nuclear means. The worst of diplomatic nightmares for the Soviet Union or the United States would be to confront an absolute choice between retreat and the use of nuclear weapons. This is the tension which led ultimately to the resolution of the Korean conflict and should in the end have the same impact in Vietnam.

In short, it is erroneous to assume that a balance of power can be achieved or maintained without deterrent balance at every level, military and diplomatic. There can be no meaning in a policy of reliance on "massive retaliation."

It is often said that the concept of the balance of power is immoral and should not be the foundation for the foreign policy of an idealistic nation. But the principle of the balance of power is the key to any system of law, domestic or international, that seeks to assure liberty in peace. It is the idea behind federalism, the separation of powers, and the anti-trust laws in American constitutional usage. For world politics it is the only alternative to international anarchy, on the one hand, or to a Roman solution for the problem of international peace, on the other. I cannot understand why international peace and its correlative principle of not interfering in the internal affairs of other states—the two basic principles of the

United Nations Charter—should be regarded as lacking in "idealism," or as an unworthy or immoral goal for the foreign policy of the United States. The balance of power remains the only available means for achieving these ends. There simply is no alternative, save prayer.

III

The magnetic field of world politics for the 1970s is arranged in different configurations from those of 1919, 1939, or 1947. The nature and the distribution of power and the character of international politics are changing, and changing rapidly. In the 1830s de Tocqueville saw that Russia and America would become giants in world affairs, as Napoleon did a generation earlier. De Tocqueville and Napoleon did not, however, foresee the development of China and Japan, the decline of Europe, the end of empire, and the emergence of many of the newer threats to the possibility of peace.

I can detect nothing in the pattern of change which would allow the United States an easy escape from the kind of policy it has pursued since 1947. Like the pain of making a living, in Dean Acheson's phrase, the job of safeguarding the interests of the nation in a changing world is endless. There is no simple cure for it, no aspirin that could make it go away. Congressional resolutions cannot repeal the fact that hostile and expansionist powers are pursuing programs that would radically alter the balance of power and leave the United States isolated on its own continent. Great shifts in the balance of power have always drawn the United States into war. There is no reason to doubt that Thucydides' maxim still applies to the affairs of men; what made the Peloponnesian War inevitable, he wrote, was not the episodes of conflict which preceded it, but "the growth of Athenian power, and the fear which this caused in Sparta."

The best, indeed the only, cure for the emergence of such fear as a fever is to prevent the convulsions which are its cause—to continue to insist on the achievement of a reasonably stable system of peace in world politics, based on a dispersal of power and the enforcement of understood rules as to the limits of rivalry.

Many who accept this premise as a valid definition of the purpose of American foreign policy often add that times have changed since the late 1940s when Truman and Acheson laid down the broad lines of the foreign policy the United States has followed ever since. They point out that the Communist movements of the world are no longer so tightly controlled as was the case then, implying that they are less of a threat to the balance of power than they were in Truman's time. Of course the division among Communist parties and nations offers Western diplomacy certain opportunities, but it by no means guarantees their success. The pressure of Soviet or Chinese ambition (or Cuban influence and example) is still felt in many parts of the world. In each case it attempts to harness to its cause local revolutionary impulses and more diffuse feelings of violent protest. That pressure, backed by arrays of conventional and nuclear force and the full panoply of political, psychological, and guerrilla warfare, has increased in intensity since the Sino-Soviet split. It is hardly obvious why the pressures arising from the rivalry of several revolutionary parties, movements, and nations should be easier for the West to manage and contain than was the case when the world Communist movement was firmly under Soviet control. Both in economics and in labor relations, competition, even among the few, is hardly less turbulent and dynamic than monopoly or duopoly.

The interplay of these factors and rivalries has become the central theme of world politics.

The primary pattern in the magnetic field of world politics for the next ten years or so is what is often called the Sino-Soviet-American triangle. It would be more accurate to describe it as a pentagon, including Japan and Western Europe as among the principals, although it should remain a primary goal of American policy to maintain, and indeed to consolidate, its alliances with Western Europe and Japan.

The Soviet Union is allied with the nations of Eastern Europe, save for Albania and Yugoslavia; with Cuba; and with Syria, Egypt, and other Middle Eastern states. It has developed and will continue to develop close relations with India. It will surely seek to establish at least a cooperative, and conceivably an allied regime in China, as opportunity may occur or be created.

It is fashionable in Western Europe and the United States to believe that the cold war is over, that détente prevails, and that the

Soviet Union is pursuing a policy of collaboration with the West, both in the field of nuclear arms and on other issues. I have been unable to find any evidence to support such a view. True, the NATO governments no longer engage in vituperation against the Soviet Union. But Soviet propaganda, at home and abroad, is still written in vitriol. We have simply stopped listening.

Limited agreements with the Soviet Union, particularly in the field of nuclear weapons, have been achieved, and others may still be achieved: it is decidedly in the Soviet interest to induce the United States to reduce its military and research expenditure—for only then could the Soviet Union limit its own armaments budget —and prevent Europe, Japan, and some other countries from becoming nuclear powers. Michel Debré, when he was Minister of Finance, once remarked that what the world needed most was a trade union of finance ministers to suppress the scientists. Like every other country, the Soviet Union complains from time to time about the rising cost of military technology.

Thus the possibility of nuclear agreement is kept alive while the Soviet Union pursues a policy of imperial expansion based on ambitious programs of military expansion, particularly striking in the fields of sea power, space technology, and nuclear energy. The build-up of Soviet sea and air power, and of nuclear and other advanced military technologies, has no parallel in world politics since the Kaiser's bid to challenge Britain on the seas during the years before World War I. Nuclear warfare has been avoided in the period since 1945 because the persistent pressure for the expansion of Soviet control has paused before an occasional American threat of reprisal with overwhelming force. But Soviet energy presses outward, patient and ingenious, flowing around obstacles, taking advantage of every opening. It can be stopped only by the calm deployment of unacceptable risks.

The underlying balance of forces is changing as the West flags. The nature of Soviet pressure is changing as well. Soviet policies of expansion are far more sophisticated and difficult to contain today than was the case in 1949, when they were no more than the glacial outward movement of a land mass—first in Iran and Turkey, then in Greece and Berlin, then in Korea. A direct invasion of Europe is not now a serious possibility, at least while there are strong NATO conventional forces in being. But Europe has been outflanked in the Mediterranean, and in the northern seas as well, by a process of penetration which poses major problems for the defense of allied interests in the Mediterranean and the Middle East, in Iceland, in Norway, and in Europe as a whole. The true Soviet goal in Western Europe, one would suppose, is not occupation, Polish style, but West European neutrality and disarmament and American withdrawal both from the continent and from the Mediterranean.

In the perspective of American policy, the conflicts in the Middle East should be viewed in these terms. The Middle Eastern crisis is not an Arab-Israeli conflict or a conflict among different tendencies in Arab politics. It is a NATO crisis, an attempt to drive the United States out of Europe, to dismantle NATO, and thus to bring the resources and energies of Western Europe under effective Soviet control. Arab hostility to the existence of Israel is exploited as a catalyst for the process of Soviet expansion in North Africa and the Near East. Unless peace on American terms is achieved in the Middle East—that is, peace under the Security Council resolution of November 22, 1967—and achieved soon, no conceivable combination of events, short of major war involving the United States, could forestall Soviet predominance in the area, which President Nixon has declared it to be a vital national interest of the United States to prevent.

In the Far East, Soviet policy has been caught up in a dilemma whose contradictions were evident in the conflicts over Korea, Indonesia, and Vietnam and are now brought into even more vivid and portentous focus by the Soviet quarrel with China. The dilemma is implicit in the basic problem of the balance of world power. If Soviet control expands too quickly or too far, as was the case in Korea, it may stir a response from the United States, Japan, and Europe, or from China, or from all together. But if the Soviet Union moves to abate the risk, it will be charged with revisionism and collusion with the West, and may lose to China, or to Communist parties oriented to China, its leadership in the world-wide movement of revolutionary impulse, which in many parts of the world is a powerful and attractive tool of imperial expansion.

The United States and the Soviet Union have parallel national interests in limiting Chinese expansion. Consciousness of those interests dominated Soviet and American policy toward India after the Chinese demonstration on the Indian frontier in 1962. That policy of parallelism ended, for fundamental reasons, when the Soviet Union supported the Indian attack on Pakistan in 1971, following the Bengali revolt in East Pakistan nine months earlier and its suppression by the Pakistani government. From the point of view of national interests, the Soviet Union should likewise have collaborated with the United States with regard to Indochina, insisting on the inviolability of the arrangements for French Indochina which emerged from the Geneva Conference in 1954 and were confirmed by the Soviet agreement with the United States over Laos in 1962. But the attractions of American misery in the Vietnam morass were irresistible to Soviet policy makers. Perhaps they concluded that the United States had been so irreparably weakened and paralyzed by its internal debate over foreign policy that its interests could be ignored. They may also have been concerned that China would have moved into North Vietnam if Soviet influence were weakened or withdrawn, as had proved to be the case in North Korea fifteen years before. In the event, the Soviets supported North Vietnam's effort to change the Geneva arrangements by force and refused to liquidate the adventure, as they did finally in Korea, when, between 1968 and 1971, North Vietnam failed to win its war.

In recent years the Soviet Union has increased both its nuclear capability and its conventional military presence on all fronts—in Siberia and Outer Mongolia, in Central Europe, in the Mediterranean, in the Atlantic and the Indian oceans. It apparently believes that it has restrained China by nuclear threats, or at least imposed limits on Chinese policy for the next few years, before Chinese nuclear weapons could constitute a major threat to the Soviet Union. To take advantage of this short period of time, the Soviet Union has been pressing a bold and risky strategy in the Mediterranean and in Europe, in order to achieve the disintegration of NATO and the withdrawal of United States forces from Europe and the Middle East before it faces the probability of a showdown with China. In Europe and the Middle East, Soviet policy has recently had a new urgency, which can be explained only as a policy of pressing for the neutralization of Europe and the end of NATO while China is still relatively weak, the United States weary and uncertain after the ordeal of Vietnam, and Europe still not genuinely united as a political and military force.

This Soviet policy, as the British say, has proved to be "too clever by half." Its consequences are potentially disastrous for the Soviets. Their tactical success in Vietnam has led to strategic failure in a larger theater. By building up their conventional and nuclear forces in Siberia to a level of clear and present threat and by expanding their presence in Southeast Asia, they forced China to turn to the United States as the only power on earth that could deter a Soviet attack on China itself. For China and the United States have parallel interests in limiting Soviet expansion, exactly like the interests the United States and the Soviet Union share in limiting Chinese expansion. The heavy Soviet hand in Siberia and the increasing Soviet threat to China from India, the Middle East, and Southeast Asia have compelled China to change its foreign policy, for the time being at least, in order to obtain American backing and thus persuade the Soviet Union that its nuclear and non-nuclear threats against China involve unacceptable risks.

In 1971 China moved dramatically to obtain American support against the Soviet Union. Naturally, it will seek to pay as little as possible for American efforts to prevent Soviet aggression against China. But it is inconceivable that help so vital to Chinese security should not involve at least a Vietnam settlement compatible with American policy, a Taiwan settlement which respects long-standing American commitments and Japanese and American security interests, and an understanding about Korea based on the principles and interests which led the West to resist the conquest of South Korea in 1950. The Chinese government has explained its approach to the United States in terms of an article by Mao Tse-tung published in 1940. Just as it was proper then to seek American help against Japan, the article contends, so it is proper now to unite "with forces that can be united with while isolating and hitting at the most obdurate enemies." [3] Thus, the Chinese argue, it is entirely compatible with revolutionary principles to obtain help from an imperialist power not now committing aggression against China in order to confront the imperialism that presents the greatest danger to the country.

This major event illustrates the classical mechanism of the balance of power at work. The potentialities of conflict between two powers, or two power groups, must take into account the possibility

---

[3] Quoted in *The New York Times*, August 22, 1971, Sec. I, p. 5, col. 1.

of reaction by a third. The Soviet Union must be concerned about Chinese reactions if it becomes dangerously involved in Europe or the Middle East, and about American, Japanese, and NATO reactions, as well as the risk of rebellions in its Central European empire, if it should undertake to destroy the Chinese nuclear establishment or become embroiled with China in other ways. Equally, China cannot expect to obtain American, European, and Japanese backing to head off the rising threat from the Soviet Union unless it accepts and respects the interests of those nations.

The most appropriate posture for the United States in this crisis is that stated by Acheson in his famous and controversial speech after the withdrawal of American forces from Korea in 1949. He said that no person can guarantee areas where there is no American military presence against attack, but "should such an attack occur . . . the initial reliance must be on the people attacked to resist it and then upon the commitments of the entire civilized world under the Charter of the United Nations"—a formula whose potential was demonstrated in Korea.

The tensions of this triangular relation, which during the next decade should also involve Europe and Japan as effective allies of the United States, offer great hope for a degree of peace which could meet the security needs of the United States. The dynamics of response and counter-response require both China and the Soviet Union to confront the fact that there are limits to imperial expansion. Under the circumstances of modern life, the path of wisdom and prudence is that of stalemate, stability, détente, and peaceful coexistence under the rules of the United Nations Charter. We must assume that these will remain the major goals of American foreign policy in the decade ahead—goals the United States will continue to seek through patient and sustained diplomatic effort, necessarily backed by force in being. Policy cannot assume that these goals have already been achieved.

IV

The goals of American foreign policy in the third world are the true center of the debate about the future of that policy. Most critics of recent foreign policy concede the national interests of the United States in protecting the independence of Western Europe and of Japan, great centers of power whose transfer to Soviet or Chinese control would affect the national safety. And most understand as well the interest of the United States in a rapprochement with China and with the Soviet Union or, if rapprochement is not possible, in achieving a state of stabilized tension in the magnetic field of their interrelationships.

But the conviction that the troubles of the third world do not concern the security of the United States is the simple and imperative theme that runs through much of the literature.

Some put the thesis in terms of power politics. These men say that the safety of the United States requires only that we keep Western Europe and Japan out of hostile hands. A few go further. They believe that considerations of security require us to prevent the hostile control only of the Ruhr Valley and similarly strategic regions. Hostile control of the rest of the world's geography could not harm us, they think. The cold war between the United States and the Soviet Union is over, or nearly over, these men say hopefully. Alternatively, they comfort themselves with the thought that the world Communist movement is no longer a "monolith" directed from Moscow. From this, they infer that the emplacement in developing countries of regimes calling themselves Communist does not raise the specter of a great octopus enveloping the West in its coils, even when those regimes allow Soviet military bases to be established. Besides, they claim, the third world is and will remain too weak to constitute a threat to the security of the United States and should not be a matter of concern even if the Communist movement regained its unity and discipline. Anyway, the world is so full of turbulence that no one hostile power or combination of hostile powers would in fact be able to dominate the third world, or at least dominate it for long.

Others reach the same conclusion by a different route. The third world is floundering, they say, and cannot achieve progress without a "revolution." From the point of view of suffering humanity, the United States should stop supporting reactionary or inadequate regimes in countries of the third world and should embrace the revolution. Writers like Carl Oglesby and Noam Chomsky support this view because they identify themselves with the idea of revolution and with that of socialism. Senator J. W. Fulbright and Hans J. Morgenthau do not regard themselves as socialists or revolutionaries, but they are inclined to think that the nonindustrialized countries need a socialist revolution.

For another group of writers, the angry conviction of third world "irrelevance" expresses racial and ethnic antipathy or disillusion with the spotty achievement of development aid programs in many parts of Asia, Africa, and Latin America. For others, it represents the view that however desirable it might be to hold back the tide of Communist advance in the third world, it cannot be done, and we had therefore better give up wasting our substance in the effort.

Whatever its source, the opinion is widespread: the United States should get out of the third world and stay out. No more Koreas, and no more Vietnams. Revoke and denounce the commitments to the third world made during Eisenhower's administration. And then let nature take its course. We should resolve to stand aloof and, like a reformed alcoholic, resist every temptation to intervene.

Men of this persuasion often start their books by pointing out that there are some reasonably stable factors in world politics today: (1) the nuclear standoff between the United States and the Soviet Union makes nuclear warfare between them unthinkable, and the shadow of nuclear escalation makes it unlikely (or most unlikely, or nearly impossible) for them to engage in conventional warfare with each other; (2) nonetheless, nuclear guarantees by the superpowers retain a certain credibility, at least when backed by the presence of conventional forces and underlined at intervals by demonstrations of will. As a result, spheres of influence genuinely exist—regions where one of the superpowers has indicated a strong state interest which the others are willing to recognize or have been forced to recognize. Thus most people assume that neither the Soviet Union nor China would use force or the threat of force in Western Europe, Korea, or Japan. And it is obvious that the corresponding assumption is safe with regard to Western intentions in Eastern Europe and, a fortiori, in China, Cuba, and the Soviet Union themselves.

In this perspective, these American and European critics say, why should our countries concern themselves with the third world? We are safe. No one will invade or bomb us, or send us to Siberia or to concentration camps. The fate of the third world is not worth the life of one of our soldiers.

Even if one accepts, for the moment, the hypothesis of indefinite standoff in the relationship between the great powers, at least so far as the use of nuclear weapons and conventional military force is concerned, what role does the third world play in the ambitions of the Soviet Union, of China, and of other Communist states dreaming about expansion?

Khrushchev once answered the question in an interview with James Reston. Nuclear wars are impossible, he said: the nuclear weapon doesn't respect class differences. After Korea, conventional warfare is too dangerous. Therefore, he concluded, Communist states must rely on wars of national liberation to carry the revolution forward, especially in the third world.

The difficulty is that many parts of the third world are protected by public declarations and demonstrations of Western interest quite as formal as the North Atlantic Treaty or the corresponding American commitments to Korea and Japan. The need for military and communications facilities, shared economic interests, long-standing historical ties, and powerful links of nationhood, religion, and tribe connect America and Europe to many nations in Asia and Africa, and of course in Central and South America as well. These connections are often suffused with the kind of emotional intensity that could detonate war—for example, the feeling in Britain, Canada, and the United States about Australia and New Zealand. And, as Professor Albert Wohlstetter has shown, technology is reducing the significance of distance as rapidly for security calculations as for economic affairs. No program of security, either by way of nuclear or non-nuclear deterrence, can today be autarchic or regional.

Thus far, however, the Soviet Union, China, and Cuba, separately, and in various combinations, have not respected Western commitments in the third world as they are sometimes assumed to respect the American commitments to Western Europe, Japan, or South Korea. They continue to sponsor or to threaten international attacks on many of the nations of the third world to whom the West has pledged its full support. Indeed, the pace of such campaigns has increased in recent years. These attacks draw on the full armory of modern guerrilla warfare, using both violence and political and psychological weapons. They involve proxy wars and guerrilla wars, kidnappings, assassinations, bombings, and bank robberies. In 1971 Mexico sent away half the Soviet embassy staff, on the charge that campaigns of this kind were being directed from the embassy itself.

Is this process of national concern to the United States, Europe, and Japan?

V

The Middle East offers a good opportunity to test the implications of the argument for an American withdrawal from the third world and for a policy of confining our overseas security commitments to Europe and Japan at most.

Every region of the third world does not, of course, have exactly the same bearing as the Middle East on the security of the United States. But they all have features in common, in different configurations, and they all raise common questions, although with differing degrees of urgency.

The Middle East is an anthology of the security problems that arise in the third world. The eastern Mediterranean—the locus of "the Eastern Question"—has always been a buffer zone, and therefore a theater of rivalry, on the international frontier between the spheres of influence of rival great powers. It has been a central theme of European security and diplomacy at least since the times of Cyrus the Great and Alexander. The Romans endured endless trouble in the East, including a bitter guerrilla war with the Jews which required a quarter of their legions. And they did not feel secure until they had invested both Carthage and Egypt and occupied the Levant. The Crusades represent one aspect of the Eastern Question for European security, the Battle of Lepanto another. The Arab invasion was as important to European history as the invasions of the Normans and the Mongols. Turkey was a problem while the Ottoman Empire was strong, and a worse problem when it began to disintegrate. Fighting and showing the flag in North Africa and the Middle East were among the earliest duties of the American navy. The competitive jostling for position of the European rivals in the Balkans led to a succession of small wars in the late nineteenth and early twentieth centuries, and then, of course, to World War I itself. After that war, Turkey lost more of its European territories and its non-Turkish possessions in the Near East were divided between France and Britain. As a result, French and British military forces were installed along the Mediterranean from Syria to Morocco, except for the Italian colony of Cirenaica, and in considerable depth beyond, especially in Jordan, Iraq, the Persian Gulf, and southern Arabia.

During the thirteen years after World War II, however, France and Britain withdrew from every one of their Mediterranean positions. Inevitably, new constellations of force appeared to fill the vacuums.

The competition of rival national claims to territory formerly within the Ottoman Empire has dominated the recent history of the region. Indeed, that story is more than a hundred years old. Now, as in earlier times, local conflicts and enmities, bitter in themselves, become irreconcilable when linked to the conflicting aspirations and fears of world powers.

The Algerian revolt against France in the 1950s and the effort of Egypt to eliminate the British presence in that country led to long and dangerous conflicts in which Soviet, American, French, and British policy played varying roles. The relative harmony of British, French, and American policy in the Middle East was shattered by the disaster of Suez, which left the Soviet Union and the United States virtually alone, for practical purposes, as great-power arbiters in the conflicts of the region. Since the end of the Algerian affair the Soviet Union has held center stage in the Middle East, playing in a melodrama—the fate of Israel—that could easily become a tragedy. There are other currents of rivalry in the Middle East which the Soviet Union has sought to exploit—Nasser's dream of Arab unity, for example, which frightened many who preferred their own nationhood. But all these themes of the story are influenced in turn by the explosive forces which radiate from the conflict over Israel.

The history of Israel and the history of Arab nationalism—the nominal protagonists—have been decisively influenced at very stage by the conjunctures of world politics. The Balfour Declaration was, among other things, an episode of World War I. During the same period Arab nationalism was given great impetus by the British campaign against Turkey and by the Arab response to the implications of Balfour's famous statement. Both movements made their political debuts in the Middle East after World War I—Zionism in the development of the Jewish community within the British mandated territory of Palestine; Arab nationalism in the politics of Trans-Jordan, Saudi Arabia, and Palestine itself. As Arab anxiety about the size and energy of the Jewish community in Palestine became more acute, representatives of nearby states became involved in behalf of the Arab Palestinians, and in their own behalf. These political moves, which helped to deepen the consciousness of Arab nationalism, were addressed both to the authorities within Palestine and to the League of Nations, which established committees to grapple with the thorny conflict.

After a period of relatively slow growth during the 1920s, Jewish immigration to Palestine increased rapidly when Hitler came to power. By the end of the 1930s the Jewish population of Palestine had reached 30 percent. The anxiety and hostility of many Arabs became more pronounced. With the end of the World War II, most of the Jews who had survived the massacre wished to leave the charnel house of Central Europe. The larger part headed for Palestine, only to confront the desperate rigidity of British immigration policy, paralyzed by the competing pressures of compassion and fear. The yearning of the displaced Jews of Central Europe for Palestine was an irresistible force. So was the resistance of the Arabs to their coming. Attacks began on Jewish populations which had lived for many centuries in North Africa and the Near East. They too began the trek to Palestine.

Violence and counterviolence made Palestine nearly ungovernable. And these developments occurred at a time when Britain was liquidating its empire and the security positions it had established to protect its imperial communications. In 1947 Britain passed the Greek baton to the United States. At the same time, it gave up the mandate it had received from the League of Nations twenty-five years earlier and remitted Palestine to the United Nations.

Anglo-American and United Nations committees studied the problem. Their deliberations were overwhelmed by passionate emotions: shock at what had occurred in the German concentration camps, just beginning to sear the consciousness of the world, and fear that too large a flow of displaced persons into their own countries could produce socially dangerous counterreactions. The war had been won at immense cost. The Western nations were not yet confident that their societies were immune to the diseases which had raged so virulently in Germany, Italy, France, and Eastern Europe.

The result, backed by the enthusiasm which the Zionist ideal has always aroused in many Christian spirits, especially in Protestant communities, was the United Nations partition resolution of 1947. The Zionists supported the resolution, which, despite its many inadequacies from their point of view, held out the vision of a Jewish state. For the Arabs, the resolution was a high-handed attempt by the United Nations to give away territory which did not belong to them, but to the people who lived there. By the laws of natural justice, by the principles contained in the Covenant of the League and the United Nations Charter, the Arabs argued, the people of Palestine, and they alone, had rights of self-determination, which the General Assembly could not abrogate or ignore. With the end of the British mandate, an inchoate Palestinian nation had come into being. The fighting was internal to that "nation," and the United Nations should not, and legally could not, interfere.

But the world community, convened in the General Assembly, reached another conclusion. History had thrust jurisdiction upon the United Nations. There was the reality of the mandate and of the Jewish community which had formed in Palestine under the protection of the League. And there was another reality as well—the prospect of war, if nothing was done, a prospect which affected the most important responsibility of the organization, that of peace keeping. It chose, therefore, to ordain a partition of the territory of the mandate, and called for the establishment of separate Arab and Jewish states, joined in economic union, and of a separate regime for Jerusalem.

By another coincidence of world politics, the Soviet Union was willing to join the United States in supporting the resolution, which the Arabs had plainly said they would resist with force. The Soviet vote in the General Assembly, and Soviet arms shipments to Israel, reflected their policies of postwar expansion and their correlative interest in pushing Britain and France out of their strong points along the shores of the Mediterranean.

Thus Israel emerged into the society of nations—an active community which had become a state. Nominally, it was established by a decision of the United Nations, acting with regard to trust territories administered under its authority. In fact, like so many other nations, it was born in the travail of war--a war which those who voted for the partition resolution should have known was inevitable unless they acted, yet with shocking irresponsibility did nothing to prevent.

The war of 1948–49 resulted in armistice agreements between Israel and Egypt, Jordan, Syria, and Lebanon—the only political documents thus far negotiated and signed by those states. The agreements were the product of conferences under United Nations auspices held at Rhodes in 1949. Those conferences, in turn, met because the Israelis made it clear that hostilities would be resumed unless the Arab nations, and above all Egypt, obeyed the Security Council's call that the parties agree on an armistice.

The war of 1948–49 had many other results, both in the Middle East and in world politics. The Arab refugee problem emerged, a burden, a curse, and a weapon of politics and of war. After the failure of the Lausanne Conference twenty years ago, the Arab policy of not making peace with Israel crystallized and became a dogma, keeping alive the dream and hope of revenge. In turn, Israel became convinced that it was surrounded by neighbors committed to its destruction and supported in their ambition by the growing power of the Soviet Union. Israel developed its defense capacities accordingly. With the defeat of British policy, the United States became more involved, both out of sympathy for Israel and as part of the process of assuming Western leadership in a cold war which had already required it to act in Iran, Turkey, and Greece, and to undertake the obligations of the North Atlantic Treaty.

In 1956, once again, the processes of macropolitics dominated events in the Middle East. The Soviet Union had changed sides since 1947. Nasser had come to power, and started on an ambitious course of nationalist expansion incompatible with British or American policy. Understanding this fact, Nasser approached the Soviet Union well before the celebrated episodes of 1955—the Aswan Dam affair, the Israeli raid in the Gaza Strip, and the American refusal of arms to Egypt—which are popularly supposed to have led Nasser to seek Soviet support. Nasser and the Soviet Union were indispensable to each other's plans of expansion, and their alliance was a matter of deliberate choice. With Soviet support Nasser could resist Western advice or pressure. He nationalized the Suez Canal, outraging both France and Britain, and he closed the Strait of Tiran, thus blockading Israel from the south. France had another grievance against Egypt—Egyptian support for the rebels in Algeria, in the tragic war which was straining the fabric of French life. After Nasser refused a French request to desist from his course, France resolved to act, and turned to Israel as well as to Britain. Thus the three states with acute grievances against Egypt came together in the ill-fated Suez campaign.

That event caused many changes in the politics of the Middle

East, and of the world. Britain and France fell back; the United States and the Soviet Union moved forward. Israel was perceived to be more formidable than many had realized before. With increasing emphasis, Nasser claimed the mantle of leadership in the cause of Pan-Arab unity, asserting his influence in many areas and arousing fear and resentment as well as exaltation in the Arab world. Thus the divisions sharpened between the radical and the traditional Arab states, with momentous change ahead in Syria and Iraq, and later in other countries as well.

This quick sketch, intended only to evoke the past, recalls the main events and trends which frame the modern Middle Eastern crisis. That crisis is now the key factor in a much larger process of political struggle.

What is the crisis about? Is it a regional quarrel which the United States, Europe, and Japan can safely ignore, or is it a matter of vital concern to their security?

The protracted conflict between Israel and some of its Arab neighbors is not the cause of the Middle Eastern crisis, but its symptom and its consequence. The heart of the crisis is the process of Soviet penetration in North Africa and the Near East. Without Soviet influence, Soviet support, and Soviet arms, there would have been peace long ago between Israel and its neighbors. The Arab states would have had no alternative but to accept Israel's right to exist.

The first goal of the Soviet campaign is to achieve strategic and tactical control of the Mediterranean, the Middle East, and the Persian Gulf area. On that footing, the next step would be to drive the United States out of Europe and the Mediterranean and to have NATO dismantled. The Middle Eastern crisis is a NATO crisis, not an Arab-Israeli quarrel. It is a fissure in the foundation of world politics—a Soviet challenge to the relationship of Western Europe and the United States, and therefore to the balance of power on which the possibility of general peace throughout the world depends.

The phrase "Middle East" is a geographical anomaly. The Middle Eastern problem extends from Morocco to Iran, from Malta, Yugoslavia, Greece, and Turkey in the north to Aden, Sudan, and beyond in the south. It is an area of major strategic importance for its oil, its space, and its utility in transportation and communications among Europe, Asia, and Africa. Those concerned with the security of Europe have always been sensitive to the dangers of hostility from Middle Eastern positions. Modern weapons and communications systems and the problem of nuclear surveillance underline the strategic pertinence of these ancient fears. Even Japan is still dependent on Middle Eastern oil, and therefore politically vulnerable to threats that its oil supply may be interrupted.

In the Middle East, as in other parts of the third world, the dissolution of empire gave rise to a large number of weak and vulnerable states, struggling to master the techniques of modern wealth and social organization. The nations of the area vary widely in wealth, political outlook, and capacity for effective self-government. They are united by ties of culture and religion, by historic memories, and above all by pride in their Arab heritage and hostility to the colonial idea. They are divided by jealousies, and their rivalries are often tinged by violence. Some are monarchies or traditional societies of an older kind; some, like Iran, Turkey, Lebanon, and Tunisia, are progressive Western societies based on capitalism; others—Syria, Algeria, and perhaps Egypt and Libya as well—are radical communities governed by one or another sect of the cult of revolution and controlled by a state apparatus which has driven older elites into exile. Almost all have military forces of increasing strength and influence, whose officers are trained either in Europe or America, or in the Soviet Union.

The most popular and inflammatory political conviction throughout the region is that the creation of Israel was an injustice to the Arabs; that Israel is the spearhead and agent of Western imperialism; and that sooner or later Israel will have to be destroyed. All must give lip service to this thesis; many believe it. In Middle Eastern conversations one is often reminded that it took a hundred years or more to drive the Crusaders away. Except for Bourguiba, no Arab leader, however moderate, dares advise his people publicly that the creation of Israel has been ratified by history and that its existence is a fact of life Arabs ought to acknowledge.

As a result, Arab policy and especially Egyptian policy since 1950 or 1951 has been one of refusal to make peace with Israel, relying—thus far successfully—on the political weight of their numbers and strategic position to induce the Western governments in the end to turn against Israel and force it to yield.

Hostility to Israel is the only political idea which can bring about Arab unity even for a short time. More important, it is a political force within every Arab community which can be used to arouse the masses and weaken or destroy moderate regimes suspected of cooperating with the West—the defenders of Israel—and of being willing to make peace with Israel. Often the show of unity, even on this issue, is superficial. Many Arab leaders would gladly make peace with Israel. They realize that the idea of revenge against Israel is sterile and self-destructive and that its true purpose is not the destruction of Israel but the radicalization of Arab politics in Jordan, Lebanon, Tunisia, Saudi Arabia, and the Persian Gulf area. But few can publicly oppose the dream of a holy war when opinion is inflamed by the call to battle.

In its modern form, the Soviet interest in the Middle East was evident in the early days of World War II. In the Ribbentrop-Molotov meeting of 1940, Ribbentrop offered the Soviets the Persian Gulf area. Molotov put his finger in the middle of the map, on Egypt. "We want this too," he is reported to have said. The first postwar crises—the warning bells of the cold war—concerned Iran, and then Turkey and Greece. But Soviet policy reached far beyond these border states, even in the period of its exhaustion at the end of the war. In 1945 the Soviets sought the mandate for what is now Libya. Then they cooperated with the United States in authorizing the establishment of the State of Israel and were an important arms supplier to Israel during its first war with the Arabs in 1948–49. Starting in 1955, Soviet policy acquired new dimensions. The Soviet Union supplied arms and later economic aid to Egypt on a large scale. In time this policy was extended to Syria, Iraq, Sudan, Algeria, and Yemen. And it led to the massive intrusion of Soviet military experts and technicians in most of these countries and, at a later stage, to a direct Soviet naval and air presence at what now seem in effect to be permanent bases in the region.

One of the Soviet Union's chief weapons in this process has been the exploitation of Arab hostility to the existence of Israel as a catalyst of turbulence and revolutionary feeling in Arab politics. There is no magic which could persuade the Arabs to give up their sense of grievance about the existence of Israel. At best, that bitter feeling will take many years to fade. It will not fade, but will become worse, if it continues to be used as an engine of radical takeover throughout the region, both by the Soviets and by their Chinese rivals.

Initially, Soviet policy was simply to push at open doors in the Middle East, as in other parts of the world. In recent years, however, it has become a much more sustained and massive affair—a genuine campaign, rather than a policy of taking advantage of opportunities on the cheap. It is no longer a shadowy feint that could be reversed without embarrassment, but a major investment of resources and prestige involving the deliberate assumption of major risks.

The Soviet arms supply and other support to Egypt were the proximate cause of the 1956 war in the area; false Soviet intelligence, coupled with massive supplies of Soviet arms, played the same role in the tragedy of 1967.

American policy in 1967 had the advantage of a comprehensive study of Western interests in the entire area against the background of Arab politics and Soviet activity. Ambassador Julius Holmes was recalled from retirement to direct the work. On the basis of that study and the policy review it precipitated, President Johnson concluded that the rising tide of Soviet penetration, and the trends in Arab politics which that penetration encouraged and fortified, threatened major American and allied interests in the region; that the Soviet presence in Syria, Egypt, Algeria, Iraq, Yemen, and Sudan already constituted a substantial threat to allied interests; and that a continuation of the process, which could involve the Nasserization of Jordan, Lebanon, Libya, Tunisia, Malta, Morocco, Saudi Arabia, and the Persian Gulf, would present the United States and NATO with a security crisis of major, and potentially catastrophic, proportions. NATO military positions were being outflanked. Communications between Europe, Africa, and Asia were threatened. A disturbing Soviet fleet roamed the Mediterranean. Oil essential to the European and Japanese economies could be used as a lever of political coercion. And the specter of an all-out attack on Israel, with its implicit risk of general war, was becoming more and more possible, even likely. The process of Soviet penetration and the phenomenon of what the Soviets call "ultra-extremism" in Arab politics were difficult to control or reverse, since penetration had rested thus far, save in Yemen, not on international aggression but seemingly on internal coups d'état, and then on political steps taken by the Arab governments themselves.

In the light of that analysis, an Arab-Israeli war was perceived not as a local conflict but as a stage in a process which threatened the security of Europe and the United States in fundamental ways. The policy conclusion that emerged was that the United States, in association with Great Britain and as many other nations as the

United States could persuade to cooperate, should undertake a major effort to prevent the war and, after twenty years of waiting, to fulfill the urgings of the Security Council, and the promises of the armistice agreements of 1949, that the parties make peace. The protection of American and allied interests—to say nothing of decency, and the moral obligations which inhere in promises on which others have relied to their hazard—demanded nothing less. Only on that footing could one hope to contain or reverse other aspects of the process of Soviet expansion threatening Europe's southern flank.

This is not the place to review the history of the Middle Eastern crisis of 1967. Suffice it to recall that the American effort to prevent the Six Day War failed, but that the analysis of the American national interest on which that effort was based became the foundation for the policy which the United States announced at the time of the fighting, and which the Security Council finally adopted on November 22, 1967.

On the first day of the Six Day War in 1967, President Johnson declared that American policy was to move not only for an end of hostilities, but for a beginning of peace. The Arab-Israeli conflict, he said two weeks later, had become a burden and a threat to world peace. The time had come to bring it to a definitive end.

This position, different from the American posture in 1956–57, has been decisive to the diplomacy of the subsequent period.

When hostilities erupted on June 5, 1967, the Soviet Union blocked American cease-fire proposals in the United Nations for several days until it realized what was happening in the field. Then, when the cease-fire resolutions were finally in place, the United States undertook a major diplomatic campaign, extending around the world, in the Security Council, then in the General Assembly, then at the summit meeting between President Johnson and Premier Kosygin, at Glassboro, New Jersey, and finally back in the Security Council.

On November 22, 1967, the Security Council passed a unanimous resolution calling on the parties to reach an agreement which would definitely settle the Arab-Israeli controversy and establish conditions of just and lasting peace in the area. That resolution was achieved after more than five months of intensive diplomatic effort on the part of the United States, Great Britain, Denmark, Canada,

Italy, and a number of other countries. The history of that effort gives the text an extremely "plain meaning."

A number of positions emerged. Their interplay, and the resolution of that interplay, are reflected in the document.

The Soviet Union and its chief Arab associates wished to have Israel declared the aggressor, and to be required under Chapter VII of the UN Charter—that is, under threat of sanctions—to withdraw to the armistice demarcation lines as they stood on June 5, in exchange for the fewest possible assurances: that after withdrawal Israeli maritime rights in the Strait of Tiran would be "no problem" (sometimes the same thought was expressed about the Suez Canal as well) and that after Israeli withdrawal the possibility could be discussed of a document that might be filed with the Secretary General, or of a Security Council resolution, that would finally end any possibility of claiming that a "state of belligerency" existed between Israel and its neighbors. (This position was asserted without regard to the fact that the Security Council had twice explicitly denied that any state could claim "belligerent" status or "belligerent" rights in the Middle Eastern conflict.)

The Israeli position was at the other extreme of the spectrum. In the Israeli view, the Arab governments had repudiated the armistice agreements of 1949 by going to war. Israel believed that the parties should meet alone and draw up a peace treaty. So far as territorial problems were concerned, Israel contended that negotiations should begin not with the armistice demarcation lines, but with the 1967 cease-fire lines. Until negotiations actually began, Israel should not weaken its bargaining position by publicly revealing its peace aims, although the Prime Minister and the Foreign Minister did state publicly that Israel had no territorial claims as such but was interested in the territorial problem only insofar as issues of security and maritime rights, and, of course, the problem of Jerusalem, were concerned. Meanwhile, Israel began its administration of Jerusalem, the West Bank, the Golan Heights, the Gaza Strip, and the Sinai Peninsula as the occupying power under the cease-fire resolutions and international law, without annexations, justifying its policies "at the municipal level."

The United States, Canada, most of the Western European and Latin American countries, and a large number of other nations supported a different approach, which ultimately prevailed.

In the taut circumstances of May and June 1967, no majority could be obtained, either in the Security Council or the General Assembly, to declare Israel the aggressor. The question of who fired the first shot, difficult enough to resolve in itself, had to be examined as part of a sequence of Byzantine complexity: the false reports of Israeli mobilization against Syria; the removal of United Nations forces from the Sinai and the Gaza Strip; the closing of the Strait of Tiran; the mobilization of Arab forces around Israel and the establishment of a unified Arab command; and the cycle of statements, propaganda, speeches, and diplomatic efforts which marked the final weeks before June 5. Before that mystery, sober opinion refused to reach the conclusion that Israel was the aggressor. In view of the political orientation of the United Nations, no serious attempt was made to obtain a resolution declaring the United Arab Republic to be the aggressor.

Secondly, the majority opinion in both the General Assembly and the Security Council supported the American view, first announced on June 5, 1967, and stated more fully on June 19, 1967, that after twenty bitter and tragic years of "war," "belligerency," and guerrilla activity in the Middle East, the quarrel had become a burden to world peace and that the world community should finally insist on the establishment of a condition of peace, flowing from the agreement of the parties.

Third, Egypt's violations of the international understandings which ended the Suez crisis in 1957 led to the conclusion that Israel should not be required to withdraw from the cease-fire lines, except as part of a firm prior agreement which dealt with all the major issues in the controversy: justice for the refugees; guarantees of security for Israel's border and for its maritime rights in the Gulf of Aqaba and the Suez Canal; a solution for Jerusalem which met the legitimate interests of Jordan and of Israel and of the three world religions which regard Jerusalem as a holy city; and the establishment of a condition of peace.

Fourth, while the majority approach always linked Israeli withdrawal to the establishment of a condition of peace through an agreement among the parties, the question remained, "To what boundaries should Israel withdraw?" On this issue the policy of the Security Council was sharply drawn, and rested on a critical provision of the armistice agreements of 1949 with Egypt, Syria, and Jordan: that the demarcation line "is not to be construed in any sense as a political or territorial boundary, and is delineated without prejudice to rights, claims or positions of either Party to the armistice as regards ultimate settlement of the Palestine question." The wording of the armistice agreement with Lebanon is slightly different, although its tenor is the same. Many other provisions of each agreement make it clear that the purpose of the armistice was "to facilitate the transition from the present truce to permanent peace in Palestine" and that all non-military "rights, claims, or interests" were subject to later settlement as part of the transition from armistice to peace. These paragraphs, which were put into the agreements at Arab insistence, were the legal foundation for the controversies over the wording of paragraphs 1 and 3 of the Security Council resolution of November 22, 1967.

That resolution, promulgated under Chapter VI of the charter—that is, as a call for an agreement of peace—finally received the unanimous support of the Security Council. It was backed in advance by the assurance of the key countries that they would accept the resolution and work with Ambassador Gunnar Jarring to implement it.

It is important to recall what the resolution requires. It calls upon the parties to reach "a peaceful and accepted" agreement which would definitively settle the Arab-Israeli controversy and to establish conditions of "just and lasting peace" in the area in accordance with the "provisions and principles" stated in the resolution. The agreement required by paragraph 3 of the resolution, the Security Council said, should establish "secure and recognized boundaries" between Israel and its neighbors, "free from threats or acts of force," to replace the armistice demarcation lines established in 1949 and the cease-fire lines of June 1967. The Israeli armed forces should withdraw to such lines as part of a comprehensive agreement settling all the issues mentioned in the resolution and in a condition of peace.

On this point, the American position has been the same under both the Johnson and Nixon administrations. The new and definitive political boundaries should not represent "the weight of conquest," both administrations have said; on the other hand, under the policy and language of the armistice agreements of 1949 and the Security Council resolution of November 22, 1967, they need not be the same as the armistice demarcation lines. The walls and machine guns that divided Jerusalem need not be restored. Adjustments can be made by agreement under paragraph 2 of the Security Council resolution, to guarantee maritime rights "through international waterways in the area" and, equally, to guarantee "the territorial inviolability and political independence of every State in the area, through measures including the establishment of demilitarized zones."

This is the legal significance of the omission of the word "the" from paragraph 1 of the resolution, which calls for the withdrawal of Israeli armed forces "from territories occupied in the recent conflict," not "from *the* territories . . ." Repeated attempts to amend this sentence by inserting the word "the" or equivalent language failed in the Security Council. It is not legally possible, therefore, to assert that the provision requires Israeli withdrawal from *all* the territories occupied under the cease-fire resolutions to the 1949 armistice demarcation lines.

This aspect of the relationship between the Security Council resolution of November 22, 1967, and the armistice agreements of 1949 likewise explains the reference in the resolution to the rather murky principle of "the inadmissibility of the acquisition of territory by war." The murkiness of the idea, stated abstractly, arises from the failure to distinguish between territorial changes brought about by uses of force which violate Section 2(4) of the charter, and those which are justified as self-defense under Article 51. Moreover, the concept is difficult to reconcile with the practice, which has almost become a rule, of basing cease-fire and armistice lines on the actual position of troops after hostilities, and then having these lines become actual political boundaries, occasionally with small modifications. This was the case in the Middle East, in Indochina, in Korea, on the Indian subcontinent, and in Central Europe. Whatever the full implications of the idea might be, as applied to the Middle Eastern situation in 1967, it would necessarily permit the territorial adjustments and special security provisions expressly called for by the Security Council resolution of 1967 and the armistice agreements of 1949.

The resolution provided that the Secretary General should appoint a representative to consult with the parties and assist them in reaching the agreement required by paragraph 3 of the resolution.

The prolonged controversy about who has "accepted" the resolution is worth noting, for it sheds light on the intentions of the parties. It was never a real issue, since the key parties to the hostilities had given advance assurance that they would cooperate with the Secretary General's representative, Gunnar Jarring, to promote the agreement called for by the resolution. Shortly after Ambassador Jarring had begun his consultations, however, the question emerged in the form of Arab insistence that Israel indicate its "acceptance" or its "implementation" of the resolution before discussions could proceed. One version of these proposals would be that Israel withdraw to the armistice demarcation lines in advance of negotiations on any other problem of the resolution. This position violates the text of the resolution, and the experience of broken promises which the text reflects. It is, however, the interpretation of the resolution from which Egypt has not yet publicly budged.

Throughout 1967 and 1968 Ambassador Jarring and the representatives of many governments sought to persuade Nasser to enter into negotiations that might result in progress toward agreement under the resolution. Given the theory of the resolution, it is impossible for the parties to take serious negotiating positions on "secure and recognized boundaries" before they grapple with security arrangements and guarantees of maritime rights. The problem of borders would look altogether different to Israel, manifestly, if it were clear that the Sinai and the West Bank were to be completely demilitarized. And other problems under the resolution—refugees, for example, and the consequences of a state of peace—require negotiations and agreement, not simply formal compliance with the resolution. But thus far each initiative has had the same outcome: in the end the United Arab Republic has simply balked, in the pattern of Egyptian policy since Lausanne, on the problems of making a definitive peace with Israel.

There is great skepticism among the parties, a skepticism altogether natural against the background of more than twenty years of history. The Arabs fear that Israel has no intention of withdrawing, even to secure and recognized boundaries; Israel fears that the Arabs have no intention of making peace. Many Israelis perceive the Arabs, and especially Egypt, as determined to destroy them, with Soviet help. Many Arabs perceive the Israelis as committed to a policy of indefinite expansion.

But Israel has said repeatedly and officially that it has no territorial claims as such; that its sole interest in the territorial problem is to assure its security and obtain viable guarantees of its maritime rights; and that, even on the difficult issue of Jerusalem, it is willing "to stretch its imagination" in the interest of accommodating Jordanian and international interests in the Holy City.

These assurances by Israel have been the foundation and the predicate of the American position in the long months since June 1967. If the Arabs are skeptical of Israeli professions, the remedy is obvious: put them to the test of negotiation. They could be sure, as Prime Minister Golda Meir remarked in 1970, that the position of the United States in the negotiating process would come more than halfway to meet their claims.

Thus far it has proved impossible to initiate the final stages of the processes of consultation and negotiation which are necessary to the fulfillment of the resolution. The reasons for the stalemate are obvious. The basic obstacles to peace have been the intensification of terrorist activities supported or condoned by Arab governments and the policy embodied in the Khartoum formula approved by the Arab states in 1967: "No peace, no recognition, no negotiations." The principal tactical responsibility for the absence of peace is the policy of the government of the United Arab Republic. It has said it is ready to carry out the Security Council resolution "as a package deal," in all its parts, yet until the summer of 1970 it refused to say it was willing to implement the provision of the resolution requiring it to make an agreement establishing peace. President Sadat then took the important step of stating his willingness to sign a peace agreement with Israel. But as these lines are written, in the spring of 1972, Egypt still rejects procedures of consultation and negotiation accepted by other parties to the dispute as a way of achieving the agreement required by the resolution. And, in words and in military actions, it still proclaims the view that the Security Council resolution requires Israel to withdraw to the lines of June 4, 1967, before it undertakes even the vaguest and most impalpable of counter-steps.

In short, the Egyptian government refuses to implement the resolution. It is backed in that posture by the Soviet Union, prodigious supplies of arms, and some 20,000 Soviet military "advisers." Egypt could not have persisted in this stand for long against the will of the Soviet Union. Under these circumstances, and in the nature of Arab opinion, no other party to the conflict can move toward peace.

It is easy to understand the Soviet position, and that of Egypt, in terms of a policy of political and military expansion which threatens not only Israel, but Syria, Jordan, Lebanon, Iraq, Saudi Arabia, and the states of the Persian Gulf. They have gained positions and aroused forces which seem for the moment to enhance their influence and diminish that of their rivals. Arab raids and Israeli reprisals have generated an atmosphere of turbulence and violence which is dissolving many sectors of Arab society and bringing more and more extremists to power.

It is not, however, a posture easy to reconcile with the terms and purposes of the Security Council resolution of November 22, 1967, nor with their professed willingness to see peace come to the area.

The absence of peace has strengthened the Soviet and Egyptian position. New and more radical regimes have taken over in Libya and the Sudan. The government and society of Lebanon and of Jordan are weakened by the pressures of anti-Israeli feeling and the guerrilla movements which have flourished as a result.

In April 1969 the Egyptian position moved far beyond a passive refusal to implement the Security Council resolution. President Nasser denounced the cease-fire proclaimed by the Security Council in June 1967—a cease-fire which he had of course accepted at the time and agreed to respect until peace was made. It was that cease-fire which stopped the remorseless surge of the Israeli armed forces in June 1967. But in 1969 Nasser proclaimed a "war of attrition" against Israel, and tried to carry it out.

Inexplicably, the United States and its allies did nothing. They did not even summon the Security Council into emergency session, to call on the parties to respect the cease-fire and meet in a conference to carry out the peace-making resolution of November 22, 1967. Nor did they concentrate their fleets in the eastern Mediterranean and put mobile reserves on the alert in Germany, Malta, and Libya, where the United States and Great Britain still had bases. The paralysis of American policy at this point strengthened the impression that the American government was controlled by a small group of isolationist senators, and that the United States would do nothing to resist the destruction of Israel and Soviet domination of the entire Middle East. From such impressions, fatal miscalculations grow.

Israel reacted swiftly to Egypt's renewal of open warfare in 1969. In a devastating series of raids, the Israelis asserted supremacy in the Egyptian air space and inflicted heavy casualties on the Egyptian armed forces. The Soviet Union, rejecting all efforts to restore the cease-fire of 1967, had already arranged to assign Soviet pilots to combat roles in Egypt and to supply Egypt with more and more sophisticated anti-aircraft missiles. Meanwhile the Arab guerrillas, especially those influenced by China, sought to prevent peace, to destroy the regimes in Jordan and Lebanon, and indeed to precipitate general war.

Nonetheless, in the summer of 1970, Secretary of State William P. Rogers obtained Soviet and Egyptian assent to the renewal of Ambassador Jarring's mission, in the setting of a cease-fire and standstill agreement for at least ninety days. The formula for a negotiating procedure accepted by Nasser in 1970 went considerably farther, in terms of the vocabulary of Arab politics, than one he had refused in the spring of 1968. According to Jarring's report to U Thant of August 7, 1970, that formula pledged the parties to join in "discussions to be held under my auspices, according to such procedure and at such places and times as I may recommend, taking into account as appropriate each side's preference as to methods of procedure and previous experience between the parties." [4] In 1968 Egypt had rejected a formula that contemplated a "conference" without specifying its modalities or giving Jarring the last word on its format. Nonetheless, for reasons which have not been revealed, Jarring has not yet used his apparent power under the new formula to convene a conference of the parties.

Why did the Soviet Union and Egypt decide, even nominally, to accept the American proposals in 1970? Military events, Chinese pressures, and Egyptian second thoughts about the risks of complete Soviet control in their country all must have played a part in the decision. The war of attrition had been a disaster for Egypt. But concern about American intervention must have been decisive. While the introduction of Soviet pilots and missiles improved the Egyptian military position somewhat, the event had aroused American public opinion. Senators who opposed the President on Vietnam publicly urged him to take a strong stand in the Middle East and pledged their support for such a policy. And President Nixon issued warnings whose credibility was enhanced by his actions in Cambodia. At a minimum, Soviet uncertainty about the future course of American policy indicated a cooling-off period.

But should one assume that there is no more to Soviet policy than a cynical zig or zag? Objectively, one should judge the conjuncture

---

[4] *The New York Times*, August 8, 1970, p. 2, col. 7.

of events in the summer and late fall of 1970 and the winter of 1970–71 to be more favorable to the possibility of peace than has been the case for many years.

The death of President Nasser and Jordan's success in suppressing the guerrillas in the fall of 1970 strengthened the chance for peace. President Sadat cannot hope to claim President Nasser's prestige in the Arab world for a long time, and he should prove more cautious, and more concerned with internal problems, than his predecessor. King Hussein's position in Jordan is stronger than it has ever been. He has demonstrated that both the military and the political strength of the guerrillas was exaggerated. As for Syria and Iraq, both countries were suddenly required to confront the reality of their military weakness before an Israeli threat. There has been a noticeable shift in the temper of Arab politics since the fall of 1970, despite the steady military build-ups along the Suez Canal. The withdrawal of Iraqi troops from Jordan is perhaps the most significant and most hopeful straw in the wind since 1967.

The details of a peaceful settlement between Israel and its neighbors have been exhaustively canvassed. There is no mystery about them. With a will for peace, they should be easy to resolve.

So far as Egypt is concerned, the problem of peace is simplicity itself. Egypt has no title to the Gaza Strip, which it occupied as a result of the fighting twenty years ago. Israel has no substantial historic claim to the Sinai Peninsula, although Egyptian title has some historic ambiguities. Israel does have a claim, under the Security Council resolution of November 22, 1967, to arrangements which would guarantee Israel's right of passage through the Suez Canal and the Strait of Tiran. And it has a claim, under the same resolution, to security arrangements, including demilitarized zones, which would assure the safety of the "secure and recognized" boundaries to which its forces would eventually withdraw.

There are many ways in which these ends could be met. The complete demilitarization of the Sinai, patrolled by United Nations forces or conceivably by joint Israeli-Egyptian patrols, would perhaps be the simplest and most effective. Short of such a solution, the leasing of security positions by Egypt to Israel at Sharm-el-Sheikh and elsewhere represents another possibility.

Perhaps the most practicable procedure would be to combine these ideas. The parties could agree to a timetable extending over a considerable period. The goal would be Israeli withdrawal by

stages, pursuant to the agreed timetable, during which conditions
of true peace would be established. Throughout the transition period and after the ultimate Israeli withdrawal, either to the armistice demarcation lines or to new borders which did not deviate substantially from them, the Sinai would be permanently demilitarized.
Such a plan would most fairly settle the dilemmas posed by the
tragic history of the last twenty-four years.

It is probably impossible to make progress on the terms of a
peace between Israel and Jordan in the absence of a movement toward peace with Egypt, although such a step is not to be excluded,
if the divisions between Egypt and Jordan become deeper. The dynamics of Arab politics and rivalry are generally thought to be too
volatile to permit such a development. But in the Jordanian case the
elements of peace are obvious: some agreed adjustments in the armistice demarcation lines, as part of the movement from armistice
to peace; demilitarization of the West Bank; an open economy and
free movement of peoples between the two countries; access to the
Mediterranean for Jordan; and a special regime in Jerusalem that
would give suitable recognition to its relationship to both countries
and to the international religious character of the holy places. Ambassador Lewis Jones has suggested that an international private
foundation be established to take administrative charge of the holy
places and to restore and preserve them as monuments available to
all the world. It is a promising idea, perhaps too sensible for the
irrational politics of the Middle East. So far as the Gaza Strip is
concerned, it could well become part of Jordan, in a context of
peace, as territorial compensation for adjustments elsewhere.

Viewed objectively, the nominal issue that blocks peace between
Israel and Egypt is pitifully trivial: a military presence in a desert
area nearly devoid of population. But it is an issue of pride and dignity for Egypt, and of life and death for Israel, which once evacu-
ated the Sinai in reliance on international promises, only to find
itself threatened from that area, and alone.

In the perspective of the campaign of Soviet expansion in the
Middle East, however, the problem takes on another cast. The
nominal issue is not the real issue. The process of Soviet expansion
has passed beyond Israel's reach. Israel cannot contain the Arab
masses if the Soviet Union arouses them to fury and provides their
air cover and cutting edge. That force can be contained only by the
credible assertion by the United States, hopefully backed by some

or all of its NATO allies, that it will not accept Soviet predominance in the Middle East. That demonstration of strength can become a political reality if it becomes clear that peace can be
achieved only on the terms the United States announced on June
19, 1967—the terms of the Security Council resolution—and that all
the Soviet efforts since that time have not helped the Arabs in any
way. The tenacity of Israeli and American policies since 1967 may
yet persuade the Arabs that this is indeed the case.

VI

The moral of the Middle Eastern drama, I suggest, is that there
is no way to isolate the quarrels of the third world from the security
concerns of Europe, the United States, and Japan. From the point
of view of American, European, and Japanese security, every part
of the third world is not exactly comparable to the vast arc between
Morocco and Iran, but most such regions have comparable potentialities, many more ominous than those of the Middle East.

Some geographical positions in the third world have inherently
important strategic implications, from the point of view of land,
naval, or air warfare, space communication, and nuclear deterrence.
Others have inescapable links to the nations and peoples of the
West, historical ties and economic importance of special weight and
sensitivity. The Western security interest in most areas of the third
world, however, is contextual. Such countries become important to
the security of other states not in themselves, but in relation to
trends and to the policies of their neighbors. It would be absurd to
say that a Communist regime in Syria would in itself threaten the
security of Europe or the United States. The security problem for
the West begins to emerge if Syria becomes a base from which guerrillas attack neighboring states and seek to provoke war among
them. It becomes radically more acute if Syria acts as a proxy for
the Soviet Union, in providing a staging area in a process of indefinite subversion, attack, and expansion. Yugoslavia presented one
set of problems to the West when it was an enthusiastic member
of Stalin's team, quite another when it established its independence of Soviet rule, and then received Western support. In both
roles, it was a Communist state.

Above all, when considering war as a psychological phenomenon—that is, as a violent response to fear and rage—episodes of this kind have to be considered in relation to each other. The German attack on Poland in 1939 was not in itself more serious as a blow to British and French security than the occupation of the Rhineland, Austria, or Czechoslovakia. But it provoked the war precisely because the sequence was finally perceived as part of a process that could only end, unless it were stopped by force, in the accumulation of overwhelming power in German hands, and hence in the domination of Britain and France by Germany.

In the Middle East all three aspects of the security problem—geographical, contextual, and psychological—are important. Middle Eastern oil is vital to the economies of Europe and Japan and of marginal use to the economy of the United States. Its strategic space is of critical importance to the security of NATO. Soviet hegemony or near-hegemony in the area would make the position of NATO vulnerable and render communication with the Middle East and the Far East expensive, slow, and chancy. As President Pompidou has said, the Soviet presence in the Mediterranean threatens "the soft underbelly" of Europe and constitutes a situation like that of the Cuban missile crisis. These are words of tremendous resonance. But they are not exaggerated. The cumulative spread of Soviet influence, country by country, over a period of more than twenty years, has created a sense of unease in Europe and America which could easily become the panic that leads to war.

Western ties with many Middle Eastern states are old and deep. And the West's relationship to Israel is complex and explosive, with powerful psychosocial dimensions on both sides. Some derive from the history of Christianity and the role of anti-Semitism in Western culture; others from the experience of genocide, so vivid in the nightmares of Western man. Ambiguities characterize Western attitudes toward Israel, and Israel's attitudes toward the West—feelings of identity, attraction, resentment, admiration, fear, and guilt. They would make a dangerous mixture if Israel were being beaten to its knees by Arab states with Soviet pilots and officers in their ranks. Whatever men may imagine in advance, I believe Europe and America, and many other countries, would not stand by were another chapter of massacre to be threatened in the strange history of the Jews.

The apparently endless troubles of the third world are the heart of the anguish over foreign policy in the West today. This is the case not because the United States wrongly applied to Asian problems the ideas of the Truman Doctrine and the Marshall Plan developed for Europe, but simply because the pressures on the West implicit in Soviet and Chinese programs of expansion—and, on their own scale, of Cuban programs as well—are intense, and are becoming more intense.

The Middle East is a case in point. Whether the Arab-Israeli conflict erupts in another outburst of open warfare or, as is more likely, is resolved by a political settlement generally consistent with the Security Council resolution of November 22, 1967, the Soviet campaign of expansion in the Middle East and Chinese rivalry with the Soviets for control of revolutionary movements in the area will be major problems of American and NATO policy for years to come. Western security interests in the area will not be guaranteed simply by an agreement of peace between Israel and its neighbors. But they cannot be safeguarded without such an agreement. The pressure will end only if the Soviet Union and China finally accept—or are forced by events to accept—the logic of détente and peaceful coexistence. In the absence of concerted and determined Western counter-pressures to achieve that end, the region will face a condition of spreading anarchy, which, on past form, would almost surely erupt in war.

If this analysis is correct, it must be assumed that the United States will continue to protect its national interests in the third world, as well as its manifest security interest in the independence of its major allies, Western Europe and Japan.

What lines of policy should be anticipated as integral to that effort?

The risk of both regional and general war would be much less, obviously, if the United States and its allies could obtain universal acceptance of Article 2, paragraph 4, of the UN Charter: that all nations "refrain in their international relations from the threat or use of force against the territorial integrity or political independence of any state, or in any other manner inconsistent with the purpose of the United Nations." In the absence of miraculous conversions, this goal could only be achieved by convincingly confronting those who would breach the rule with the certainty that the rest of the international community would contest such violations, in the pattern of the Korean war, or go further, if the habit of breach is not broken, by reprisals against those responsible, and by a clear threat to denounce Article 2, paragraph 4, as it applies to themselves, unless it is honored reciprocally.

"Spheres of influence" is the traditional name for a second, and perhaps more practicable, policy of peace. Its shortcoming, if the reasoning presented here is sound, is that it must be nearly universal to be effective. The dynamics of Balkanism, now evident throughout the third world, would require a policy of spheres of influence to approximate that of enforcing the UN Charter. It has proved nearly impossible thus far to define a workable policy of peace with respect to the third world, save for short periods when rules of mutual restraint were respected, as in the Congo crisis of the early 1960s. Any alternative, as the experience of Korea, Vietnam, and the Middle East attests, is necessarily so ambiguous, and its signals and alarm bells so liable to be misinterpreted or ignored, as to be nearly unworkable.

The West has tried both peace through universal rules and peace through mutual respect for spheres of influence. Neither approach has worked. The rules of the charter were breached over and over again. And, while the West refrained from interfering in the affairs of Eastern Europe, the Soviet Union has not respected the interests or the commitments of the West in Berlin, Cuba, Korea, Vietnam, or the Middle East. It is by no means self-evident that Soviet policy would even respect the manifest state interests of the United States in the continuity of its relationships with Western Europe and Japan.

Under these circumstances, what is to be done?

In 1968 I published a short book, *Law, Power, and the Pursuit of Peace*. Its theme was that we were in the midst of a major crisis in international affairs, like those of the decades before 1914 and 1939: a crisis of perception and will at this stage, but one which could not be aborted without the most serious efforts by the United States and its allies. I argued that change was urgently required in the foreign policy of the United States and its allies "if its great aim, the achievement of peace, is to remain in our grasp." [5] In the shadow of Korea and Vietnam, American opinion was in revolt against the burdens the nation had carried since 1947. No one could tell how far that revolt would take policy. But the American deterrent, the sole force keeping the general peace since 1947, had been put in

---

[5] P. xiii. University of Nebraska Press and Harper & Row.

doubt, while the pattern of events was more ominous, and more difficult to control, than was the case in the late 1940s and early 1950s.

The argument of *Law, Power, and the Pursuit of Peace* was that the minimal security of the United States could be protected only by establishing a new balance of power in the world and achieving the reciprocal acceptance of rules of restraint which could limit conflict and assure the nations that the underlying equilibrium of force would be respected; that thus far neither the Soviet Union nor Communist China had accepted this prudent idea as the basis for a policy of coexistence, although neither one had declared full-throated war against it, either; and that while the United States could not be expected indefinitely to respect these rules without reciprocity, the strategy of our foreign policy should continue to press both China and the Soviet Union to accept the logic of peaceful coexistence.

Under these circumstances, I contended, there was only one prudent course capable of containing the pressures of Soviet and Chinese expansion and preserving the hope of peace. It was to achieve closer concert in our alliances, both in Europe and in Asia, and a more equal sharing of their burdens and responsibilities. For reasons that may or may not be rational, American opinion will accept collective responsibility just as ardently as it resents having to do the job alone. Therefore the remedy for the isolationist yearnings of the American soul, and in any event the equitable principle of dividing the costs of security over the long run, was a process of transforming our alliances. Through political understandings of this kind, I urged, the United States should "become in fact the junior partner in regional coalitions to assure stability and development in areas of the Free World now threatened with conquest or chaos." [6]

Formally, the transformation of our alliances was in train in 1968. But the process moved slowly, given the continuity of social habits and the grip of old ideas on men's minds. Both Europe and Japan hesitated to take on the burden of equal responsibility. The political costs of such an effort at home were great, and public opinion did not fully understand the political and military implications of the nuclear stalemate. Despite their economic and social recovery, Europe and Japan were more dependent on the United States, because

[6] *Ibid.*, p. 116.

of the nuclear problem, than was the case twenty years ago. But Europe and Japan took nuclear protection to be the order of nature. If the American nuclear umbrella offered impregnable safety, why undertake the difficult course of sharing the tiresome and expensive ordeal of confrontation at the conventional level? It was all too easy to understand the reluctance of Europe and Japan to join in policies of full collective security.

These perceptions were the heart of Johnson's strategy. Nixon has now made them the central feature of the Nixon Doctrine.

To achieve this transformation of our alliances, I contended, would indeed require the most serious kind of effort on the part of the United States and its allies—intellectual effort, in the first place, and, secondly, an emotional willingness to act on intellectual conclusions. Taking drastic action on merely intellectual grounds is among the most difficult tasks men can ever undertake, when the pressure for change in policy lacks the volcanic impulse that flows from events like Pearl Harbor or the invasion of Poland in 1939.

My more recent review of the problem has not led me to a different conclusion. On the contrary, it confirmed its urgency. I should still contend that the United States and its allies have no real alternative but to renew their commitment to the line of policy they have followed since 1947. The acceptance of reciprocal rules defining the outer limits of conflict must be pursued as the explicit goal of that policy. Given the strength of national and ideological ambitions at work in world politics, such acceptance can be achieved only by the patient and restrained firmness which has characterized Western insistence on its rights in Berlin and on the defense of Iran, Western Europe, Korea, the Middle East, and South Vietnam.

One can hope for better and more sophisticated handling of the political and military applications of that policy in the future. One can try to convince the Soviet Union and China that there is no workable alternative to the policy of the United Nations Charter, which forbids not only traditional imperial expansion, but international support for revolution. One should use the major opportunity opened up in 1971—China's request for American assistance to deter an ominous Soviet threat—as the basis for bringing this conviction home to both countries.

Another factor works in the same direction—the fear of nuclear proliferation and the implications of the Non-Proliferation Treaty. The treaty imposes an obligation on the Soviet Union, the United States, and Great Britain to protect non-nuclear signatories against nuclear threat. The United States would face the issue in its most acute form if the Soviet Union made an overtly nuclear threat against a non-nuclear signatory. But this dimension of the treaty emerges from the shadows whenever the Soviet Union threatens a non-nuclear power. The treaty would become a curse if it were to be used as a screen behind which non-nuclear powers are systematically invested, through "wars of national liberation" or otherwise. The treaty can survive only if it reinforces the pressures for accommodation and leads to a degree of political cooperation among the nuclear powers and an end of expansionist adventures like the Soviet program in the Middle East.

But success in these efforts is by no means assured. And at best it will be slow. What success requires is not trivial, after all: it is nothing less than acceptance of the UN Charter, and therefore abandonment of the idea of international support for revolution.

It follows that a strengthening of the NATO alliance system and a corresponding change in the structure of American relations with Japan are essential to any strategy which would have more than a token chance of success. Rightly or wrongly, American opinion resents the fact that so large a part of the burden of defense for the last twenty-five years has been borne by the United States, while many of the beneficiaries of that effort have been able to concentrate their resources and energies on economic development. The explosive character of the changes in American economic policy announced on August 15, 1971, derives from this bitter feeling. Unless such change in the structure of our alliances is achieved soon, the risk of irrationality and imprudence in American policy will increase, with consequences that are beyond prediction.

Alfred Marshall used to remind his students that trees do not grow to the sky. Economic trends, he said, should never be projected indefinitely along straight lines. Marshall's metaphor applies also to the problem of peace. The prospects for peace are not uniformly bleak. The pressures of Soviet imperialism have called strong counterforces into being—first, NATO and the security arrangements of the Eisenhower Era, more recently, the dramatic change in Chinese policy, which is echoed in many other parts of the world. If the United States and its allies continue to stand fast, despite the clamor of opposition, it is not beyond hope that the Soviet Union and China will accept the logic of genuinely peaceful coexistence. No one can promise success in such an effort. What can be said is that there is no hope for peace without it.

Chapter 3

War and Peace in the Middle East: An Israeli Perspective

Saul Friedlander
and
Edward Luttwak

In a world of dependent small powers, Israel is more dependent than most. Its physical survival has required sophisticated weapons from major powers, and its economy relies on generous grants and loans to finance heavy burdens of immigration, absorption and defense expenditure. In spite of this dependence, successive Israeli governments have resisted enormous pressures from friends and enemies alike and have remained masters of Israel's fate.

Israel has maintained its independent course by clinging stubbornly to some basic tenets of policy, in the expectation that they would ultimately be endorsed by at least one of the major powers. To date, that expectation has been realized. French acceptance of fundamentals of Israeli policy was essential during the 1950s; American acquiescence in them is vital now and for the years ahead. The United States has become Israel's sole supplier of sophisticated weaponry, and the bulk of the aid which sustains Israel's economy also originates in the United States. Still, the United States has not been able to dictate Israel's policies. Israeli governments have maintained their own view of Israel's situation and have not renounced policies and objectives which they considered fundamental; they are likely to go to extremes to preserve that posture.

The Politics of the Conflict

Ideology and Interests

On the character of the conflict, as on most other questions, Israelis hold a wide range of views. Some of them are rooted in ideology and ideological assumptions. For many Israelis, Arab hostility to the idea and later to the fact of a Jewish state is easier to explain than the persistence of Arab governments in radical policies which have proved economically and politically costly. For there is no clash of material interests between Israel and most Arab states, and specific issues with adjacent Arab states are generally regarded as of secondary importance; even the very real issue of the territories occupied by Israel since the Six Day War in 1967 has not proved to be the main obstacle to a settlement. A "cultural" explanation of the conflict, therefore, has been increasingly accepted. Starting with the plausible assumption that Arab policies are conditioned by sentiments and values of Arab nationalism, there is a remarkable consensus among orientalists both in Israel and the West on the following propositions:

That Arab nationalism is essentially a secularized version of traditional and reformist Islamic ideas. Christian Arabs too, inasmuch as they adhere to the tenets of Arab nationalism, identify with Islamic values.

That the ideal self-image of the Arab Muslim in relation to the non-Muslim is one of superiority not only in spiritual but also in political and military matters.

That the military "success story" of early Islam is part of the Muslim's religious consciousness, particularly intense among Arabs since they were the heroes of that story.

That for the Arabs, who believed that they were members of a powerful and victorious community, the intrusion of the Western powers in the Middle East presented a profound cultural as well as political problem. It was all the more acute because of the apparent suddenness of this intrusion, following the delayed but then rapid decline of Ottoman power.

That the ebb of Anglo-French imperialism in the Middle East was interpreted by the Arabs as being much more than a windfall in their political circumstances; it was seen rather, in the phrase of a well-known orientalist, as a "rehabilitation of history" by which the state of the world again became compatible with the Arab world view. Furthermore, Arabs interpreted the retreat of Western imperialism as of their making and discounted the importance of developments outside the Middle East.

That this restored and indeed reinforced self-image prevalent among the Arabs was shattered by the Israeli victories of 1948 and 1967. The continued existence of Israel presents an acute psychological and cultural problem to those Arabs in whom Arab nationalism and its Islamic source-ideas generate significant emotions.

The Israelis who believe that these propositions approximate reality therefore discount Arab statements which portray the causes of the conflict in material terms, such as compensation to Arab refugees. They also discount the Marxist/Maoist stance now fashionable in certain Arab milieux as mere packaging intended to appeal to foreign opinion. They consider that the Arabs are concealing their real motivation, which would hardly appeal to non-Islamic opinion, and they point to the difference in style and content between Arab statements meant for Arab audiences and those addressed to non-Arabs.

This "cultural" view of the conflict, of course, shapes Israeli attitudes and policies. If cultural and emotional factors are basic, with material issues only the medium for their expression, a "quick fix" settlement cannot succeed. Other wars have been terminated by settling the material issues in anticipation that the parties' emotional fervor would eventually abate, but such a settlement of the Arab-Israeli conflict would adjust only peripheral matters; the causal factors would remain. Israelis who hold this view therefore oppose concessions to the Arabs, especially territorial concessions, since they believe that Israel's emotional intrusion upon the Arab world is not commensurate with its geographic extension. (This does not mean that these Israelis oppose all territorial concessions, but they would regard them as concessions to Israel's allies rather than to her enemies.)

From this view of the conflict, every Arab demand short of the elimination of Israel is seen as strictly tactical, and nothing can be gained by conceding to it. While an indefinite prolongation of the conflict is hardly to be contemplated with equanimity, only long-term cultural change will affect its basic causes. However, even some

who hold this cultural view of the conflict believe that political realities might force the Arabs to a political accommodation, if only
for the short term.

Egypt remains the dominant power among Israel's Arab neighbors. By the mid-1950s the Egyptian leadership had adopted pan-
Arab ideals as its own, evoking a powerful response from much of
the urban population, which had been conditioned by the purposeful pan-Arabism of Palestinian propagandists and by the Muslim
brotherhood. The policies that followed also suited the regime's internal circumstances, justifying the development of large and costly
armed forces to serve as its political base. During the 1960s, however, the Egyptians maintained that an immediate military solution
to the Palestine problem was not possible, though Nasser did not
go so far as to recognize Israel's military superiority, raising instead
the specter of Israel's powerful allies. After the defeat of 1967
Egypt's declared policy was based on the principles enunciated at
the Khartoum conference of September 1967: no peace treaty with
Israel; no recognition of Israel; no negotiations with Israel; and no
bargaining about the future of Palestinian territory and people. But
an immediate military solution was also expressly renounced.

The "political solution" promoted by Egypt called for political
pressures on Israel, mainly from the great powers. Meanwhile,
Egyptian military strength was to be developed, both to intensify
the pressures of the major powers on Israel and provide an alternative if the political solution failed. Many Israelis, particularly those
who held the cultural view of the conflict, saw Egypt's apparent acceptance of the continued existence of Israel within its pre-1967
borders as temporary and tactical, just as during the May 1967 crisis
the Egyptian goal seemed to be the pre-1956 status quo or, by the
eve of the war, the pre-1948 status. Another segment of Israeli opinion, however, held that the Egyptian policies were face-saving and
that Nasser was trying to achieve a genuine settlement of the conflict based on the pre-1967 borders and providing for substantial
compensation to the Palestinian refugees.

From 1967 until 1970, as the war after the war developed, Egyptian military strategy went through several distinct stages, but the
corresponding political strategy appeared to remain unchanged.
From time to time, whenever some new tactic seemed promising,
the Egyptians leaned toward the military option, but in each in-

stance the Israelis recaptured the initiative by mobile operations which the Egyptians could neither deter nor defeat from their static posture.

In the spring of 1970, however, the construction of a Russian-manned missile and fighter air-defense system in Egypt raised the costs of Israeli action in the air and introduced new and unpredictable risks in land operations. Although the Egyptian position along the Suez Canal deteriorated further even after that development, the new missile deployments of August 1970 and the standstill cease-fire appeared to reverse the situation. At the present time it seems to most Israelis that the value of the military option has been enhanced in Egyptian eyes and that struggle for power inside Egypt may become a further stimulant to Egyptian military action.

Jordan

The 1967 war and its immediate consequences placed King Hussein of Jordan in an exceedingly difficult position. Only a separate peace with Israel could have ensured the prompt return of substantial parts of the West Bank, which in demographic and economic terms was more than half his kingdom, but such a settlement was opposed by other Arab governments and by many of his own citizens. This opposition was reinforced by the growth of the Palestinian military organizations in the second half of 1967 and even more by Hussein's financial dependence on other Arab governments.

Hussein's policy after 1967 seems to have been based on two guiding principles: a political alignment with Egypt and maintaining residual links with the United States. This external balance was paralleled by an internal one in which Saudi military and economic support offset radical pressures within and from outside his kingdom. The crisis of September 1970 showed that Hussein's policies worked up to a point: his earlier alignment with Nasser probably eased somewhat the political problems of confronting the Palestinian military organizations, while the United States was instrumental in stopping a Syrian invasion of Jordanian territory.

Egyptian support for Hussein wavered and finally ceased at the critical phase of his conflict with the Palestinians, but Egypt's refraining from early and outright condemnation perhaps proved helpful to the king. At the same time, the Saudi military presence in the south of Jordan certainly simplified the tasks of the Jordanian army. Hussein benefited from another source of support: quiet but credible Israeli threats effectively neutralized Iraqi forces in Jordan, who desisted from helping the Palestinians. Hussein thus survived that crisis too, but from the Israeli point of view his policies, though fairly successful in their own terms, represent a poor second-best to a political settlement with Israel.

The Palestinian Military Organizations

The new Palestinian military organizations were formed in reaction to Egyptian policies enunciated at Arab summit meetings in 1964–65, which advocated careful preparation for a decisive conflict with Israel and the achievement of Arab political unity as a necessary preliminary condition. The then-existing Palestinian military organization, the Palestine Liberation Army (PLA) of the Palestine Liberation Organization, was, like its parent body, entirely dependent on official funding by a number of Arab countries and subject to Egyptian political control. Al Fatah represented a new departure: the Palestinians, who had concentrated on focusing pan-Arab sentiment on the struggle against Israel, were now to operate independently. The leaders of Al Fatah realized that neither their own embryonic movement, nor any conceivable Palestinian organization, could defeat Israel whether by conventional or guerrilla warfare, but they believed that the Arab states were sufficiently powerful to defeat Israel and that Egypt's policy of further hesitation was unjustified. Al Fatah therefore consciously adopted a catalytic role to bring about an Arab war against Israel. In January 1965 it started a campaign of border sabotage by infiltration and over-the-border shelling. (At that time, Al Fatah was dependent on Syrian funding, weapon supply, and training; the Syrians seemed to view it as a useful instrument in their continuing but muted struggle against Nasser's dominance of the Arab scene.)

It is difficult to assess the importance of Al Fatah's role in bringing about the war of 1967, but the fact that the war occurred fulfilled its aims, though the outcome of the war, of course, did not fulfill its expectations. Although it could not claim any combat successes during or after the war, Al Fatah grew very quickly during the postwar period of confusion and anguish in the Arab world. It obtained funds from official Arab sources and developed propaganda

and fund-raising organizations which used social pressure and sometimes physical coercion to exact contributions from the middle-
class segment of the Palestinian diaspora in the Arab world. But the
development of these fund-raising techniques quickly broke Al
Fatah's monopoly: soon new organizations developed, each with its
own fund-raising effort, and by September 1970 there were more
than fourteen of them.

The slow political work required to establish a subversive base in
Israeli-controlled territory proved to be too exacting for the Palestinian organizations. Except for planting a few cells of urban terrorists, which Israel quickly dismantled, their activity was limited
to armed infiltration across the cease-fire lines to sustain a guerrilla
campaign, and the military and political impact on Israel was
rather small. The political strength of these organizations soon declined, but the September 1970 crisis in Jordan temporarily restored
their prestige among Palestinians in the occupied territories. Their
main source of strength remains the support of certain Arab governments, but the Palestinians living in Jordan itself provide a strong
political base as well as recruits for the salaried jobs in the organizations' ranks.

The leaders of the Palestinian organizations have promoted different ideological blends of Marxism and nationalism, but they are
in full agreement in rejecting the current American peace initiative.
In fact, their declared goal, the "liberation of Palestine," implies a
rejection of any conceivable negotiated settlement, however unfavorable to Israel. Their position is therefore in sharp contrast with
that of the Egyptian and Jordanian governments, and parallel to
that of the Algerian, Iraqi, and Syrian governments. But, as the
events of September 1970 have shown, the Palestinian military organizations enjoy a measure of political support even from Arab governments with whose policies they differ. This, and the active help
of the Syrian government, proved sufficient to enable them to survive the Jordanian onslaught, although the conflict exposed their
military insignificance, and their political standing as credible antagonists to Israel was much eroded.

There will probably continue to be at least one Arab country adjacent to Israel or Jordan which will provide the Palestinian organizations with secure bases and communications facilities and enable
it to survive as a political force in the Arab world. But their inability to develop the instruments of revolutionary war in Israeli-occu-

pied territory will probably relegate them to a secondary role, as tools of inter-Arab conflict.

Syria

Syria's position reflects both the more extreme policies of its leadership and a greater degree of operational control over its military forces than is the case with Egypt. While declared Syrian policies have been entirely uncompromising, the Syrian-Israeli cease-fire line has been the quietest. On several occasions Egyptian armed forces have appeared to be acting outside the framework of any reasoned policy, thus impairing the effectiveness of Israeli deterrence by retaliatory threats or reprisals, but that same Israeli strategy has functioned quite well in the case of Syria. Every Syrian military action along the cease-fire line has had an obvious political motivation. On each occasion the Syrian army made a purposeful military move to coincide with some political event in the Arab world; in each instance there was a prompt Israeli response to which the Syrians did not react, and the exchanges were followed by relatively long periods of inactivity. Such rationality of action and full control over all the forces operating on its territory does not exist in the other Arab states adjacent to Israel. But Syrian policy remains the elimination of Israel, and the Syrian leadership has repeatedly rejected any political settlement of the conflict. Syria is thus the only Arab state adjacent to Israel whose immediate goal in the conflict is identical with that of the Palestinian military organizations.

Iraq

The present Iraqi leadership reflects the decline of political life following the disintegration of the Baath party into a number of warring factions. But the Iraqi leadership is even more determined than Syria's to make political capital vis-à-vis Egypt out of its refusal to accept a negotiated settlement of the conflict with Israel. Its military power, however, is pre-empted by the threat from Iran and potential threats from dissident elements within Iraq itself. The contrast between the vociferous Iraqi support of the Palestinians prior to the crisis of September 1970 and the total inactivity of the Iraqi contingent caught in the very midst of the fighting exposed the weakness of Iraq as a factor in the conflict.

Saudi Arabia

The death of Nasser may have resurrected King Faisal's abortive attempt to establish leadership over some parts of the Arab world, but the factors which disqualified him earlier are still in force. Faisal has taken a consistently uncompromising attitude in the Arab-Israeli conflict, but unlike other Arab leaders who take that position he has not even tried to implement it either in military or diplomatic terms. The role of the Saudi contingent in the September 1970 crisis in Jordan showed that in practice Saudi policy is principally to contain radical forces in the Arab world.

The military insignificance of Saudi Arabia and its passive diplomatic role with respect to American peace initiatives indicate that it will remain a secondary factor in the Arab-Israeli conflict, whether in peace or in war.

The Policies of the Great Powers

Given Britain's minor and equivocal role in the present phase of the conflict and the limited scope of French policies, such attention as Israeli decision makers have given the outside world has focused largely on the United States and the Soviet Union. While there is still a tendency to attribute some grand design to the Soviet leadership and a parallel tendency to regard American policy as indecisive, official Israeli opinion is not informed by any coherent vision of the goals of either power and the options open to them. Prime Minister Golda Meir's off-the-cuff remark in the summer of 1970 that the Cabinet had not even discussed the possibility of a Soviet response to Israel's interdiction bombing near Egyptian cities tells its own story.

The Soviet Union

Israelis have been guided by three assumptions about Soviet policy. First, they believe that the Soviet Union does not seek the prompt and utter destruction of Israel. Second, they have gradually become convinced that the dominant faction in the Russian leadership values very highly its newly established position of influence in Egypt and that it would not agree to any resolution of the conflict unless it reinforced that position. Third, they assume that any Soviet moves would be conditioned by expectations as to the American response.

Until the spring of 1970 the Israelis believed that Soviet involvement in the conflict would stop short of deploying combat personnel. After that took place in April 1970, without United States response, Israeli apprehensions as to the direction and firmness of American policy intensified and, of course, affected Israeli assessments of Soviet behavior. At that time there began a more intense search for ways of deterring Soviet military involvement by means other than American containment. While this scheme was largely fanciful, given the early and firm Soviet decision to side with the Arabs, at least one rather more realistic plan did receive a hearing at the highest political level. In essence, this amounted to buying off the Soviet Union by offering a prompt reopening of the Suez Canal in exchange for an indefinite standstill and cease-fire. As far as is known, this plan is still being considered, which would indicate that in some Israeli quarters it is thought that the Soviet Union is primarily interested in developing its presence in the Indian Ocean and points farther east and that it might be willing to sacrifice some of its political influence in Egypt to that end.

Soviet acquiescence in if not promotion of the cease-fire and standstill agreement of August 1970 caused some segments of official Israeli opinion to think that the Soviet Union was trying to achieve limited political gains by obtaining a settlement of the conflict which would be seen by the Arabs in a positive light. Others thought that the Soviets had indeed focused their ambitions beyond the Middle East. Some, however, regarded the Soviet move as a ruse, and only these were not shaken by the Egyptian violations of the standstill, in which, it was accepted, the Russians were directly involved.

The United States

Since the 1967 crisis Israeli perceptions of American policy formation have become more sophisticated. It is now widely realized that American policy is shaped by the interplay of official and other pressures at moments of decision. Partly for that reason there is a tendency in Israel to regard American policy as more indecisive than it really is, and probably too much attention is accorded to the administration's trial balloons, to senatorial pronouncements, and to press campaigns.

Israeli decision makers see American policy as guided by three considerations: the protection of Israel against the threat of annihilation, the preservation of the remaining American political and economic interests in the Arab world, and the avoidance of a direct confrontation with the Soviet Union. The first two aims essentially conflict, given the declared policies of most Arab countries, but the tension between them became really acute when the United States became the sole supplier of sophisticated weaponry to Israel as well as its only advocate among the major powers.

After the 1967 war the United States appeared to the Israelis to be promoting peace plans increasingly favorable to the Arabs, and Israeli commentators displayed exasperation with the course of American policy, in which they saw a gradual erosion of American commitments to Israel. But it was not until the aftermath of the August 1970 cease-fire that many Israelis began to see American policy in an almost sinister light. When the Israelis informed the United States that the Egyptians were violating the standstill agreement, they expected either firm American diplomatic action or compensatory arms to Israel or both. When the Nixon administration chose instead to cast doubts on the validity of Israeli complaints, a major crisis of confidence developed. This extended, naturally, to the entire American quest for a peace settlement, and devalued American standstill guarantees that were to be Israel's main compensation under current American plans for settlement. This crisis did not last very long, however. The firm albeit covert American moves which contributed to the prompt Syrian withdrawal during the September 1970 crisis in Jordan, and Russia's apparent acquiescence, enhanced American credibility in the region. At the same time, American promises of arms supplies to Israel became far more generous than ever before.

Since then, Washington's new and harder policy has caused fresh anxieties among many Israelis, principally over the degree to which Israel can rely on the United States to deter further Soviet intervention in the conflict. There appear to be at least two currents of policy in Washington. The first, expressed by Presidential adviser Henry Kissinger among others, seems to indicate a willingness to confront the Soviet Union over the specific issues arising from its military involvement as well as its general intent in the Middle East.

This willingness has not yet been reflected sufficiently to give repose to Israeli anxieties. *Many Israelis feel that in the last analysis the United States will fail to prevent the relentless growth of Soviet power in the region.*

A second current suggests that the United States will try to provide Israel with the wherewithal to meet Arab military threats independently. The big question is whether this policy applies to the Soviet threat as well. The authors of this paper are pessimistic enough to suspect that the United States may be tempted to deter the Soviet Union by massive arms shipments to Israel, and by these means alone. The costs and dangers of such a policy for Israel need not be enumerated.

A further anxiety derives from Israeli fears that the United States might be ready again to appease the Arabs at the expense of Israel. They fear that Israel might be forced to relinquish most of its territorial gains (including, in particular, those which strengthen its strategic posture), not in exchange for Arab political concessions or credible third-party guarantees, but only for arms, which would merely raise the "entry price" of Soviet military intervention: a low-cost, low-risk containment policy for the United States. Israel would rather have smaller arms and supplies and retain strategically advantageous parts of the occupied territories. With the United States pursuing what may effectively be an imposed settlement, it is likely that Israeli-American relations will be punctuated by recurrent crises. But most Israelis are aware that a major incentive for a conciliatory American stand toward the Arabs has waned: it would now be very difficult to convince most Arabs that any pro-Arab settlement had indeed been secured by the United States, and it is the Soviet Union rather than the United States which would profit from such a settlement.

Israel's diplomatic area of maneuver is exceedingly narrow. It can do little more than attempt to persuade the United States to harden its policies vis-à-vis the Russians, and to resist the erosion of the American resolve to obtain political concessions from the Arabs in exchange for Israeli territorial concessions. There seems to be no prospect of Israel being supported by the United States beyond this point, unless major political changes within the region itself were to intervene.

More recently, Israelis have learned that the United States has been reevaluating Soviet intentions globally, and have some hope that this may induce the United States government to modify its policies with respect to the Middle East. Israelis are acutely aware, however, that American policy in the Middle East is formed in an institutional setting unfavorable to Israel. They see the Secretary of State as determined to achieve a solution in the one region which White House policy makers have left to his department. The State Department has consistently pressed for softer policies toward the Arab world, and in this instance it is not offset by the Defense Department, for it too advocates policies unfavorable to Israel. With these two key departments aligned as they are, the scope for Presidential and congressional influence more favorable to Israel is necessarily limited.

The Military Balance

Since the 1967 war the strength of the Egyptian armed forces has increased by a considerable margin. The number of combat soldiers has gone up from some 180,000 in June 1967 to more than 450,000 in April 1971; the number of supersonic fighters and attack aircraft has increased from some 200 to more than 450; the number of tanks and assault guns has gone up from about 1,200 to more than 2,000. At the same time, equipment lost during the war has been replaced, with significant upgrading in quality: MIG-15 and MIG-17 fighter-bombers have been replaced with far more effective SU-7s; MIG-19s have been replaced with MIG-21s, and T-34 tanks of World War II vintage with T-54/55s. Moreover, the presence of a large number of Soviet technicians and advisers has brought a substantial improvement in the training, organization, and management of the Egyptian army.

For static warfare, then, the increase in Egyptian military capabilities has been impressive. But as far as mobile operations are concerned, it is thought in Israel that the basic weaknesses of the Egyptian army have not been remedied. The success of military forces in a mobile war critically depends on effective command and control, and it is believed in Israel that the cultural-educational background of most Egyptian officers militates against this. It is also thought that the bureaucratic atmosphere of the Egyptian armed forces discourages risk taking and low-echelon initiative in general, which are also essential in a fast-moving war. The Egyptians recognize these two inherent weaknesses, and their method of command is highly centralized in order to lessen their impact, but a highly centralized command prevents rapid response to the fleeting dangers and opportunities presented by a war of movement. The Russian-inspired strategy of static defense (with offense by fire-power alone), reflected in the Egyptian deployment on the west bank of the Suez Canal, is therefore seen by Israelis as efficient, given the relative capabilities of the Egyptian and Israeli armies.

There is little doubt among Israeli experts that a large-scale Egyptian crossing of the Suez Canal would be defeated by the Israeli armored formations deployed in the Sinai Peninsula. In fact, reinforcement of these forces would be required only if the Israelis themselves decided to effect a large-scale crossing of the canal in order to destroy the artillery and air defense forces on the Egyptian side.

As for the other Arab armies, only Syria's has more than nuisance value. Soviet arms deliveries to Syria have been very large, and the number of tanks and combat aircraft deployed has doubled since 1967. But the Syrian armed forces are still poorly trained, and worse led, and it is thought that they could neither threaten Israel nor defend Damascus against a determined attack.

Over the years the military balance has moved in Israel's favor as the increased sophistication of the weaponry deployed on both sides has given greater weight to Israel's superior manpower. The Middle East is now entering the era of semi-automatic weapons systems, but their operation remains dependent on human choices and maintenance. Thus the relevance of Israel's cultural-educational advantage over the Arabs will become still greater. Whether this will remain so when fully automatic weapons systems are deployed is an open question.

In the medium term, then, the "improvement potential" of the Israeli army will be greater than that of the Egyptian army, as it has been in the years since 1967. In 1967 the second echelon of the Israeli army went to war with reconditioned bolt-action rifles of 1890 design; much of its field artillery consisted of pre-1939 British field guns, and even the air force's equipment was inadequate. (The preemptive strikes against Arab airfields on June 5, 1967, were carried out by an air force whose total payload per strike did not exceed 300 tons.)

Although much of the obsolete weaponry has been replaced since

1967, the capabilities of the Israeli army could still be increased substantially if it were supplied with better equipment. The same cannot be said for the Egyptian armed forces; their potential for improvement by simple reequipment was largely achieved after 1967.

The Soviet Union could, of course, supply still more advanced weaponry, but that would predicate the commitment of more Soviet combat personnel, since training of the Egyptian forces in its use would be slow.

Since an easy path toward a rapid increase in military capability is denied to the Egyptians, their improvement depends on qualitative upgrading of their manpower. Improvement in performance cannot be routinized; it must depend on cultural changes, which can only result from long-term modernization of Egyptian society. But in the medium term the relative balance of military power will depend critically on the nature of the war to be fought, the capability gap between the two sides being far narrower for a static war of attrition.

Guerrilla Action

Immediately after the 1967 war many qualified observers on both sides expressed high expectations about the potential of Arab guerrilla action against Israel. Those estimates apparently reflected the success of many guerrilla movements elsewhere in the 1960s rather than any local reality. In fact, in the five years since the end of the war Arab guerrilla action has failed to play a significant role in the military confrontation between Israel and the Arab states, primarily because of the failure of the Palestinian military organizations to develop subversive bases among the Arab populations in Israeli-controlled territory.

Considering that a large number of men living in the occupied territories have received military and guerrilla training, and considering the ready availability of assorted weaponry left over from the war, the volume of guerrilla and sabotage activity inside Israel has been very small. Indeed, for Israelis who recall the 1936–39 "disturbances" it appears almost insignificant. The fact that each string of sabotage actions remains localized and ends when the security services announce the arrest of those responsible shows that the networks involved were improvised with poor planning and worse security.

Since the Palestinian organizations have failed to develop the political support and terrorist compulsion required to establish a subversive base within Israel, they have remained dependent on infiltration across the cease-fire lines. Initially the Israelis controlled infiltration with mobile patrols and improvised installations. Although apparently only small numbers of infiltrators got through, in the course of 1968 the Israelis suffered some tens of casualties in fire fights. By the second half of 1969, this border had been effectively sealed by a combination of surveillance equipment and physical barriers, and since that time very few infiltrators have succeeded in crossing the Jordan Valley. It should be noted that throughout this counter-guerrilla campaign the Israeli army had ways of knowing rather accurately the number of infiltrators who crossed the Jordan.

Having failed to develop the instruments of revolutionary war, the Palestinian organizations were forced to resort to less effective forms of military action: the shelling of Israeli territory from the other side of the cease-fire lines and shallow penetrations at the Lebanese border. But the Israeli army was able to control these attacks by striking at the guerrillas in the Gilad area on the other side of the cease-fire line, and the sporadic intervention of Jordanian and Iraqi artillery was effectively discouraged by controlled Israeli retaliatory shellings and air strikes.

In the latter half of 1969 the Palestinian organizations gave up even this area of activity and shifted their main effort to the Lebanese frontier. Since then they have continued to use Lebanese territory for rocket attacks against Israeli settlements adjacent to the border, and the exposed "Northern Road" has been the scene of border ambushes. Subsequently periodic Israeli military patrols operating on both sides of the border have brought this form of attack under control too.

The progressive reduction in the scope of Palestinian guerrilla activity may be one of the reasons why only a very small proportion of the guerrillas have been active at any one time. It has been estimated, for example, that a force of one hundred guerrillas could have carried out all the operations conducted since 1967, even allowing for generous periods of rest. This means in effect that the active guerrillas never amounted to more than one percent of the so-called trained fighters on the organizations' payrolls.

There is no reason to expect an increase in the guerrillas' capabilities within the framework of the present cease-fire lines. But the projection of the present pattern of transborder shellings onto a Rogers-plan map of Israel causes a great deal of apprehension among Israelis. It is this, as well as the political impact of the Pal-·estinian guerrillas on Arab opinion, which gives the movement such significance as it has.

Military Intervention by the Soviet Union and the United States

The deployment of Soviet air-defense contingents in Egypt in the first months of 1970 naturally increased Israeli anxieties about Soviet military intervention in the conflict. More recently, however, there has been a return to the more sober view that full-scale military intervention remains unlikely. It is pointed out in Israel that the sheer size of the forces deployed by the warring countries of the region would require a very large initial commitment of forces from an outside power if it were to intervene in a decisive manner without using nuclear weapons. Specifically, several Soviet armored divisions with corresponding air support would be required to effect a crossing of the Suez Canal in the face of determined Israeli resistance. Official Israeli opinion holds that Soviet military planners would not contemplate such an intervention because logistic channels would be exposed to Israeli attack and the possibility of American response would present yet greater dangers.

The Soviets could, of course, deploy a powerful air force in Egypt or elsewhere within striking range of Israeli territory, but it would have to be on the order of several hundred aircraft to support a full-scale Egyptian invasion. Lesser Soviet support is not unlikely, however. At least one air battle between Soviet and Israeli aircraft has already taken place, and the fact that five MIG-21s piloted by Russians were shot down by the Israelis against no losses of their own has not allayed Israeli anxieties. Though the Israelis hope to deter active Soviet intervention by their own means, the ultimate deterrent against such intervention remains the United States.

The United States could intervene very quickly by giving a measure of air support to Israeli ground forces from carrier-borne and land-based aircraft redeployed on Israeli airfields. But the capacity of the latter is limited, and the Sixth Fleet as presently constituted disposes only of some forty-eight air-superiority fighters (F-4Js) and some ninety attack aircraft (A-6s and A-7s). Even without discounting for fleet-defense requirements, this force is not of overwhelming magnitude given the scope of any probable conflict. In a war situation, moreover, the use of the Sixth Fleet against, say, Egypt would involve the risk of a local Soviet response. As for land-based aircraft, well-known political constraints would reduce the deployability of U.S. aircraft in the eastern Mediterranean if U.S. action against the Arabs were considered.

Strategic Advantages of the Occupied Territories

Pre-1967 boundaries presented a number of exceedingly difficult problems for Israeli defense planners, in terms of both "basic security" and "current security" against small-scale infiltration. These boundaries were disproportionately long, so much so that while the area of Israeli-controlled territory more than trebled after the 1967 war, the length of the land perimeter actually decreased. The long and tortuous pre-1967 border meant among other things that infiltration could not be prevented by defensive installations and patrols, as is now being done, and reprisals, designed to have "feedback" effects (which did not always materialize), had to be resorted to instead.

Another "structural" weakness was the large salient formed by the "West Bank," which reduced central Israel to a narrow strip some ten miles across. So long as only Jordanian forces were deployed there, this salient was not seen as a possible bridgehead for a strategic attack against Israel, but the entry of other armies into Jordan would have been a *casus belli* for Israel.

The configuration of the West Bank also meant that two of Israel's major airfields, and Jerusalem itself, were within easy range of artillery deployed there. In fact, the Jerusalem area was so vulnerable geographically that even the relatively weak forces available to the Jordanians could have cut it off from the rest of the country. (Both airfields, Jerusalem, and the most densely populated area of the country, the Tel Aviv area, would also have been within easy range of the Soviet-built artillery rockets now available to the Palestinian military organizations.)

Neither the Lebanese nor the Syrian border presented problems of basic security, but the Syrian presence on the Golan Heights threatened Israel's water supplies, and Syrian shelling of Israeli settlements was a constant problem. Here not only were defensive measures impossible, but topography rendered offensive action costly and difficult.

All this changed in 1967, but the most significant improvement in Israel's strategic position has been vis-à-vis Egypt. The Sinai Peninsula provides Israel with an extensive protective glacis, and controlling it has increased warning time against air intrusions from main Egyptian airfields. (Aircraft would have to reduce their payload sharply if they were to use dispersal airfields or evasive low-level flying tactics.)

The Suez Canal and the fortifications built along it provide Israel with fixed defenses supporting the defensive capabilities of the forces deployed in Sinai. This means, among other things, that the Israelis would not have to resort to either a preemptive attack or protracted mobilization in the event of a full-scale Egyptian deployment. The canal is all the more valuable as a strategic asset because there are only three routes leading eastward from it toward pre-1967 Israel. And control of the east bank of the canal enables Israel not only to maintain a defensive posture in the face of a major enemy deployment but also to repel an invasion without necessarily having to control the skies over the area adjacent to the canal.

Nuclear Weapons

According to press reports which have become frequent since the early sixties, Israel has the technical know-how and the facilities required to manufacture nuclear weapons. There has been no explicit Israeli definition of the circumstances under which the Israeli government would manufacture and use nuclear weapons, but successive Israeli governments have stated that Israel would not be the first country to introduce such weapons into the region. It is clear that if nuclear weapons were to be deployed by any Middle Eastern power their command and control arrangement would be crude and delivery systems would be few in number and vulnerable to preemption, with destabilizing consequences.

One might consider the consequences of several eventualities. If Israel acquired nuclear weapons but the Arab countries did not, Israel would have an absolute advantage, since its enemies could no longer risk launching an all-out attack. The threat of military destruction by the Arabs would then disappear, although guerrilla warfare could, of course, continue. A nuclear guarantee to the Arab countries by the Soviet Union would partially neutralize Israel's advantage but would not eliminate it.

If the Arabs also succeeded in acquiring nuclear weapons, a balance of terror might develop in the Middle East, so that large-scale military action as in June 1967 would be largely precluded. Israeli reprisals against guerrillas would also involve greater risks than before. But in the state of tension likely to prevail, the Israelis would find it difficult to predict the behavior of Arab governments, and for that as well as for technical reasons nuclear deterrence would be unstable and a nuclear war originating in a preemptive move would be a distinct possibility.

The third possibility, that the Arabs would acquire nuclear weapons while Israel had none, is unlikely, but that eventuality would involve the danger of extinction for Israel.

If press reports on Israel's technological capabilities are to be believed, its government faces the following options:

(1) To acquire nuclear weapons and ensure its military security for the foreseeable future, at the risk of being caught in an irreversible process leading to general destruction should the Arabs acquire the same weapons.

(2) Not to acquire nuclear weapons, in order to avoid the danger of an eventual nuclear war. That choice would assume that the Arabs will not obtain nuclear weapons if Israel does not have any, and that Israel will continue to maintain its non-nuclear superiority. Such a decision could also result from pressure from the United States rather than from any Israeli calculations, since any foreseeable U.S. administration is likely to be set against such an expansion of the nuclear club.

If it has the means, Israel would probably try to acquire or to manufacture nuclear weapons only if it became apparent that the Arabs were about to obtain them or that the non-nuclear military balance was moving in favor of the Arabs. Such a development is also possible if the divergence of views between Israel and the United States reaches the point where Israel needs a substitute for U.S. arms supplies and no longer has to take an American reaction into consideration.

If both sides were to acquire nuclear weapons, Israel's physical survival would depend upon Arab actions. Should nuclear weapons be introduced into the Middle East, the strategic importance of the territories now occupied by Israel would become minimal, though the Sinai would perhaps be more suitable than the Negev for nuclear tests, and very useful for the deployment of short-range missiles.

The Present Round of Peace Negotiations

Most Israelis believe that the Arabs will accept Israel's existence only when they are convinced that it cannot be destroyed by force. Most Israelis would remain skeptical of any unilateral Arab declarations of nonbelligerence or similar move short of full recognition and direct negotiations with appointed representatives of the Israeli government. (Unilateral Arab declarations are discounted as rapidly reversible and, with respect to Arab public opinion, easily denied.) In the absence of full Arab recognition of Israel, Israel's immediate defense needs have a clear priority and far outweigh long-term preoccupations about peaceful relations with the Arabs; in fact, ultimate peace is more likely to flow from effective defense than from limited and ambiguous political concessions on the part of the Arabs.

The prevailing impression in Israel is that most segments of Arab opinion believe that the destruction of Israel by military means is an attainable objective. While prior to the death of Nasser some marginal groups in Israel argued that the Egyptian leadership no longer regarded the elimination of Israel as feasible, almost all Israelis agree that it would fulfill an aspiration which is uppermost in Arab minds. Most Israelis therefore accept a basic operational rule: nothing which contributes to the security of the nation should be abandoned until it has been ascertained that the Arabs really intend to recognize the existence of Israel and to live at peace with it. This attitude operates as an important constraint on Israeli policy with respect to peace negotiations.

Until 1970 brought Russian intervention alongside the Arabs, there was another set of attitudes held by the Israelis which militated against peace negotiations. Many Israelis have generalized feelings of superiority over the Arabs, which enable them to accept the Arab denial of coexistence with equanimity. They consider Arab society as backward and even degenerate in contrast to the Jewish society of Israel, which is seen as modern and dynamic. In individual terms such feelings of superiority are expressed in everyday Arab-Israeli contacts; in political terms this attitude is expressed in the common feeling that Israel can wait until the Arabs eventually come around, and if the Arabs try to use force again, they will be beaten again.

Y. Harkaby, a well-known specialist on Arab affairs, has written an accurate description of such Israeli attitudes, published shortly before the June 1967 war: "We have a tendency to pay no attention to those of our actions which we dislike, and conversely, to place the whole burden of accusation on the Arab's shoulders as if we on our part had only good intentions toward them. Our identification with Zionism, the pride which we feel in its achievements and ethno-centrism peculiar to every human group, are all elements which may impair the objectivity of our vision. All the virulence of our criticism is reserved for our opponents while our self-criticism remains weak." [1]

The outcome of the Six Day War naturally reinforced such attitudes of superiority, while the Arab rejection of Israel's repeated peace offers has intensified Israeli distrust of long-term Arab intentions. The years since 1967 may have increased Israeli tolerance for the social and personal costs of protracted warfare, but they have also reinforced the Israeli belief that the economic and military requirements of protracted warfare will in the end always be forthcoming. Quoting Arthur Ruppin, a Jewish leader of a generation ago, General Moshe Dayan said in September 1968, "The Arabs refuse to recognize our achievements. If we want to continue our work despite their attitude, we cannot avoid the sacrifice of human lives; fate imposes upon us perpetual war with the Arabs. This may not be a desirable situation, but such is the reality." [2]

For a number of reasons, of which the structure of the coalition government is only one, Israeli attitudes to the recent rounds of peace negotiations are expressed in response to plans formulated by others rather than in official Israeli plans. (Several partial Israeli plans have been publicized but none of them has been adopted by the government, so political positions have not polarized around them.)

While all the factors in the conflict can hardly be said to have become stabilized, Israelis see a crystallization in the positions of

---

[1] Y. Harkaby, *Les Temps Modernes*, No. 253 bis, 1967, p. 473.
[2] *Ha'aretz*, Nov. 22, 1968.

the two big-power protagonists as reflected in their stated goals relative to the American peace initiative: the United States advocates the return of the occupied territories in exchange for Arab political concessions and third-party guarantees; the Soviet Union would limit the *quid pro quo* to third-party guarantees and would provide for no substantial political concessions on the part of the Arabs. Twenty years of experience with international and third-party guarantees in the Arab-Israeli conflict leads most Israelis to discount their value, and they therefore tend to seek Arab political concessions as the necessary payment for Israeli territorial concessions.

One can quickly dispose of the marginal positions. The pro-Soviet Communist party, Rakah, whose supporters are mainly Arabs, follows the Moscow line on peace negotiations as on all other issues. Matzpen, a very small group whose membership is in the hundreds, also advocates the return of all the occupied territories without negotiation or compensation. A number of other small political groups, including Uri Avneri's Ha Olam-Ha-Ze (the local version of the New Left) and the Maki Communist party (which does not follow the Moscow line), also advocate extreme conciliation of the Arab world. At the last general elections, in October 1969, these four parties together polled some 6 percent of the vote, half of which was accounted for by Arab votes. At the other extreme, there is only one avowed annexationist group, known as the Whole Land of Israel, which failed to win a single seat in the October 1969 elections. But almost 30 percent of the votes were cast for one major and two minor parties which are also opposed to territorial concessions: Menahem Begin's Gahal party, and the State List and Free Center parties. Both the National Religious party and the Ahdut Ha'avoda faction of the Labor party also include sizable elements which opposed territorial concessions. Indeed, the legendary stability of the party structure, which has remained unchanged through all the upheavals of the last generation, appears to be threatened by the debate over the return of the occupied territories.

On the other hand, the strong longing for peace which is a feature of Israeli life was expressed in public opinion polls after the government's rejection of what could be called a concrete peace initiative. In the spring of 1970 the Israeli government refused to allow the president of the World Jewish Congress, Dr. Nahum Goldman, to meet President Nasser as an authorized representative; almost

40 percent of the population disapproved of the government's decision.

The Israeli government has at no time defined its policy beyond stating that Israel is prepared to make substantial territorial concessions in exchange for full diplomatic recognition and a peace treaty. It has also insisted that the new frontiers, as well as being recognized, would have to be defensible.

Until October 1968 the Israeli government insisted that negotiations should be direct from the very beginning. Since that time, in a process which has sometimes been described as erosion, the government has gradually accepted a greater and greater degree of indirectness. This was reaffirmed in the 1971 round of the Jarring talks and did not lead to any defections from the coalition government. (The Gahal party left the coalition because of the explicit acceptance of the principle of territorial concessions.) But the government maintains its insistence on direct negotiations at some later stage and a peace treaty to follow.

East Jerusalem is not usually discussed as being negotiable, but owing to the possibility of a compromise in its juridical status it is not likely to be the key issue. The major territorial issues involve the Golan Heights, the Jordan Valley, the Eilat and Rafiah junction areas, and Sharm-el-Sheikh. One segment of the government follows the Defense Minister Moshe Dayan in his insistence that Sharm-el-Sheikh, together with the road linking it with Eilat, should remain under Israeli control. The Deputy Prime Minister, Yigal Allon, has formulated a plan for a permanent Israeli military presence in the Jordan Valley which would not entirely cut off the West Bank from the Hashemite Kingdom and which would not preclude an Israeli withdrawal from most of the West Bank. That the Gaza Strip is to be within Israeli military control is implied in the demand for an Israeli military presence in the Rafiah area, but its ultimate disposition is not now an issue.

It is characteristic of the motivation of these supposedly "strategic" territorial plans that Allon has not commented on Dayan's demand on Sharm-el-Sheikh while Dayan has not commented on the Allon plan beyond indicating repeatedly that Israel should do nothing to reinforce the distinction between Israel and the West Bank.

Israeli political attitudes on how to contend with United States pressures have not crystallized, since no specific American demands have been made. The events leading up to Israeli acceptance of the

August 1970 peace initiative indicate that the government's policy will be shaped by internal political and external military factors at the time, rather than by United States pressure as such.

Unilateral Policy Choices for Israel

Disposition of the Occupied Territories

Israel's administrative policy in the occupied territories has been remarkably coherent since the last months of 1967, largely because Moshe Dayan has been able to control the policies and machinery of the military administration. Because none but symbolic decisions have been made about the ultimate disposition of the occupied territories, Dayan has succeeded even in limiting the intervention of other members of the Cabinet and, through them, of the various Israeli pressure groups concerned with the territories.

Dayan's policy has been based on three elements: (1) preventing organized political opposition and terrorist or guerrilla activities; (2) minimizing the significance of the armistice lines separating pre-1967 Israeli territory from the occupied territories, and (3) to the extent consistent with the first and sometimes overriding the second principle, interfering as little as possible with the lives of the local inhabitants.

Striving for "normalcy" has meant preserving local governmental power structures and bureaucracies, maintaining the status quo in legal and religious matters (with one significant exception), and permitting an "open door" between the occupied areas and the rest of the Arab world. Students from Gaza are allowed to attend universities in Egypt, West Bankers move freely to and from the East Bank of Jordan, and travelers from the Arab countries are allowed to visit the occupied areas. In the West Bank these policies have succeeded in large measure: living standards have increased and the security has been satisfactory, while the net costs of the occupation have been very low.

This liberal policy has not succeeded, however, in the Gaza Strip. There the policy has not had the benefit of the West Bank's tradition of vigorous municipal politics or the personal prestige of Moshe Dayan among many of its people. Further, living standards on the Gaza Strip are no higher and indeed may be a little lower than they were before 1967. Security in the strip has remained poor, though terrorist action is localized and the area has not become a base for guerrilla activities in the Sinai Peninsula or in Israel proper.

The coherence of Israel's occupation policy dissolves, however, when it touches on the ultimate disposition of the territories. Annexationist sentiments do not appear to have become more explicit, but there is little doubt that in the past five years a web of interests has grown in support of continuing the status quo. Dayan's policy has been consistent in discouraging the development of Israeli economic enterprises in the occupied territory, but some marginal Israeli interests have been established, and access to the Dead Sea by way of Jericho, to Hebron, and to certain transit routes across the West Bank has induced strong desires to preserve such access in the future.

Annexationist sentiment, on the other hand, is discouraged by demographic realities. There are now some 1.3 million Arabs living in Israeli-controlled territory, including the 300,000 Israeli Arabs (and the 350,000 dwellers in the Gaza Strip, an area which evokes no sentimental attachment). The absorpiton of an additional 1 million Arabs, with full citizenship rights like those which Israeli Arabs now enjoy, would fundamentally alter the character of Israeli society. Israel would no longer be a Jewish state, but only a Jewish-dominated state. Further, owing to the higher Arab birth rate, and in the absence of mass immigration from the United States or the Soviet Union, the Arab population would exceed the Jewish one in about thirty years.

Long-range demographic projections have no significant impact on Israeli public opinion or governmental policy, but the immediate population problem weakens the annexationist stand, particularly that of the left-wing annexationists in the Ahdut Ha'avodah party. They are aware that the reservoir of potential working-class immigrants, i.e., Jews from underdeveloped countries, is almost exhausted and that future immigrants from the West are hardly likely to go in for manual labor; their ideal of "Jewish labor" would be compromised by the absorption of a large Arab working class.

Since 1967 various voices both in Israel and the occupied territories have advocated the creation of a Palestinian political entity. Basically, the idea is to form a central government out of the existing municipalities of the West Bank, which would collect taxes, provide public services, and eventually assume full rule over the

West Bank and the Gaza Strip, and, in some versions, also the Golan Heights, as a possible site for refugee settlement. According to
some proposals this Palestinian state would gradually become independent, taking over responsibility for internal security, external defense, and foreign relations.

At first sight, this is an attractive proposition to many Israelis,
since it holds out the prospect of continued control of the occupied
territories without annexation. But some members of the Cabinet,
led by Prime Minister Golda Meir, have consistently opposed this
idea. They believe that the Arab states would not recognize an autonomous or even an independent Palestinian state if it were linked
to Israel by treaty or even informally. The creation of such an entity, then, would bring peace no nearer, while complicating the second best alternative, the indefinite continuation of the present situation.

In the West Bank itself, the relentless opposition of both King
Hussein and the Palestinian military organizations deterred several
municipal leaders from associating themselves with these proposals.
In any case, the West Bank municipal leaders have never had any
significant influence over the populations or the weak municipal
structures of the Gaza Strip, and their influence in the West Bank
has declined, while the emergence of a younger and more representative leadership has been impeded by the lack of representative political structures. The September 1970 crisis in Jordan and Moshe
Dayan's explicit rejection of the proposals have further dimmed the
prospects of a Palestinian entity.

Rehabilitation of the Palestinian Refugees

Most Israelis reject the belief, apparently widespread elsewhere,
that the basic cause of the Arab-Israeli conflict is the problem of
the Palestine refugees. They believe that the refugee problem is
rather a symptom and instrument of the conflict, and point to the
fact that most Arab "host countries" failed to cooperate with the
UN Relief and Works Agency (UNRRWA) insofar as it sought
to resettle rather than maintain the refugees. Nevertheless, the continued existence of refugee camps in and around present Israeli territory is certainly not in Israel's interest.

Since 1967 the rehabilitation of the refugees has been the subject of several reasoned proposals and at least one fully elaborated plan. While the general economic recovery of the occupied territories and the employment of tens of thousands of refugees in the Israeli economy has certainly raised living standards, the refugee problem is essentially what it was in 1967. Paradoxically, one reason is that most refugee camps have become rather like villages. The West Bank camps are productive economic units with a large number of small commercial and craft enterprises, including cooperatives. The vast majority of the refugees do not subsist on rations alone, but work in agriculture, retail trade, and even as entrepreneurs in small-scale manufacturing. In Lebanon and Syria, too, the camps provide only a fraction of the housing services and food consumed by the refugees, who earn the difference in the local or refugee economy. Only in the Gaza Strip is the standard of living approximately what UNRRWA rations allow.

Rehabilitation, therefore, means providing better housing and better jobs for refugees whose standard of living is already close to that of the local population, or in the case of the Gaza Strip, above that standard. It is complicated by the need to plan it (perhaps refugee new towns, scattered units in nonrefugee environments, and financial compensation) in such a way that the rehabilitated refugees will cease to be a political problem. It is only since 1969 that the Israeli government has begun to consider seriously implementing large-scale rehabilitation programs. It is too early to say much about this new policy, except that its low priority indicates a governmental consensus that the problem of the Palestinian refugees should be solved multilaterally in the context of a peace settlement.

Seeking a Partial Peace

Since its antagonists refuse to negotiate with Israel, the government has never had a choice between a direct settlement and a great-power resolution of the conflict. It has been suggested, however, that Israel should seek a separate peace with Jordan, where there does exist an area of mutual interest and possible agreement. The Israelis might be willing to make generous concessions in order to establish the principle of peaceful coexistence between Israel and at least one Arab state, and the Jordanians could minimize the political risks of going it alone by obtaining what is patently a very good deal. Such a settlement would require, however, that King

Hussein be able to withstand strong pressures both inside his kingdom and from the Arab world in general, and that the Israeli government make concessions which would provide Hussein with real incentives to reach an agreement and would minimize his risks.

Hussein's long-delayed but very successful offensive against the Palestinian military organizations appears to have increased the chances for such a separate peace. On the other hand, Hussein has apparently been unable or unwilling to pursue it, presumably because he wishes to retain "legitimacy" with the other Arab regimes. But time has also reduced the value to Israel of such a settlement, since Hussein's acceptance of the principle of coexistence is now worth much less. Unofficial Israeli contacts with the Jordanian regime, however, have been initiated, and at the "working level" the chances of an agreement seem to be good.

Initiatives to Deescalate the Conflict

Most Israelis are acutely aware of their government's limited area of maneuver in the present, internationalized, phase of the conflict, and it has been suggested that Israel should act unilaterally to reduce tensions and widen the range of its options. One proposal is that the government should renounce the requirement for direct negotiations, declare Israeli willingness to return practically all the occupied territories (with small stated exceptions), and state its expectation that this ought to lead to the eventual signing of peace treaties.

Another proposed initiative, and one which may be marginally more realistic, is directed at disengaging the Soviet Union from the conflict by allowing the reopening of the Suez Canal. The plan advocates a simultaneous withdrawal of Israeli and Egyptian forces to identical distances from their respective sides of the canal. The canal, it is assumed, would be cleared and used while peace negotiations proceed in an appropriately dilatory fashion. The proponents of this plan assume that reopening the canal is, or could be, the overriding Soviet policy objective and that to achieve it the Soviet Union would be willing to absorb substantial political losses in Egypt. This plan, however, has since been appropriated by a deft Egyptian initiative which turned it into a vehicle for seeking a partial Israeli withdrawal.

The Israeli Military

With the death of Nasser the future course of Egyptian policy has become even less predictable than hitherto, but the cease-fire and the associated negotiations present a number of well-delineated options to the parties involved. These boil down to a choice between the status quo, a partial settlement, and a renewal of the fighting.

If the cease-fire is terminated or broken, Israel will face three distinct military threats from Egyptian ground forces along the canal and the associated Soviet-Egyptian air-defense system:

(1) The Egyptians could mount a static artillery offensive, possibly supplemented by harassing commando operations. This appears to be the most probable development, and one dangerous to Israel. Although Israeli strongholds along the canal are virtually shellproof, casualties would occur, and even if limited to some tens per month, would exceed the level that Israel regards as acceptable.

(2) The Egyptians could mount a limited offensive aimed at seizing the east bank of the canal, possibly in order to reopen it under Soviet auspices. But the antiaircraft missiles could not protect Egyptian ground forces for more than a few miles beyond the canal, and that is insufficient for a secure hold on the waterway as would be required for clearing it. A missile-based air defense, moreover, cannot provide tactical air support, so such an offensive would lead to a straight fight between Israeli and Egyptian armor, a prospect which the Egyptians would not contemplate with equanimity. This Egyptian option looks much better if a swift crossing of the canal were followed by an immediate cease-fire which would establish a new status quo, but that diplomatic feat does not seem feasible, assuming continuing American support of Israel.

(3) Under cover of Soviet air-force deployment, on the order of several hundred strike and interceptor aircraft, the Egyptians could mount a full-scale invasion of the Sinai, with or without the participation of Soviet ground forces. But Soviet air-force contingents in Egypt at this time could not sustain such an operation, and Egypt's own air power is inadequate to the task. Soviet military intervention of this order is one of the imponderables of the crisis, but not an immediate emergency.

The principal threat, then—an artillery offensive—is both sufficiently dangerous and sufficiently probable to cause great anxieties to Israeli defense planners. They appear to have three basic options to deal with it:

(1) Absorb the Egyptian artillery offensive and reduce its impact by additional protective construction and other countermeasures. This low-risk option may cost some tens of casualties per month.

(2) Stage one or more ground offensives across the canal, by either commandos or mechanized forces or both, to dislodge or disrupt the Egyptian artillery. This could be supplemented by counterbattery fire. (Until recently Israeli artillery was grossly outranged by the Soviet-built high-velocity guns which were supplied to the Egyptian army in large numbers.) The thick antitank and antiaircraft defenses around Egyptian artillery batteries, which include some hundreds of antitank guns, would make this option rather costly. And the Israeli operation would have to be conducted in the course of a single night; otherwise, the Israelis would be subject to daylight air attack once they penetrated beyond the first line of Egyptian SAM missiles.

(3) Attack the air-defense system first and then use continuing air strikes to control Egyptian artillery fire. This looks like the most probable option in the light of what is known about the basic tactical approach of the Israeli Defense Forces, but is not without its problems. Even with deception and electronic countermeasure equipment and radar-seeking missiles, the destruction of all missile batteries may cost dozens of aircraft. A partial offensive would be almost as costly and far less useful, since tactical bombing cannot be performed efficiently in a hostile air environment. Further, the Soviet-Egyptian air-defense system over the Nile Valley could be used to shelter preparations for a new missile deployment (which could be established in a single night), so the costly air attacks would have been for nought. The intervention of Soviet-manned fighters cannot be discounted either, especially since the introduction of Flagon and Foxbat high-performance aircraft.

A coordinated night operation by commandos and mechanized forces against the missile batteries would also be costly in human lives, and it could trigger the intervention of Soviet-manned interceptors during the daylight phase of the operation, when Israeli aircraft would have to follow up the ground-force attack. The Egyptians and their Soviet colleagues seem to have taken this possible response most seriously: the SAM batteries are protected by large numbers of antitank guns, as well as entire battalions of antiaircraft guns and infantry.

There are, of course, a number of other tactics which could be used, but Israeli planners have to take into account the fact that the SAMs could be replaced in the course of a few hours. The Egyptians could simply move forward columns of mobile SAM batteries prepared under the shelter of the inner air defenses, which include Soviet-manned interceptors. A radical response would therefore require a phased attack against the forward SAM deployment and then against airfields, missile batteries, and ground-control facilities throughout Egypt, including those manned by the Russians. Such an attack would involve risks that the Israeli government is not likely to accept and which the American government is not likely to underwrite.

The Possible Outcomes

As to the possible evolution of Arab-Israeli relations, two extremes can be excluded because their probability in the next ten years or so remains very low: a general peace with harmonious relations between Israel and its Arab neighbors, or the physical destruction of Israel. If we consider the future, then, in terms of continuing conflict, the trends outlined in this survey permit a number of extrapolations, though there are also a number of imponderables. In the authors' view, the following prospects are likely:

(1) A strengthening of the extremist elements in the Arab world and a corresponding weakening of the pro-Western regimes.

(2) Continued Israeli military superiority over the Arab world as a whole and Egypt in particular, as long as substantial Soviet forces are not directly involved in offensive operations.

(3) The continued inability of the Palestinian military organizations to affect Israel's power in economic or military terms.

The two major imponderables are the possible evolution of Soviet military intervention or the imposition of a makeshift settlement by the United States and the Soviet Union. If such a settlement were to be imposed, a real, albeit impermanent, deescalation of the conflict cannot be excluded. If, however, a settlement is not imposed from the outside, the present situation might continue for several years with occasional and limited military activities along the cease-fire lines.

A prolongation of the conflict may lead to an unsettled situation in the occupied territories, but it would also lead to an increasing degree of administrative and economic integration. This development would enable Israel to undertake long-term unilateral projects for the rehabilitation of Arab refugees living under its control, which, in turn, may lead to a softening in the attitude of some Arabs toward Israel. In any case, prolongation of the present situation would probably imply a further strengthening of Israel in relation to the Arab world and, failing a real peace, that is clearly the most desirable alternative for a large majority of Israelis.

But the probable strengthening of extremist elements within the Arab world might induce the Arab states, and Egypt in particular, to take military initiatives which could lead, directly or indirectly, to another general war. Without the active intervention of the Soviet Union, Israel would no doubt win again. But it is hard to believe that, given its present degree of involvement, the Soviet Union would allow the Arabs to suffer another defeat without intervening directly. In any case, the authors of this paper believe that another victory against the Arabs would not bring peace any nearer.

Part III

Israel

Chapter 4
Inside Israel
Chaim Adler

The most important and pervasive influence in the life of Israel in the 1970s probably will be its international relations. Since the inception of Israel, its internal structure has been determined largely by the precarious political balance it maintains with its Arab neighbors. Fundamental changes wrought by the 1967 war in the state's security and international position will have deep and far-reaching impact on almost all facets of Israeli society. Of crucial importance will be whether the coming years bring an indefinite prolongation of the current stalemate, with Israel continuing to occupy Arab territories; whether war will break out again on a continuous or sporadic basis, and with what consequences; or whether there will be a peaceful political settlement of the conflict.

This attempt to anticipate social developments in Israel can offer only preliminary hypotheses. It is assumed that considerable tension between Israel and the Arab states will continue, but with serious attempts to avoid all-out war. If these conditions continue, one would expect existing trends in internal social development to continue as well.

It seems correct to classify Israeli society as a revolutionary society, for insofar as the essence of a revolution is the establishment of a heretofore nonexistent social order, Israel today is the product of a social revolution. With the creation of a politically independent, economically advanced, and culturally creative modern Jewish society, based on concepts of social justice and equality, a new social order was founded. Zionism, the basic ideology of this new society, calls for immigration as a form of demographic growth, which gives the revolutionary process an unfinished and ongoing form.

As in most revolutionary societies, Israel's growth in the past fifty years has drawn legitimacy from a "prophetic" revolutionary ideology. Israel's basic ethos, at whose core is the pioneering ideology of

147

the early settlers, has created a high degree of consensus and social unity. It gave rise to an Israeli version of a "frontier society" which by and large was willing to forgo material rewards and comforts.

The revolutionary-pioneering spirit has remained a feature of Israeli life to the present day, though with varying degrees of intensity. The Six Day War in June 1967 revitalized somewhat the flagging frontier spirit. Lasting peace in the Middle East, or even a political settlement short of peace, might kill part of this spirit by eliminating the problem of survival. Thus the coming years will probably witness tension between a desire to perpetuate the revolutionary spirit and a tendency to institutionalize the existing norms of a relatively affluent society.

A second feature of Israeli society also stands to be challenged during the decade. Unlike most new small nations, but like some of the major revolutionary systems, Israel in the early years of its existence successfully avoided the pitfalls of an inner-directed parochialism and a self-centered identity. Its multidimensional relations with world Jewry, its international contacts in scholarship, science, the arts, and music, its socialist alliances, as well as its complex network of technical assistance programs in Asia, Africa, and Latin America, gave the Israeli people an openness and orientation to world events. Israel thus enjoyed international standing beyond its numerical strength and political weight and, though geographically removed from major world centers and encircled by hostile neighbors, it developed a wide range of interests and relationships.

In recent years, and especially since the Six Day War, there have been the beginnings of a disturbing counter-movement. As a victorious and "conquering" nation, Israel is being increasingly shut out by the international community, even by some of the groups that were formerly its principal contacts with the rest of the world. Apparently, despite growing tourism in both directions, meaningful international exchange and communication have been reduced. As a result of criticism of Israel after the war, many Israelis have tended to withdraw and to concentrate on local issues. This withdrawal coincides with the advent of a generation of Israeli-born youth and an increase of citizens of Middle Eastern origin. Generally, neither of these groups has been oriented toward relations with international reference groups. It seems safe to hypothesize, then, that both Israel's current international position and the changes in its demography make it vulnerable to "provincial chauvinism" [1] based upon self-satisfaction and inward orientation.

A third feature of Israeli society is its quick growth rate. The first two decades of Israel's statehood saw enormous growth in almost all spheres of social, economic, political, and cultural life that far surpassed the normal expansion that could be expected from mere population increase as a result of immigration. Growth became one of the landmarks of the society, an integral part of its ideology. But this growth was not accompanied by corresponding social change and innovation. An examination of the institutional structure of Israeli society (particularly in the political sphere), its ideologically defined goals or purposes, or its patterns of cultural and social activities reveals a high degree of stability and continuity.

The reason may be sought in the development of Israeli society. The social revolution wrought by Zionism in Palestine reached its peak in the 1930s, underwent consolidation in the 1940s, and culminated in the establishment of the state in 1948. In the early years the revolutionary spirit, as well as the know-how that went into the establishment of this society, came from the young European settlers. By the 1950s and 1960s the early pioneers had grown older and become the central elite. With emotional commitments to, and vested interests in, the "revolution," they tended to become conservative and unsympathetic to change.

Perhaps the one major exception has been Zahal, the Israeli defense forces, which has grown and at the same time undergone adaptation and change. This included ideological flexibility as well as change in military doctrines, training and educational techniques, and scientific and technological innovation. In fact, it is claimed that one of the important characteristics of the Israeli military is its rapid and effective adaptation to new and changing conditions. One could suggest that a principal reason for the limited changes in Israeli society is that most of the motivation for innovation has been absorbed by the military. Zahal has thus become the locus in which the Israeli-born younger generation can find an outlet for youthful change-oriented energies and meaningful self-expression.

No doubt, there will be an ever-growing need to direct Israeli youth into spheres other than the military, even if the present *aliyah*

---

[1] A term coined by S. N. Eisenstadt, professor of sociology at Hebrew University.

(immigration) of educated and skilled immigrants continues. Peace in the Middle East would make it possible to divert energy and talent into different social spheres. But if current political conditions persist, there probably will be a scarcity of change-oriented elements in Israel's institutional life. In view of the demands for social change and institutional innovation that the next decade will almost inevitably bring, such a scarcity might pose serious problems for the further development of Israeli society.

Bold and rational confrontation with the real social issues of Israel, however, could mobilize its society for change and innovation, revive its future-oriented pioneering spirit, and avert the dangers of parochial, chauvinistic complacency by linking it to parallel developments abroad. It is our purpose here to analyze some of these issues.

Social Integration

It is fair to assume that during a stalemate in the Arab-Israeli hostilities, and certainly under conditions of peace, Israel's foremost problem will be social integration. In the pre-state Yishuv (community) social integration was a minor problem, for the community was demographically homogeneous and displayed strong solidarity, engendered by the future orientation of large sectors of its members. In the first two decades of statehood the physical absorption of the newcomers and external military pressures helped integrate the society. This is no longer happening. The current cease-fire and apparent diminution of the military threat have permitted the rise of disintegrative forces, among them feelings of discrimination and dissatisfaction by the lower classes, which have found expression in strikes and demonstrations. One must expect that such disintegrative trends will increase, especially when class differences can no longer be attributed to recent-immigrant status and in fact appear only *after* society has overcome the initial difficulties of absorbing immigrants. These tendencies may develop into a major problem for Israeli society in the next decade.

The background of the problem can be readily appreciated. As a result of the large waves of Jewish immigration from the Middle and Near East, especially during the 1950s, the demographic and cultural composition of the society was drastically changed. While in 1948–49 only 15 percent of Jewish settlers in Israel came from Oriental countries, by 1967 that figure had risen to 48 percent. There can be little doubt that, in historic perspective, this immigration will be one of the most significant and even heroic stories of Israel: under conditions of war, this small and poor society tripled its population within the first fifteen years of its existence and launched a most impressive process of absorption and rehabilitation.

Before the establishment of the state, disadvantaged groups, mostly Jews of Oriental origin, were a small minority. And, because of the rather low standard of living of the general community then and the high degree of political-ideological solidarity, these pockets of disadvantage did not have a disintegrative impact. Since the establishment of the state, close to 50 percent of the immigration has come from underdeveloped, semifeudal, traditional societies in the Middle East, the newcomers composed mostly of large families headed by uneducated or poorly educated adults without financial resources. Significant sections of the Oriental Jewish community, then, were from the beginning ill equipped socially, politically, and economically to meet the requirements of the progressive, technological, and largely modern Israeli society. While housing, free education, employment, health services, and social welfare programs prevented chaos, they did not bridge some of the gaps between these immigrants and the more advantaged veteran elites and European newcomers.

These conditions made for two great dangers: that social and economic differences along ethnic lines would emerge and split the previously highly integrated society, and that the society might lose its modern and democratic features. Israel would then face serious problems of survival and of further growth, as well as difficulties in preserving a meaningful dialogue with other Jewish communities in the Western world.

Israel coped with these dangers in two ways. A series of social welfare programs ensured that no one suffered from real hunger, malnutrition, or lack of some kind of housing; very few adults experienced long periods of unemployment, and very few youngsters remained without schooling. Social institutions open to all, primarily the army and the school system, gave the new groups, and especially the marginal ones, some sense of social participation. There can be little doubt that in the last two decades Israel has succeeded in giving the immigrants from Oriental countries a considerable sense of belonging as well as the basic conditions for a more or less decent existence.

Nevertheless, this period has been marked by two parallel and somewhat connected developments which may interfere with the integration of the society. First, there has grown quite a large and disturbing stratum of poverty on the fringes of society, comprised mainly of Jews of Oriental origin. In 1969, for example, there were more than 365,000 people at poverty levels or on welfare, and an additional 266,000 near poverty.[2] That year, 6.5 percent of the families of Oriental origin lived four or more persons per room, as compared with only 1.1 precent of the families of European or American origin.[3] In 1968, 66 percent of the Jewish families receiving aid from the Social Welfare Bureau were of Oriental origin, although this group constituted only 27 percent of the total Jewish population.[4] Nine percent of families are large, having 40 percent of all children; 90 percent of these families are of Oriental origin.

There is, then, clearly a high correlation between poverty and ethnicity. A very high proportion of the poor are of Oriental origin, though by far not all people of Oriental origin are poor. But it is not the correlation between origin and poverty that is the cause of disquiet. As in many other parts of the world where ethnicity and poverty are related, here too it is poverty itself that is provoking unrest. Ethnicity is a background characteristic of this poverty, not its cause.

At the same time, however, Israeli social policies and the process of absorption have brought about considerable change and mobility among Jews of Oriental origin. For example, a startling rise in the possession of durable goods by Oriental families took place between 1958 and 1969: from 8.2 to 94.9 percent for electric refrigerators; from 14 to 90.6 percent for gas ranges; from 3.1 to 41.5 percent for electric washing machines.[5]

There was also a considerable decrease in the size of the "ab-

---

[2] R. Rotter and N. Shamay, *Patterns of Poverty in Israel, Preliminary Findings* (*Social Security,* Journal of Welfare and Social Security Studies, National Insurance Institute, No. 1, Feb. 1971, Hebrew).

[3] *Statistical Abstract of Israel 1970* (Jerusalem: Central Bureau of Statistics), No. 21, Table F/17, p. 181.

[4] *Statistical Abstract of Israel 1969* (Jerusalem: Central Bureau of Statistics), No. 20, Table B/17, p. 44.

[5] *Statistical Abstract of Israel 1969, op. cit.,* Table F/21, pp. 185–86.

sorbed" Oriental family. While Oriental mothers with no schooling had 6.6 live births in 1967 (compared to 4.0 among mothers of European or American origin), the rate dropped to 4.6 for those with elementary education or less, and reached a low of 3.1 for those with 9 to 12 years of schooling and 2.5 for those with 13 or more years.[6]

There was also a marked increase in the rate of "interethnic" marriages, certainly a sign of absorption and change. While in 1952 only 5.6 percent of all marriages were between an Oriental bride and a non-Oriental groom, and 3.4 percent between a non-Oriental bride and an Oriental groom, these percentages rose to 7.6 and 8.6, respectively, in 1968.[7]

Another indicator of change is the rise in the rate of students of Oriental origin in post-elementary education, from 17.1 percent of the total student body in 1956–57 to 42.6 percent in 1969–70.[8]

Finally, considerable change has taken place in political life as well. There has been only a slight increase in the number of Knesset members of Oriental origin, but a most significant mobility into political roles on the local level.

Yet despite these changes, large sectors of Oriental Jewry perceive their position in society as marginal. For them the crucial want is no longer the achievement of decent living conditions and minimal participation in society. Rather, they wish to carve out for themselves avenues of access to the center of society, and active participation in it—a desire which is, of course, fertile ground for feelings of ethnic exclusion and discrimination. The result is an apparently paradoxical situation, but well known elsewhere: at a time when most of the basic needs of the Oriental newcomers have been satisfied, their awareness of their collective position in society is sharpening. In fact, initial economic, political, and educational success gives greater importance to the remaining gaps in these very fields and plays a decisive role in shaping an ethnic identity containing elements of dissatisfaction.

These developments, then, will constitute the core of the integra-

---

[6] *Statistical Abstract of Israel 1969*, No. 20, Table C/30, p. 84.

[7] *Jewish Marriages in Israel* (Jerusalem: Central Bureau of Statistics), special publication No. 194, Table 19, p. 24; *Statistical Abstract 1970, op. cit.*, No. 21, Table C/13, p. 71.

[8] *Statistical Abstract*, No. 14 (1963), Table 16, p. 641; and No. 21 (1970), Table S/19, p. 560.

tion problem during this decade. If no significant breakthrough occurs in the coming years to give the Oriental Jews a sense of participation in society, serious social disintegration may be expected.

The phenomenon of poverty calls for a carefully planned and ongoing Israeli version of the "war on poverty," i.e., for a redefinition of priorities and a reallocation of resources in accordance with the new priorities. Even with the present severe economic burdens, there could be a shift of resources, for example, from investment in public housing for new, usually Western, immigrants to investment in housing for the poor or in the construction of facilities which would relieve dense housing conditions (e.g., community centers, playgrounds and parks, public space where youngsters could do their homework, etc.). Similarly, new tax policies could limit the rising standard of living of the more affluent and allocate more financial resources to the poor. Finally, it seems necessary to introduce birth-control techniques among the poor, for nowhere in the world have the poor really changed their social condition so long as they continued to have large families. Since there is no moral or political justification for the perpetuation of poverty, there seems to be a need for reevaluation of the religious emphasis on large families. It should be stated that none of these proposed policies is aimed at a particular ethnic group; all are aimed at eliminating the sources of poverty.

In addition, Israel will have to provide for Oriental Jews more direct means of access to the center of society. This may require massive mobilization of yet untapped social and cultural resources within the Oriental community; granting more freedom to express cultural pluralism; facilitating professional advancement of the educated; and providing for greater political representation on all levels.

Israel has a fair chance to succeed in such an approach to its problem of social integration, for several reasons. Continued immigration, to which there appears to be rather wide commitment, will tend to bring about some social openness and acknowledgment of differences. Also, unlike other ethnically diverse societies, Israel has no history of enslavement of one group by another or of official discrimination against any group. Neither has poverty in Israel led to human degradation, hunger, or social degeneration. Finally, the immorality of prejudice and the illegitimacy of expressing discriminatory views, together with the powerful governmental integration programs and the solidarity engendered by external pressures, mainly the Six Day War, raise hope for the success of Israel's struggle for integration.

Education

Like most other institutions in Israel, education too has its roots in the pre-State Yishuv. The State of Israel inherited an educational system that was open, uniform, and demanding: it was open because of the socialist ethos of the founding fathers; it was uniform to facilitate the welding of a new nation out of the many newcomers from different parts of the world; it was demanding in keeping with the Yishuv's dedication to its European heritage and its commitment to found a new, modern, progressive social order. The establishment of an educational system which rather successfully fused universal openness and uniformity of content and structure with an emphasis on high standards was made possible by the great degree of social, educational, and cultural homogeneity of the community.

This heritage found expression in the dramatic expansion of the educational system in the first two decades of statehood.[9] Israel instituted a nine-year course of compulsory elementary education covering one year of kindergarten and eight years of elementary education and a largely academically oriented high school system.

In the first half of the 1950s it became evident that more than expansion was needed if the educational system was to fulfill its envisaged role. Even more than in the pre-state era, education was now looked upon as the main tool for the social, cultural, and political absorption of the huge waves of new immigrants. It was to weld the diversified groups of newcomers into one society and at the same time create for all students equal opportunity to participate in that society. But a disturbing disparity emerged between the educational achievements of Oriental students and those of European or American origin, as a result of which the first were

---

[9] The increase between 1951 and 1969 in the number of students in different types of schools was as follows: post-elementary schools, from 25,000 to 125,500 (a 5-fold growth); vocational schools, from 4,300 to 43,-500 (a 10-fold growth); academic institutions, from 3,700 to 32,400 (a 9-fold growth). This increase considerably exceeds the expected growth rate for the threefold increase in Israel's population during that period. *Statistical Abstract 1969, op. cit.*, No. 20, Table 5/12, p. 557.

significantly underrepresented in secondary schools, and even more so in higher education.

Admitting the shortcomings of taking only administrative measures—principally expansion of the system—Israeli policy makers faced a dilemma: Should they give up the emphasis on the high quality of education and retain uniformity of standards and universal openness, or should they compromise their devotion to a uniform and open system and attempt to keep as many pockets of high-quality education as possible?

They attempted to do both. Measures were adopted to cope with the disparity in achievement and educational mobility between students of Oriental origin and those of European or American origin. Many different programs of compensatory education were instituted, mainly in the elementary schools, where attendance is compulsory and where makers of educational policy thus had the most legal leverage. On the secondary-school level, various kinds of schools were opened; they differed mainly in length and type of program. Most of the new or modified programs were scholastically less demanding than the curricula in academic high schools, though some, mainly boarding schools, were geared to the gifted disadvantaged students to enable them to make the transition from high school to university.

There was extreme reluctance, however, to tamper with the content and quality of academic high school and university education. Thus the academic high school became rather elitist—another bottleneck to the achievement of social mobility for the disadvantaged —mainly Oriental Jews.

The rise in the percentage of students of Oriental origin in post-elementary education was much more rapid than that in their relevant age groups in the general population. In 1956–57, 17 percent of all students in post-elementary education were of Oriental origin; by 1969–70 the figure was 43 percent. In academic high school a similar growth was indicated, from 10.5 percent in 1956–57 to 30 percent in 1969–70.[10] However, a comparison of dropout rates of students of Oriental origin and of other students in 1968–69 shows the following: [11]

---

[10] *Statistical Abstract* No. 14, 1963, Table 16, p. 641; and No. 21, 1970, Table S/19, p. 560.

[11] *Educational Statistical Bulletin*, No. 26, October 1969, Table 16, p. 103.

Origin of Students	Grades			
	9	10	11	12
		(Percent)		
Oriental	35	31	28	23
European or American	54	59	64	69

An analysis of the projected developments seems to indicate several trends. Elementary education has more or less exhausted its potential for compensating for disadvantage. (As in other parts of the world, in Israel, too, compensatory programs tend to be offered in neighborhood elementary and, therefore, segregated schools where most students are disadvantaged and in need of such programs.)

Despite the efforts at compensatory education, and despite the system's success in preventing a widening of the education gap, however, no significant breakthrough has occurred over the last years in the rate at which students of Oriental origin qualify for academic high schools or attend universities. In view of the considerable mobility achieved by the Oriental community, the educational system, in which elementary schools remain relatively segregated along ethnic lines and high schools and universities have student bodies with Oriental Jews still significantly underrepresented, has inevitably come under growing criticism and pressure for reform.

In 1968 the Knesset approved a plan to extend compulsory schooling one year, up to the age of fifteen, and to reduce elementary education to six years. (The decision stipulated that the compulsory school age be raised to sixteen a few years later.) Accordingly, all Israeli children will attend a six-year elementary school and a three-year junior high school. The latter will be a part of a six-year comprehensive school, or of a six-year academic high school, or of a six-year vocational or agricultural school, or it will function as an independent institution. Junior high school districts will not coincide with elementary school districts, so that junior high schools will tend to be integrated. The implementation of this major reform has been slow, largely for financial reasons, but the coming years doubtless will see it carried through.

In theory at least, this reform provides the solution for some of the existing problems. It will ensure that all adolescents, including the disadvantaged, have at least some high school education. And the integrated junior high schools will enable increasing numbers of youth of Oriental origin to share educational experiences with the others. The general availability of at least some high school education will also be important for meeting the manpower needs of the rapidly growing Israeli economy and the anticipated serious shortage of skilled labor. The salient questions regarding the school reform are: Will it succeed in making the educational experience more meaningful for children of all sectors of society? Will the extension of uniform education seriously lower standards of achievement?

In time, other changes and reforms can be anticipated. Once integrated schooling on the junior-high level gains momentum, there will be pressure to integrate the lower grades. (Should that succeed, integration at the junior-high level might be smoother and less tension-provoking.) The trend toward integration, however, will not do away with compensatory education; in fact, successful compensatory education may be a necessary condition for integrated schools, lest students of disadvantaged origins find themselves in a competition with which they cannot possibly cope. New approaches to compensatory education, then, are likely to emerge during the decade, perhaps through mobilizing community resources to provide informal education and by expanding social programs aimed at strengthening the disadvantaged family.

At least as much as in the past, Israel's educational system in the coming years will have two contradictory facets. It will be expected to contribute to the integration of a society which has undergone far-reaching diversification. At the same time, and in an almost opposite direction, Israel's school system will be expected to produce a high rate of well-trained technicians, administrators, professionals, scientists, and educators. In view of the high percentage of adolescents now attending high school, the anticipated expansion of the system will require much ingenuity and sophistication if it is to absorb the ever-growing number of students of disadvantaged origin. Ingenuity will be needed to cope with the need for continuing education among those groups in the population which usually do not attend schools.

Youth

A consideration of Israeli youth, their values, behavior, and associations, is essential for a prognosis of the state of the society in the coming years.

There has been a widespread and mistaken notion in Israel that Zionism reached its fulfillment with the establishment of the state; in other words, that the revolution has been successfully carried out. The result is that the ideological pioneering youth movements, which were once considered the main institutionalized patterns for youth activity, have lost much of their prestige, momentum, and impact. Nonetheless, Israel has been spared almost completely both the aggressive hedonism common among American and West European youth in the 1950s and the political activism of radical student-protest movements which spread over many parts of the world in the 1960s.

That unique phenomenon has been puzzling many analysts of the Israeli scene. It is usually suggested that recurrent wars have developed a sense of solidarity among Israeli youth, have given them a goal, and offered an outlet for their energy. Universal military service before university studies, for both young men and women, certainly makes for a motivated, more career-oriented student body, and the tensions and horrors of war certainly make for a more rapidly maturing student body. (The approximately 10,000 freshmen in 1969–70 in institutions of higher education constituted some 20 percent of their age group; this percentage generally decreases after the first two years of study to 12 to 15 percent, largely due to dropout.) One may add that in a society in which higher education is still a privilege, students will be reluctant to jeopardize their chances to graduate by engaging in politically motivated confrontations with the authorities.

However, there appear to be other explanations for the behavior of Israeli youth. The Israeli "establishment" is perhaps unique in that it has not yet given youth serious grounds for alienation. In other words, unlike many of the political orders in the West, the Israeli establishment has retained its credibility on the important issues and has not betrayed its declared goals: it has provided successful leadership to ward off the threat of physical destruction to the society, and it has made possible continuous growth and social advancement in the face of enormous handicaps.

Israel also differs from most Western countries in that the educational process has not led to huge anonymous bureaucratic establishments serving the perpetuation of the status quo. Quite the contrary: for many an Israeli, education offers the possibility not only of creative expression and a rewarding standard of living, but also the means for influencing the system. Education, together with military service, thus gives the Israeli student a sense of full participation in society. For this reason, Israel may not be fertile ground for student unrest, for, unlike the situation in other parts of the world, Israeli students do not suffer the frustration of confronting an apparently meaningless future oriented to the status quo, with no chance of influencing the course of events.

Still, the possibility of some unhappy developments cannot be dismissed. It is precisely the universality of military service that has been aggravating the persisting differences between the disadvantaged and other youths. The Oriental youth perceive a sharp contradiction between their lack of equality in society and their full and equal participation in the country's military efforts. This discontent helps explain the current social tensions, engendered almost exclusively by youth and which have ethnic overtones and occasionally result in violence.

Israel is now witnessing a dramatic transition among its Oriental youth from passivity to aggression. If the current military situation should persist, and certainly under conditions of real peace, violent outbreaks directed at the establishment might well become stronger. But Israel's leadership, extremely sensitive to criticism and completely inexperienced in dealing with violent expressions of such criticism, will probably give serious attention to launching new policies designed to eliminate the social causes of violence and ensuing social polarization.

Middle-class youth have been moving more and more toward a consumer-oriented youth culture. This is not necessarily a new trend, but rather a deepening of an ongoing process, one that must be expected in times of mounting affluence, expanded educational opportunities, and relative peace. These trends will probably continue during the decade. On the other hand, Israel's universal army service for all young men and women is responsible for a maturation process fundamentally different from that in any other modern society, and this is not likely to change even under conditions of real peace. Military service gives the average Israeli youth the opportunity to share in a highly prestigious task while participating in a future-oriented and ethnically integrated youth culture whose values are mutual help, equality, and excellence. The Israeli army is therefore one of the most powerful correctives for the limitations of the educational system; it is an actively engaging and socially integrating experience which imparts to the young Israeli a strong sense of acceptance and participation.

The Family

The family is the one institution with which Zionist ideology hardly concerned itself. Matters such as family structure, age at marriage, and personal relationships were not dealt with in the philosophy of the revolution. The one exception, perhaps, was family size: since the early days of the Yishuv, emphasis was put on a high birth rate as a means of making the nation grow in numbers and strength.

This emphasis became more pronounced after the Holocaust and the establishment of the state, symbolized, for example, by a decision promoted by Prime Minister David Ben-Gurion in the early 1950s to award a prize of 100 pounds to mothers upon the birth of their tenth child. (Although this was a substantial sum at the time, it did not enable poor families to care for their children properly.) The simplistic notion of judging national strength by numbers, however, soon began to be viewed with growing ambiguity, especially with the growing awareness that high fertility is almost exclusively characteristic of the poor, inevitably perpetuating their social and economic disadvantage. Some years ago a public commission was established to investigate the problem of fertility, and recently the Center for Demographic Planning was founded.

The most striking quality of the Israeli family is its stability. Neither the country's considerable dynamism nor the inflow of more than a million immigrants has brought signs of breakdown. On the contrary, the number of divorces has decreased from some 2,500 in 1951 to 2,370 in 1969, or from 1.7 to 0.8 per 1,000 population.[12] And

---

[12] *Statistical Abstract of Israel, op. cit.*, No. 21, Table C/1, p. 60.

whereas one tends to view far-reaching or radical social change as a potential cause for family breakdown, Israel's experience does not bear this out. The rate of divorce has not been high even where social conditions are most difficult, in the crisis-prone families in the Oriental community.

It would be hazardous to predict whether this remarkable stability of the Israeli family will persist. Perhaps the central position of the family in Jewish tradition will continue to be a basic feature of Israeli society. It could also happen, however, that in the more disadvantaged sectors of society frustrations over social marginality will cause deviation, including family breakdown.

Another important dimension of family stability is, of course, relations between the generations. While in the society at large there was far greater continuity between generations in the pre-state Yishuv than in Israel today, no comparable judgment is possible about intergenerational relations within the family. In the Yishuv there was only minor emphasis on the family, which was regarded as a remnant of the social order of the Diaspora. (This may be considered another "revolutionary" feature of the society, for revolutions tend to conceive of the family as an institution representing the social order of the old regime.) There was little reason, therefore, for youth of that period to rebel against parental values. In fact the family, probably more than any other institution, represented the ongoing and developing "revolution." The parents laid the foundations for the new society; the children generally accepted them and built upon them. The early youth movements enabled many young people to turn the tensions and anxieties of growing up in a new immigrant society toward collective goals and values.

Upon the foundation of the state, youth movements lost their central place. Today they are viewed as harmless leisure-time activities leading to social mobility. But with the changing character and reduced social significance of youth movements, intergenerational conflict has increased.

The most serious conflicts have occurred in families of Oriental origin. Initially, tensions occurred because of the far-reaching cultural changes experienced by most immigrants from the Middle Eastern countries, as regards, for example, the status of women, the concept of childhood, and the relations between the generations in the family. There were, of course, some factors mitigating tensions:

the generation gap was lessened as a result of the rapid mastery by all of at least the basic elements of the Hebrew language; there was a remarkable tendency to abandon cultural traits which could be tension-provoking; and in most of these families there was common commitment to education and the army. Many Oriental families, in fact, have displayed considerable permissiveness toward change among the young, thus ameliorating intergenerational tensions and disruptions. This can also mean, however, that the family loses its function as an effective mechanism for guidance and social control: the rate of juvenile delinquency in these families is considerably higher than in the rest of the population.

In sum, then, Israel exhibits an interesting and rare fusion of modernity and familism. It is an industrialized, mostly urban society which at the same time invests the family with functions toward its children and, in this way, seems to prevent serious family disruption. No doubt this "modern familism" results in part from the character of the land and of life in it. The country is very small, so that leaving home never means going very far. External pressures tend to increase solidarity, so that in a way the entire country is "home." Also, the rhythm of the society is governed by the Jewish calendar, in particular the Sabbath and the holidays, and their focus is mainly the family. Among the middle class particularly, the family is crucial to children for economic assistance and social contacts. There seems to be no reason to expect that these forces will cease and that the central role of the family in the social fabric of Israel will diminish.

Religion and "Jewishness"

Religion is another Israeli institution having notable stability. The religious and nonreligious sectors have been cooperating in almost all realms of social life since the mid-1930s. Their covenant has persisted for two reasons: both sectors agreed to avoid clear definition of some basic issues, for example, "who is a Jew" in the modern Jewish state; and major segments of the nonreligious majority voluntarily relegated several important areas in the life of the individual and the community to the sole jurisdiction of religious law, for example, marriage and burial, which are legally defined as religious functions and may not be performed by civil authorities.

It is, however, far from certain that this covenant will not be broken. Almost any kind of settlement with the Arabs will doubtless call for the return of all or most of those occupied territories to which the religious population feels particularly deep attachment. The great likelihood therefore is that peace would bring a rift between the two groups. Moreover, should some of the external pressures abate, it may well appear that the concessions to the religious minority in the crucial areas of national identity, legal authority, and institutional arrangements have contributed nothing to Jewish unity and have even sown the seeds of division. A continuation of the status quo under peaceful conditions could provoke a serious *Kulturkampf*, while an attempt to modify the by now deeply institutionalized status quo would arouse militant objections by the religious sector.

Religion in Israel is a major political issue. Since the 1930s most religious Israelis have tended to belong to or vote for religious political parties. Matters of religion have consequently always been issues in the political struggle, and parliamentary rulings on religious matters have been among the most important political achievements of the religious parties for their electorate. But the social significance of religion in Israel transcends the political. Whenever internal or external developments force the society to define and symbolically express its collective identity, it finds its inspiration in its religious heritage: the past is evoked to illumine the present.

What are the main issues of discord between the religious and nonreligious sectors in Israel? [13] One is the principle of the legitimation of society: the definition of its boundaries and the criteria for belonging to it. A second is the religious sector's desire to lend a religious texture to the state by legislating a Jewish life style among all citizens, e.g., regulating Sabbath activities and banning the breeding of pigs. A third is the religious groups' demand for maximum autonomy through separate institutional arrangements, as in education, and in the allocation of human resources, as in the exemption of yeshiva students from military service. The remarkable achievements of the religious groups are largely due to the fact that they have always been agreeable coalition partners: in return for

---

[13] For a more detailed discussion, see S. N. Eisenstadt, *Israeli Society* (London: Weidenfeld and Nicolson, 1967).

concessions they have supported most policies of the labor movement.

This delicate political balance is also one of the main reasons for the absence in Israel of a powerful and politically significant non-Orthodox religious movement—Conservative, Reform, Liberal, or other. Since Orthodox Judaism has become a political vested interest, the emergence of a strong non-Orthodox movement would be a potential threat to the established religious groups. Actually, the identification of religiosity with institutionalized Orthodoxy causes a slow but steady movement to the right by the religious parties. In their competition for votes, the more liberally inclined groups find themselves having to appease the right in order to retain support among the most committed of the religious population. As a result, Orthodoxy and its institutions, which otherwise might have undergone liberalization, tend to become more rigid.

Contrary to frequent claims, this state of affairs does not contribute to the unity of the Jewish people throughout the world. The Orthodox element has not gained strength in the Jewish communities of the West. In the West the Jewish community is variously constituted and defined, but Orthodox legal definition or identification with Orthodox observance is hardly the universal or dominant criterion. Most Jews outside of Israel, moreover, live in societies where there is substantial separation of church and state, where the church enjoys at most a limited share in the state's power and where the government as a rule refrains from legislating in matters of faith. Where Israeli society reveals its Jewishness, then, it tends to deviate from the democratic, open, and universalist society that is the accepted norm in the West.

In the one area where many Jews in the Western world express their Jewish identity—the synagogue—they can find communality of experience, symbols, and spirit only with that one quarter of the Israeli population which practices religion and belongs to synagogues. And in view of the almost exclusively conservative Orthodoxy of Israeli religious life, this communality is largely formal and therefore ambiguous. The nature of religion in Israel is thus likely to estrange from Israel an ever-growing number of young Jews elsewhere in the modern world.

It has been argued that the status quo contributes to unity in Israel. It is certainly true that a sustained struggle between the religious and non religious elements would have a disruptive effect. But it is also true that more and more young Israelis reject the state of affairs that permits the religious minority to impose laws, norms of behavior, and institutional arrangements on the majority of the population as a result of political arrangements that have little relevance to religion. Among non-Orthodox youth this doubtless contributes to family tensions. While in the short run, then, the status quo makes for cooperation and coexistence, it will probably have a disruptive effect in the long run.

Continued immigration from the democratic West and the influx of professionals from both the Middle East and the Soviet Union will doubtless affect the state of religion in Israel. These newcomers are bound to make common cause with the young sabras who are not Orthodox and have no emotional commitment to Jewish law or tradition. One must therefore expect a sharpening of the conflict over the Jewish essence of Israeli society and the role of religious law in defining the life style of the people.

If tension between the religious and secular sectors should develop into overt conflict, the religious group will increasingly turn inward; it will keep retreating from the original principle of religious Zionism advocating joint social institutions for the religious and secular alike. Then, the already existing pressure of the ultra-conservative wing upon the more liberal elements will probably increase, and the entire religious group will move farther to the right. Another possibility is that the strife could cause a split within the religious group, with the more liberal elements aligning with similar religious groups in other Jewish communities. A more likely development would be a change in relationship between the religious and secular sectors. The increasingly inward-oriented religious community might relinquish its pressure on society at large in return for the allocation of much-needed resources. Then, well-defined spheres of influence and cooperation could be established between the two camps, thus reducing the potential for conflict.

Related to the religion issue is the question of the nature of the Jewishness of the Israelis in general and of Israeli-born youth in particular. Though most young Israelis grow up having no identification with the religious institutions—there being no institutional or philosophical alternatives to Orthodoxy—they share an intense identification with Jewish culture. Hebrew is their mother tongue, a rich resource for their creative and cultural expression. They study the Bible, the most heavily stressed subject in the school curriculum, with such intensity that it becomes the foundation of their cultural and spiritual identity. The young Israelis roam the land of their forefathers, breathing the atmosphere of the ancient Hebrews and vividly imagining the deeds of the heroes and the world of the sages. They absorb Hebrew prophecy and Jewish mysticism and philosophy from their literature, theater, and even the mass media. They study the history of the Jewish people as an integral part of world history and develop a commitment to oppressed Jews everywhere. And, of course, the rhythm of Israeli life is largely dictated by the Jewish calendar.

Thus Israel appears to have produced a new type of modern Jew, one who has few doubts regarding his Jewish identity, who feels part of the Jewish people's past and is committed to its spiritual and cultural values, but who as a rule feels no need to lean on religious institutions. There is then little reason to fear that the younger generation of Israelis will lack Jewish identity. On the contrary, there is danger of parochialism or folkish narrowness in the strong emphasis on Jewish creativity, the centrality of the Jewish calendar in the life of the people, and the nation-oriented basis of Jewish identity.

Finally, the fact that the Jewish identity of most young Israelis is largely secular in character could lead to an interesting and fruitful dialogue with Jewish youth all over the world. The current retreat from ideological internationalism toward greater interest in their own identity among growing sectors of Jewish youth on both sides of the Iron Curtain should present a challenge to Israelis to engage them in an articulate and sophisticated debate. Contacts of this kind would help broaden the Israelis' view of their identity to include international dimensions; it would introduce Jewish youth in other communities to a working model of a modern, secular, but deeply Jewish way of life. Such encounters are already beginning on the Israeli campuses, and their development and spread could have a significant impact on the political relationship between the religious and secular segments of Israeli society.

Political Structure

Israel's political institutions show remarkable stability and continuity despite the fact that the political arena has been the main locus of internal strife from the beginning. In the first decade of Israel's existence as a state disagreement among political groups centered on issues crucial to Israeli society, especially on the role of religion in the state and on the structure of government and ways of controlling it. The need to develop a civil service to cope with population growth raised issues over the limits of state power. The transition to a centralized administration was especially tension-provoking, since the political system of the Yishuv had been diversified and voluntary. The first dispute was over the exclusiveness of Zahal as a military force and the consequent disbanding of both the "dissident groups"—the Irgun, or Etsel, and the Freedom Fighters ("Stern Gang")—and of the Palmah, the only full-time quasi-army unit of Haganah, the Yishuv's underground defense establishment. The next dispute was over education, and led to the establishment of a state school system in 1953. (In the Yishuv education had been politically partisan.) Another controversy concerned the right of all citizens to employment, which led to the establishment of a national labor exchange.

There was also conflict between those groups pressing to retain voluntary organizations and those advocating state structures and nationalization of services. This tension continues, since many of the voluntary institutional arrangements are politically partisan and consequently particularistic, and there is fear that an expanded state machinery would curtail the citizen's options and kill the spirit of voluntarism characteristic of the Yishuv. This tension will doubtless persist; the next dispute will probably arise over the nationalization of health services.

An important new characteristic of Israel's political life developed during the second decade of statehood, when for the first time security and foreign relations became matters of political dispute. The original dispute, known as the "Lavon affair" (after a key figure in an aborted intelligence undertaking), in fact dominated the entire decade, and cut across established party lines and even caused a split in the largest party, the Mapai, now the Israel Labor party. Its primary significance probably was that it removed taboos regarding political controversy over defense policy.

The economic recession of the mid-1960s dampened disputes over the direction of the society, and especially over defense matters. However, the Six Day War and, most of all, frustration over the absence of a foreseeable solution to the Arab-Israeli conflict revived political dispute over military and defense policies and gave it unprecedented volume and intensity. Again there was realignment of political forces across party lines.

One must assume that defense and peace with the Arabs will be the central issues in the political struggle in the 1970s. There will probably be two factions: one favoring annexation of all or most of the occupied territories for defense reasons or out of a conviction that the Jewish people have "historical rights" to those areas; the other advocating the return of all or most of these territories because, in their view, the Six Day War created a unique opportunity for a peace settlement with the Arabs. Any clear indication of Arab willingness to recognize Israel's existence and to reach a settlement would probably precipitate a political dispute between the two camps unprecedented in fierceness and depth.

After the mid-1960s recession the development of the economy became the first priority in Israeli political life. A society that, because it is forced to sacrifice some 30 percent of its national product for defense, is not able to balance payments for essential imports with export production must develop new ways of coping with its economic situation.

Israel's massive import of capital, which imposes a heavy burden of debt on this and the next generation, is not only for defense spending. It is also used to maintain the high, and still rising, living standard of at least the central groups in society, to help prevent hunger and degrading poverty among the lower classes, and to implement reasonable welfare standards and national insurance programs.

While Israel feels justified in using imported capital to improve living standards, it has attempted, through economic planning, to curb inflation and limit dependence on outside resources. But the weak sectors of society have suffered most from attempts to curb governmental expenditure, to keep salary increases as low as possible, and to limit allocation of tax money for public expenditures. It seems inevitable therefore that during this decade, when defense spending is bound to remain high, the political struggle over the distribution of resources not earmarked for defense will reach unprecedented dimensions, particularly in view of the growing awareness of poverty.

What is perhaps most remarkable is that there has been no breakdown of the political system despite the fact that the population has tripled, that three wars have been fought, and that the internal composition of the community has undergone radical changes. One criterion of political stability is orderly changes in leadership. Thus far Israel has had four: from David Ben-Gurion to the late Moshe Sharet, and back to Ben-Gurion, then to the late Levi Eshkol, and finally to Golda Meir. The transition from Ben-Gurion to Eshkol was probably the most painful, for it took place in the midst of the political upheaval produced by the Lavon affair, in which the very legitimacy of the system was questioned, by no other than Ben-Gurion himself. So far, however, all leaders have come from the same age group and socioeconomic class, and from the same ideological sector of the labor movement. This presumably will not always be the case, and future transfers of leadership will test the system's stability.

An important reason for the stability of the party system in the past was that it was a kind of federation of political groups, each having a powerful hold over a segment of the electorate through control over a wide variety of resources. Recently the grip of these groups on the voters has diminished drastically as power has shifted from voluntary partisan groups to the state's executive machinery, as the new immigrants' economic condition improved, and as more affluent immigrants arrived.

Israel's major political parties have been in existence since the days of the Yishuv, but there are new alignments. In the labor camp the former main party, Mapai, and the more left-wing offspring, Ahdut Ha'avoda, united and formed Avodah; it was joined by Rafi, the splinter group established by Mapai during the Lavon affair. Avodah and Mapam, the most left-wing Zionist party, formed a parliamentary voting bloc, "The Alignment." The right-wing Herut party and the more moderate Liberal party also formed a voting bloc, called Gahal, a number of years ago.

The recent alignments suggest that future political conflict will probably arise in several areas: international relations (compromise vs. annexation of the occupied territories), religion ("established" religion vs. secularism), and the economy (private vs. state enterprise). But the likelihood is that only two of these, international relations and religion, will seriously divide voters in the coming decade. Ideological dispute over economic policy seems to lose momentum, and one can expect full support for measures aimed at the continued improvement of the standard of living and the channeling of resources to the poor sector of the community.

In the areas of serious controversy, then, the probable alignments would be: religious groups and groups favoring annexation of the occupied territories; secularist groups and annexationists; secularists and groups advocating compromise with the Arab world. No drastic political-ideological change should be expected, since the secularist-compromise camp could afford neither a secularism that is too extreme nor compromises on the Arab-Israeli conflict that are too far-reaching, lest they lose too much power to the two other camps.

One must ask, of course, whether political stability is not the result of political stagnation. This does not seem to be the case. The main emphasis in Israel has always been on national unity and social stability to withstand external military pressures and to weld a new nation. It is an emphasis making for compromise, whether among parties or within them. Since the 1930s the social democrats of the Mapai party have been the main proponents of compromise, and Mapai's policies have therefore promoted continuity and stability. Israel's political system has also shown exceptional adaptability, which may have been nurtured by its very stability and continuity. It is responsive to new ideas, as in economic planning, and is a means by which new immigrants and the young are introduced into the society. The Israeli political system, then, is not stagnant at all; it is merely changing slowly and not necessarily in keeping with ideological commitments. But the change is often contrary to declared ideologies, and there is danger that ideology may be used to obstruct change and that a widening gap between ideology and reality may become fertile soil for protest.

An example of how the absorption of new social elements serves to introduce change into the system is the political representation of the Oriental Jewish communities. These rapidly growing communities never seriously attempted to form a national ethnic party; they established ethnic parties only on the local level. This suggests that the official ideology of absorption and unity was effective: the new social groups sought channels of political expression within the existing system, not outside it. Whereas local politics have undergone change in style, organization, and even ideology, on the national level there was merely expansion to accommodate representatives of the Oriental community. There was no major move toward giving them a share of power in national politics, and it is that which the Oriental communities are now demanding.

It is safe to predict that the political establishment will be more or less successful in perpetuating the system's stability by insulating the central political issues from ethnic-community interests and by co-opting the mobile elements of the more marginal sectors. The main focus of political pressure from these sectors will likely be for a substantial increase in representation. If new elements are not absorbed into the political center in the normal way, through education and acculturation, but only in response to mounting political pressure, they would be likely to bring into it different norms, values, intellectual techniques, and cultural commitments, thus considerably changing the nature of the system.

Here some reference to the Israeli defense forces is necessary. Zahal, the National Defense Force, we have said, has been one of the most powerful symbols of collective identity and one of the main instruments of social integration. It has absorbed much of the young people's vigor and idealism, and has given them opportunity for self-expression and self-fulfillment. Because of the army's emphasis on constant innovation, military careers are relatively short. Each year it releases a number of ranking officers in its quest for continuous change and renewed motivation. When they return to civilian life, they usually go into careers in economics, administration, education, diplomacy, or politics.

One could, of course, say that Zahal thus has succeeded in infiltrating all phases of civilian society. But the distinction between military and civilian life is somewhat artificial in a society where all men are potential recruits up to the age of fifty-five and where younger men, upon completing three years of military service, continue in the reserves for up to two months each year. One might rather suggest that, under these conditions, civilian norms and interests are bound to prevail. In view of the growing professionalization in most occupational fields, preparation for the transition from military to civilian careers will have to be built into the military process of socialization, and the civilian bases for the absorption of ex-officers adapted to the process.

Political life too, it should be emphasized again, will be shaped by the political-military developments in the Middle East: whether there will be a continuation of the present stalemate, a return to alternating war and cease-fires, or a permanent political settlement.

Continued stalemate, with continuing danger in the event of a change in the military situation, would leave the executive branch of the government in its relatively powerful position and would ensure the perpetuation of the unity-oriented political system. It would create substantial immunity to pressures for change and innovation, yet would allow change at a "safe pace." And it could encourage evasion or postponement on crucial questions.

Developments under conditions of renewed warfare are more uncertain. No doubt, support of a strong central authority would increase and perhaps lead to a restoration of the National Unity Coalition, encompassing all major political parties. In such a coalition arrangement, however, the parties would have to agree not to engage in partisan politics and to postpone resolution of crucial national issues, and such a neutralization of party lines carries the seeds of political stagnation.

The possibility of a political settlement is remote from any previous experience, and predictions are therefore difficult. It is safe to assume that such a settlement will be preceded by an extended period of nonwar to allow for preparation and adaptation. But it is impossible to say whether the political center will command the necessary consensus to lead the nation toward peace at a time when the external unifying factors will recede. It seems self-evident that a rather long transition to peace will be desirable to prevent a possible breakdown of the political machinery and erosion of the legitimation of the system.

Minorities

Arabs constitute the largest minority in Israel, and their situation during the decade will depend almost entirely on Israel's relations with the Arab states. Most of them are Moslems, the rest Christians. The non-Jewish population of Israel in 1969 was 423,000, of whom 314,500 were Moslems.[14]

The twenty-four years of Israel's statehood appear to have imposed on its Arabs considerable political apathy. Only a dramatic development—one not in their power to bring about—could have changed their situation. A peace settlement, for example, would have given them the opportunity to be loyal citizens of Israel with-

---

[14] *Statistical Abstract of Israel, op. cit.,* No. 21 (1970), Table B/11, p. 23.

out necessarily alienating themselves from the rest of the Arab world. Or, military defeat of Israel would have made possible their political reintegration into the Arab world. Of course, the striking Israeli victory in the Six Day War led to neither; it probably aggravated their already difficult position. Whereas all Arab states fought in the war, and some Palestinian Arabs thereafter, the Israeli Arabs did not participate at all in this inter-Arab effort.

The Israeli victory and the death of President Nasser probably made the Israeli Arabs even more apathetic, and their regular contact with the Palestinians of the occupied territories tends to reinforce their ambiguous status: many Palestinians treat the Israeli Arabs with suspicion, considering them "too Israeli." The Israeli Arabs are indeed reluctant to relinquish some of the Israeli dimensions of their identity. They are caught between cultural and religious identification with the Arab world and a reluctance to give up the obvious economic and cultural advantages derived from Israeli citizenship. It also seems that the Israeli Arabs, more than any other group in the Arab world, have a realistic view of Israel and accept the fact that it is here to stay. The Israeli Arabs, then, are at present neutralized with regard to possible efforts to improve understanding and cooperation between Israel and the Arab states. But they could play a crucial role in such an endeavor in the event of a political settlement in the Middle East.

As to possible developments, peace would certainly help bring about the social and cultural consolidation of the Israeli Arabs, an improvement in their ecnoomic conditions, and their integration into Israeli society. It can be expected that they would then serve as mediators between the Jews of Israel and the Arabs of the neighboring states and be of considerable help in implementing programs for the resettlement of Arab refugees, which is certain to be an element in any peace settlement.

Under conditions short of peace, the outlook for the Israeli Arabs is, unfortunately, bleak. The perpetuation of the status quo, with or without renewed warfare, inevitably places them in a situation in which meaningful existence is difficult and social and cultural development hampered. For while they are citizens of Israel and participate in certain aspects of its life, the overwhelming majority of them naturally identify religiously, ethnically, and even politically with the rest of the Arab world. Under conditions of conflict, they are bound to suffer from the dilemma of dual loyalty.

There is little doubt that a prolongation of conditions prevailing for the last twenty-four years would deepen the political and social apathy of most Israeli Arabs and would intensify the militant political opposition of fringe groups among them. The situation would be still more difficult if Israel decided to annex most of the occupied territories; this would increase Israel's population by close to one million Arabs, making the ratio between them and Jewish citizens about two to five. This would not only seriously jeopardize the Jewish character of the society but would also impose severe limitations on its democratic character. Territorial annexation would almost certainly preclude full social participation for the Israeli Arab population, and they would be excluded from politics as potential collaborators with the enemy. The annexation of territory would thus be a questionable move from the purely internal point of view.

On the other hand, full incorporation of Jerusalem into Israel, which would make the residents of the eastern sector of the city full-fledged citizens, could somewhat alleviate the situation of the Israeli Arabs. In East Jerusalem and vicinity there is a large concentration of intellectuals, professionals, and a well-educated middle class who could give the mostly rural Israeli Arabs much-needed social and political leadership. This could be of crucial importance in giving the Israeli Arabs a meaningful identity for building an autonomous and creative community that could live with the Jewish majority and cooperate with it. Intergroup cooperation and respect in a pluralistic society is predicated on a positive sense of identity among minority groups. Therefore, if the Israeli Arabs are expected to function as a bridge between the Jews and the Arabs of the neighboring states, a strengthening of the Israeli Arab minority will be required. Any temporary difficulties that the incorporation of East Jerusalem would cause the Israeli authorities would be offset by this long-range positive impact.

Aliyah

Israel is in need of *aliyah* for several obvious, and crucial, reasons. It is a means of assuring essential social growth. It may balance the demographic composition of Israeli society. It may also contribute financial resources and educated manpower. *Aliyah* may have impacts of a more subtle nature as well. It may reinforce the society's international orientation. It also may have a liberalizing effect on such institutions as religion or the somewhat authoritarian educational system.

Perhaps the most interesting hypothesis is that immigration from the affluent West may help revitalize the pioneering spirit in Israel. There seems to be similarity between the ideologies of some of the new social movements among young Western Jews and the pioneer movements at the beginning of this century, largely among East European Jews: the leaning to a leftist ideology, construed in somewhat romantic terms; the desire to build a better world based on a return to the simple, "natural" life; the rejection of material benefits and the quest for "redemption" under ascetic conditions; the search for meaning and purpose in the individual's life, even if it calls for sacrifice.

A unifying spirit of this kind is essential for strengthening the nation under conditions of war. In the event of peace, Israeli society will most certainly strive for rapid development, maximal technological progress and membership in the club of postindustrial societies, and reinforcement of its unique characteristics. An *aliyah* from the West would seem to be an essential condition for such developments.

Conclusion

Inevitably, this discussion has dealt with possible developments under conditions of peace. It would be wrong to look upon peace as the "messianic era" and simply wait for it. One of the most heroic features of Israeli society has been that it fought its wars as if nothing else mattered, and worked toward social and economic improvement as though there were no war. It is crucial to maintain this attitude, even to lend it renewed vigor. This not only is an important means of limiting the danger of Israel's deteriorating into a garrison state; it also strengthens those Israeli characteristics that are essential for a developing Jewish society in the Middle East.

However, there are a few important requisites. Israel will have to strike a balance between continuity and innovation, to make a choice between seeking mere social, political, and economic expansion and encouraging the emergence of new patterns in these and other areas. It will have to develop ways of coping systematically with such conflicting goals as rapid development under conditions of war, making "war on poverty" at a time when resources are also needed for the absorption of new immigrants,[15] and fusing a modern social order without destroying the pioneering spirit that brought it into being.

Beyond this, Israel will have to deal in a more systematic way with resolving dilemmas between its essence and image. It will have to encourage the creation of indigenous cultural patterns in preference to the current growing Levantinism and pure imitation of a Western lifestyle. And while it must maintain its strong ties to the Jewish past and to the Jewish people everywhere, it must safeguard against a provincialism that would isolate it from important happenings outside Israel.

The present decade will certainly be one of great dangers, but of even greater challenges and potential triumphs.

---

[15] From a long-range point of view, there is no contradiction between the two; on the contrary, a professionaly trained *aliyah* will produce the necessary resources for eradicating poverty.

Part IV

Jews
In Other
Lands

Chapter 5

Western Europe

Zachariah Shuster

For centuries Western Europe was the center of world civilization and world military power. Its population and resources today are comparable to those of the United States or the Soviet Union, and some think it might become a third force. Its influence everywhere, not least in the Middle East, is not to be dismissed.

The Jews of Western Europe are not an entity and do not have a common character. Differences among them reflect differences in their political, intellectual, social, and moral environment. The well-being of all Jews in Western Europe, however, will be directly affected by developments in the region as a whole: its stability and welfare; its move toward political and economic unity; its relations with the United States and the Soviet Union and its possible development as an independent force in international politics; the growth or decline of radicalism of the left or right; the changing influence of transnational forces, for example, the Catholic Church and other churches, international Communism, and the New Left.

More than 1.2 million Jews live in this part of Europe, about one million in France and Great Britain, and the rest dispersed throughout seventeen other countries. The Jews of Great Britain, of course, escaped the Holocaust and welcomed refugees from the war-torn countries. Those Jews who returned to their homes at the end of World War II and those who had to find new homes managed to rebuild their personal lives in countries affording them full equality. (France has also received many Jews from North Africa.) Individual Jews have largely maintained their identity, and the State of Israel, particularly since the Six Day War in June 1967, has greatly enhanced Jewish identification. But despite strenuous efforts to reestablish Jewish institutions, the situation in most of Western Europe does not augur well for a vigorous Jewish community life.

General Conditions in Europe

The countries of Western Europe are liberal democracies whose people enjoy equality, individual liberty, personal security, political and social integration, and economic well-being.

Assuming peace and general stability in Europe, there is no reason to expect any developments that would bring serious deterioration in the condition of the Jews during this decade. Western Europe will seek to stabilize and "normalize" relations with the Eastern bloc, without terminating their alliance with the United States. The countries in the region will continue to develop their industry and technology, to extend social reform, to expand and strengthen their community in economic and social matters, and, if possible, to move toward some political community so that Western Europe can become an independent force on the world scene.

There has been some progress in these directions. The treaty signed in summer 1970 between Germany and the Soviet Union, with the full approval of the NATO powers, and subsequent accords on Berlin formally fixed the boundaries established by World War II; they acknowledged the division of Germany into two separate states, recognizing the former Russian Zone as a sovereign state with an equal claim to a seat in the United Nations and other international bodies. A European security conference will probably be held. With the entry of Great Britain, Ireland, Denmark, and Norway, the European Economic Community will embrace ten nations, with a population of more than 250 million and control over 40 percent of world trade.

Of course, both East-West stability and Western European unity are far from achieved. No clear understanding exists, even among the Western countries, on the kind of "European security" arrangements they would like to see. Germany and Great Britain are thinking in terms of parallel reduction of military forces by East and West; France, on the other hand, insists on retaining full freedom to determine its military strength and seeks agreements limited to economic and cultural areas. Nor is there agreement among Western European governments as to what the Soviet Union is after. What is the purpose of a European security conference, which seems to have high priority on the Soviet Union's political agenda? Will the Soviet Union attempt to bring about a genuine arrangement among the countries on the Eurasian continent to eliminate East-West tensions so that it would then be free to give attention to problems in Asia and to its domestic concerns? Or is it concealing a desire to break up the North Atlantic alliance? What will be the role of the United States in a European security conference, and what might a conference achieve, particularly with regard to military power on both sides? What will coexistence or détente between East and West mean for Eastern Europe? Will there be no recurrence of events like the invasion of Czechoslovakia, because the smaller Eastern countries will be allowed to choose their own course? Or might they happen again, because the Western powers have made it clear that they will not intervene?

There are even greater uncertainties about the prospects for integration in Western Europe. Will it strive to become a single, federated state or an alliance of sovereign states for specific purposes? Some hope to transform Western Europe into an entity which would act as one on all major political and economic problems. It is far from that today. The Common Market is primarily a customs union. France is pursuing its independent policy, being in NATO politically and cooperating with it but rejecting military integration within the organization. It is trying to develop special economic relations with the USSR so as not to be outdone by Western Germany. Great Britain still hopes to maintain its special relationship with the United States. West Germany, unlike France, still considers the U.S. military presence its major protection.

Nonetheless, the trend is toward cooperation and integration, in keeping with the conviction that only thus will Western Europe be able to face the great blocs—Communist Eastern Europe, the United States, and the Asian continent, with China emerging as the dominant power—with some control over its own destiny. But few expect to see giant steps in that direction during the 1970s.

Meanwhile, the countries of Europe are undergoing rapid, fundamental change characterized by unprecedented growth of the national economies; modernization of industry and trade; merger of small and middle-size enterprises into larger ones, some of them cutting across national boundaries; and greater dependence on American capital investment, now amounting to some $9 billion and controlling assets of $30 billion.

Democracy in Western Europe

The welfare of the Jews living in the countries of Western Europe will depend on their continued stability and adherence to Western democratic ideas. There is every reason to expect that those happy conditions will continue throughout this decade.

There are important societal and political changes in progress. The assumption of a homogeneous nation-state, having one ethnic identity, one dominant religion, and one set of traditions, is gradually giving way to recognition that every society is a complex multi-faceted organism. Rapid mass travel, radio, and television have brought awareness of the diversity of ethnic origin and religious belief and forced acceptance of the pluralistic society. Now more than ever, the ordinary Frenchman is aware that there are Jews, Protestants, and Greek Orthodox in his own country and Germans, Italians, and Englishmen right next door.

To be sure, the countries of Western Europe have far from digested the more than eight million immigrants who have come since the end of World War II to settle or to work. The three million foreigners living and working in France, and particularly the North Africans, have not been accepted as part of French society; the 500,000 Italian and other workers in Switzerland are still regarded as a potential menace to the nation, although they are indispensable to the economy. The same applies to the more than one million "guest workers" in Germany. But the intermingling among racial, religious, and ethnic groups must in the long run change basic attitudes, perhaps the very texture of society. (The war between Protestants and Catholics in Northern Ireland and the language battle between the Walloons and the Flemings in Belgium have their origins in the past and reflect differences in social background and power distribution rather than differences over religion or language.)

Political Parties

The pattern of political rule, on the other hand, has not changed since the initial postwar period. Except for the Iberian peninsula and Greece, the governments of Western Europe are founded on the principles of liberal democracy and all citizens, regardless of ori-

gin and religion, enjoy fundamental rights. In most countries power
has been held by center parties (usually designated Christian Democratic), by left-of-center parties (primarily Social Democratic or
Labor), or by center-left coalitions. West Germany now has a Socialist coalition government of the Social Democratic party and the
small Free Democratic party. Austria is run by a Socialist regime
and a chancellor, Bruno Kreisky, who was born of a Jewish father,
though himself not an identified Jew—no mean development for
one of the most Catholic countries in Europe. In the Scandinavian
countries the Social Democrats have been in power for decades,
though the Socialists in Sweden, who lost their majority in the recent election, will continue in power only with the support of the
small Communist party. Great Britain and France, where the mass
of European Jews live, are not exceptions, for the Conservatives and
the Gaullists are center parties, committed to democratic principles and institutions, and in both countries Jews live in full confidence that their fundamental liberties are secure.

Transcending boundaries as a force for democracy is the non-
Communist left, primarily the Social Democratic and Labor parties. Although these no longer constitute a strongly cohesive transnational force, they have a common objective: the building of democratic societies based on nondiscrimination, equality of opportunity for all, and far-reaching social and economic reforms. The Socialists are either the dominant party in government, as in Germany, Austria, and the Scandinavian countries; or share power
with a center party, as in Italy; or are the strongest opposition party,
as in Great Britain. (An exception is France, where the non-Communist opposition is split into a variety of groups.)

Fear of radical change, which had prevented the emergence of
strong Socialist parties, ended after World War II, for two reasons:
the liberal center parties themselves advocated social reform, and
the Socialist parties broke with dogmatic Marxism, at least as interpreted and applied by Communist regimes.

Transnational Bodies

Of substantial importance for the protection of democratic rights
are the transnational structures created after the war as a step toward European integration and old institutions which have developed fresh outlooks.

Of special interest is the Council of Europe, an intergovernmental organization established in 1949 to deal with political affairs, particularly with human rights. Membership, now counting seventeen states, is open to any European country willing to adhere to the provisions of the Council statute and the principles of "the rule of law and the enjoyment of all persons within its jurisdiction of human rights and fundamental freedoms." This excludes the authoritarian states of the Iberian peninsula and of Central and Eastern Europe; Greece recently resigned, as it was about to be expelled.

The Council's major weakness is that each member state, no matter how important, has only one vote in the decision-making body, the Committee of Ministers, while the Assembly, in which the member states are proportionately represented by 147 parliamentarians, has only deliberative functions. The vision that the Assembly will eventually become the popularly elected legislative body, or parliament, of Europe is not likely to become a reality in the present decade. Still, the Council of Europe is the nucleus of a future framework for forging common policies, as well as a source of a European consciousness based on humanistic values and a factor in the formation of a multinational, multireligious society.

The most notable achievement of the Council of Europe is the European Convention of Human Rights and Fundamental Freedoms, which came into force in 1953 and has since been extended. Based on the United Nations Universal Declaration of Human Rights, it defines the rights of the citizen in a democratic society: the right to life, liberty, and security of person; freedom from torture, slavery, and servitude; the right to a fair trial; the right to privacy; freedom of thought, conscience, and religion; freedom of expression, assembly, and association. The Convention also provides for international machinery to assure their protection, principally the European Commission of Human Rights and the European Court of Human Rights. The rights and freedoms enumerated "shall be secured without discrimination on any ground such as sex, race, color, language, religion, political or other opinion, national or social origin, association with a national minority, property, birth or other status" (Article 14). Although many rights under the Convention bow to the needs of public order and other national interests, the Convention and the implementing institutions are an additional important safeguard for Jewish rights in member countries.

Among other transnational bodies centered in Europe and having various potentials as instruments for democracy are UNESCO (United Nations Educational, Scientific, and Cultural Organization), which has made important contributions in the fight against racism and religious prejudice and in the promotion of a spirit of universalism and rapprochement among world religions and civilizations; the International Labor Organization, which has sought not only to promote the welfare of labor but also social and economic rights generally; and the Office of the UN High Commissioner for Refugees, which provides legal protection and modest financial assistance for refugees in the countries where they have been admitted.

The Vatican and the World Council of Churches

New insights with regard to basic tenets of faith have profoundly altered the conservative, and at times reactionary, role of the Catholic Church. Vatican II made permanent changes in theology and liturgy that cut the theological ground from under anti-Semitism in Christian countries.

In regard to such matters as celibacy, birth control, and mixed marriage, however, there is continuous tension between progressive and conservative forces within the Church. The conservatives fear that rapid changes in theological principles, liturgical practices, the teaching of catechism, as well as alignment with left-of-center trends, will undermine the authority and structure of the Church. The ferment is particularly acute in the Netherlands, where there is a crisis and danger of a schism; in Belgium, where Primate Leo Cardinal Suenens is leading a movement for restructuring the Vatican institutions and revising papal authority; in France, where many young priests have formed an active opposition; and in Germany, where the leading Church authorities, still imbued with conservative political ideologies, are gradually losing their influence outside the Church proper.

On the whole, however, the Catholic Church in Western Europe has become more aware of the need for adjustment to new trends and is speaking out on social problems. Though opposed to extreme tendencies in the European churches, the Vatican has slackened discipline and control over them. Since the Ecumenical Council it has become active in various social and humanitarian areas. It takes an active interest in world peace; seeks cooperation with transnational bodies like the Council of Europe and others; and no longer engages in political party struggles in Italy, except where they involve religious principles, e.g., in the recent debate on divorce. Under the impact of the growing participation of clergymen in social conflict, these progressive trends will probably gain strength in the 1970s, especially if there should be a new pope.

The World Council of Churches (Protestant and Eastern Orthodox) has lately shifted emphasis from activities designed to create a spirit of interfaith cooperation based on the acceptance of religious pluralism, to "third world" problems, development of relations with religious bodies in Communist countries, and, generally, a radical conception of interaction between religion and social movements. The World Council appears to be losing contact with the major Christian countries and concerning itself more with the Middle and Far East and with African countries. Its recent decision to give financial aid to extremist and guerrilla movements shocked the strongholds of Protestantism. If the World Council continues in that direction, it may gain importance as a link with the rest of the world but lose much of its significance in the Western Hemisphere. (The attitude of the churches toward Jews and Israel is discussed below.)

Dangers to Democracy

Forces opposed to the liberal democratic system do exist, in groupings of the extreme right or left and occasionally in other segments of society.

Neo-fascism

The National Democratic party (NPD) was until recently the most important group of its kind in West Germany. Its followers are unrepentant Nazis, discontented socioeconomic groups, particularly farmers and the lower middle class, and some conservatives who are ill at ease with the permissive tendencies in German society today. Its leadership consists of two elements: post-fascists, former Nazi officials and members of the radical right-wing organizations of the 1950s who have no political goals but aim to gratify personal ambitions, and neo-fascists, mostly younger men who openly pursue nationalist goals but dissociate themselves from crimes committed by the Nazi regime.

When the Socialists (SPD) came to power, the NPD began to lose ground. The people generally support Chancellor Willy Brandt's economic policies and his initiatives toward a settlement with Eastern Europe. Critics of these policies no longer need join the NPD to show their discontent. They now can join the Christian Democratic Union (CDU), the major opposition party, which conducted a rear-guard struggle against the treaties with the Soviet Union and Poland. As a matter of fact, the CDU is not averse to accepting as members former Nazis (Kurt Kiesinger is not the only example) or other authoritarian-minded elements, although the party generally is sincerely committed to the principles of parliamentary democracy.

In the last parliamentary elections the NPD failed to get the 5 percent minimum vote required for representation in Parliament, and it lost heavily in the Diet and municipal elections. The party was further weakened by internal strife, which led to the forced resignation of its vociferous leader, Adolf von Thadden. Certainly, the NPD has no chance of becoming a major political factor as long as the economic situation does not take a sharp turn for the worse and Germany continues its present foreign policy. And it is doubtful whether either the CDU or the SPD, neither of which has been strong enough to form a government without support of a smaller party, would ever agree to a coalition with the NPD.

The problem in Germany is not so much the danger of possible emergence of organized neo-Nazism; it is rather that the fundamental relationship between citizen and state, ruler and ruled, on all levels of society, has not changed. The ordinary German's political concept has remained largely what it was in the monarchy, the Weimar Republic, and the Third Reich: the state, as supreme authority, regulates and orders the life of the citizen in every sphere—including education, the judicial process, and even the political party. A related concept that has prevailed for a century is that, next to regulating the citizen's life, the state's function is to aggrandize itself and increase its power in international affairs. These notions are deeply embedded, and attempts at re-education, either by the occupation powers or the German authorities, have thus far not brought substantial change.

All responsible politicians in Germany are acutely aware of the

vigilance by democratic countries, and particularly by the Jews, and
of the incalculable harm that any sign of a return to the old ways
might do at a time when West Germany is making every effort to
take its place as a full-fledged member of the international community.

In Italy the extreme right is organized primarily in the MSI (Mo-
vimento Sociale Italiano), which obtained 1.5 million votes, or 5.2
percent of the total, in the last parliamentary elections. Like the
NPD in Germany, it tries to create the impression of being a conservative and patriotic movement, rather than radical fascist. Anti-
Semitism is not emphasized, and its leadership claims it took over
from Mussolini only the "good" things. But nobody doubts that the
MSI's basic orientation is fascist and that in time of crisis it would
throw off the mask of conformity. There is also a motley of splinter
groups that use physical violence (primarily in the universities),
publish inflammatory booklets, and are openly anti-Semitic.

The Antidemocratic Left

A distinction must be made between the Moscow-oriented Communist parties and the various other movements of the left, which
though small in number are highly articulate and significant in relation to Israel.

The major weight of the Communist parties is concentrated in
France, where they regularly receive at least 20 percent of the vote,
and in Italy, where the figure is about 27 percent. In both countries the political left is divided between Communists and non-
Communists, neither of whom are in a position to form an enduring partnership with the center parties. In Italy the non-Communist leftist regime is constantly battered by the Communist opposition, which controls the trade union movement. In France the
Communist party holds the first position on the left, while the
non-Communist parties of the left—François Mittérand's Socialists and the Unified Socialist party, a small though articulate
group with one deputy in parliament—are paralyzed because they
cannot agree on a common program. The Communists' drive for
the creation of a United Popular Front was disrupted by the invasion of Czechoslovakia, but a working arrangement between them
and some non-Communist groups may yet be made. In the foresee-

able future, however, the Gaullist majority will probably remain in power, facing a divided leftist opposition.

Elsewhere in Europe there has been a steady decline of support for the Communist parties since the initial postwar period; in the last Belgian parliamentary election it was only 3.3 percent and in Norway 1.4 percent, and the figure is not much higher in any of the other countries.

The New Left deserves special attention, not because of its numerical strength but because its sharply articulate voices, expressed in many books and periodicals and on public platforms, are echoed in wider circles of students and intellectuals and because of its total commitment to the anti-Israel cause. The movement totally rejects industrial society as it exists in both the capitalist and Communist worlds, decrying the social and moral premises on which it rests.

The New Left is divided into many splinter groups and several ideologies: anarcho-syndicalist, Trotskyist, Maoist; their heroes are Mao Tse-tung, Ché Guevara, Franz Fanon, Fidel Castro, and more recently, Yasir Arafat and George Habash of the Palestinian liberation movement. Some advocate violence. Their vocabulary is identical to that of their counterparts in the United States.

In sum, democratic government seems stable and secure and is likely to remain so during this decade. Antidemocratic forces, on the right or the left, will not achieve power or—in respects that concern us here—even have substantial impact on those in power, to undermine the domestic situation of the Jews or influence the governmental policies in regard to Israel.

The Changing Condition of the Jews

The bulk of the Jews living in Western Europe is concentrated in England and France, with communities of about 450,000 and 550,000, respectively. But there is no country without organized Jewish life; a new community even emerged, almost from the void, in Spain, which counts about 10,000 Jews.

While West European Jewry is fourth on the list of Jewish population blocs—after the United States, the Soviet Union, and Israel —its significance is much greater than the figures would indicate.

Jewish communities in Western Europe continue to maintain po
sitions acquired over centuries of living in the centers of Christian
culture and Western civilization. It is difficult to imagine Rome,
Amsterdam, Antwerp, or Strasbourg without Jewish life. The Jews
of Western Europe represent a bridge between Jews in Central and
East European countries, from which many Western European
Jews originate, and the large Jewish communities overseas, in the
United States, Canada, Australia, and South Africa.

To be sure, European Jewry today is not what it was before
World War II. German Jewry, with its unique resources that have
enriched Western culture for centuries, is practically gone. The approximately 30,000 Jews who now live in West Germany are not
even a symbolic remnant of the close to 500,000 of only forty years
ago. The same is true of Austrian Jewry, reduced to a little more
than 8,000, from 200,000 before the war.

Comparable devastation has taken place in the Dutch community, which had been a prime example of Jewish traditional living
in a state of emancipation and tolerance, and whose strength has
shrunk from 157,000 to about 30,000. By their very existence, however, the Jews in Amsterdam and Rotterdam help keep alive the
concern of the Dutch people with Judaism, Jewish needs, and Israel.
Few countries have seen the development of such profound studies
of Jewish religion and culture by Protestant and Catholic clergymen, scholars, and teachers, who have made knowledge of Judaism
an integral part of their own culture and have been in the forefront
of the struggle to safeguard Israel's existence.

In lesser degree, the same can also be said of the approximately
25,000 Jews in the Scandinavian countries. Finland has only some
1,500 Jews, but they exemplify in miniature form the qualities of
Jewish life in Russia at the beginning of the century. Norway has
about 750 Jews, whose very struggle to maintain the framework of a
community in a totally tolerant society ought not be overlooked.
Sweden's Jewish community numbers 15,000, and Denmark's 6,000.

West European Jews are generally integrated into the political,
social, and economic structures of their national societies. No major
political party or social movement advocates discrimination against
Jews. The mass media not only are generally free from prejudice,
but they bring to public attention Jewish cultural and religious
events and traditions.

Economically, the Jews of Western Europe belong principally to the upper- and lower-middle classes. They pursue business careers and, in line with general developments in these countries, are substantially represented in the liberal professions—engineering, medicine, law, technology, research—and in administrative areas. Jewish diamond workers in Antwerp (where the industry is still largely owned by Jews), Jewish textile workers in London, and Jewish fur and leather workers in Paris are almost at the vanishing point. The children of the Jewish lower-middle and working classes in France, including those of new Jewish immigrants from North African countries, are entering secondary schools and universities in order to prepare for communal, technological, and managerial positions.

The Changing Anti-Semitism

Latent and diffused anti-Semitism continues to exist among substantial segments of the Western European population and will doubtless respond to active agents. It finds expression in the spoken word, wall inscriptions, anonymous tracts, and even in outbursts of mass hysteria. Two manifestations of this kind, though brief and without serious consequences, occurred in the postwar period. A rash of swastika smearing, which began in January 1960 in Cologne, West Germany, spread like wildfire throughout the world.

A more recent incident, now called the "rumor of Orléans," occurred in that city, located in central France. Its population of 88,000 is typical from every point of view. In May 1969 a fantastic rumor spread overnight that several Jewish owners of women's clothing shops were engaged in white slave traffic; that they injected customers in the dressing rooms with drugs and then moved them to underground cellars for transport to distant lands for the purpose of prostitution. This rumor prevailed for several days, although not one woman in Orléans was reported missing. The city authorities were quite embarrassed by this revival of legend, which died as quickly as it was born.

A team of sociologists investigating the case observed that the medieval-like readiness to believe such fiction revealed predispositions rooted in contemporary conditions—in social mutation, Communist anti-Semitism, and the Arab-Israeli conflict. It also indicated that European society is no longer inhibited by the sense of guilt and shame which prevailed in the immediate postwar period.

Latent anti-Semitism derives from various sources: traditional teachings about the beginnings of Christianity; myths about Jewish riches, power, and domination; jealousy of the position of Jews in the economy and the professions; and general bewilderment at the persistence of a Jewish group with its own religion and mores in an "alien" culture. A very different factor, potent even today, is the belief that Jews are leaders in rebellion against the established social order.

In the May 1968 student revolt in France, for example, attention was focused on two of its leaders, Daniel Cohn-Bendit, who was French-born but a German citizen, and Alain Geismar. The demonstrators' slogan, "We are all German Jews," adopted in answer to anti-Semitic slurs against Cohn-Bendit, probably helped attract attention to the role of Jews in this movement which traumatized France for about two months, and is still not forgotten. The fact that the same group later proclaimed "We are all *fedayin*" did not dispel the impression of Jewish leadership of the revolt, just as anti-Semites were never embarrassed to blame the Jews for the rise of both Communism and capitalism.

Anti-Semitic book production, too, continues in a number of countries, particularly in Germany and France. In France, Henri Coston, a veteran in the field, is inexhaustible in issuing pamphlets and books on well-trodden themes, as the titles indicate: *The Unknown Origins of the Bolshevik Revolution, Judaism and Communism*, and *Europe of Peoples and Europe of Bankers*. However, this literature probably serves more as mental sustenance for inveterate anti-Semites than as an instrument for making new ones. Its semifictional character, its fanatical stress on Jews as the source of all evil, its manner of presentation, all so out of tune with the current mood and style, betray the authors as relics of an earlier era. The financial resources of these enterprises remain somewhat of a mystery; links between such groups in Europe, the United States, South Africa, and Latin America are apparent and cannot be ignored.

There is little likelihood that under normal conditions such attitudes will erupt into serious attacks against Jews. Organized anti-Semitism is usually the stock in trade of the extreme antidemocratic right, whose strength in the foreseeable future will not represent a serious menace. The work of uprooting these deep-seated prejudices would require long-range planning of the kind that the West European Jewish communities are not yet prepared to undertake, though there are various groups in European society which would be willing to cooperate in such an enterprise.

It is not necessarily anti-Semitism that brings problems for Western European Jews as regards the State of Israel, though anti-Semites are quick to exploit the issue. The Jewish community is fully committed to the maintenance and advancement of Israel. Relationships between Jews and their neighbors therefore must of necessity be affected by positions and perplexities with regard to Israel.

Throughout Europe governmental policy as well as public opinion with regard to Israel have undergone considerable change since the Six Day War. One indication is that, of the major political parties in the region, only the Social Democrats and the center parties now express pro-Israel views, and even they do so less frequently and less warmly than before.

Cooling attitudes to Israel have created some tensions for Western European Jews. More disturbing, however, are the massive anti-Israel campaigns by extremist groups. In some countries elements of the extreme right have recently joined with the Communists in condemning their governments for supporting Israel. A pro-Israel policy, they say, is inimical to the national interest, which calls for friendship with the Arabs. Thus the unofficial neo-Nazi weekly, *Deutsche National-Zeitung*, with a circulation of more than 100,-000, is devoting more and more space to the warning that Germany will lose its position in the "third world," and particularly in the Middle East, as a result of its positive attitude toward Israel. (Israel was recognized not by the present regime, but by Chancellor Ludwig Erhard's Christian Democratic government.) The two NPD publications, *Deutsche Nachrichten* and *Deutsche Wochenzeitung*, similarly claim that Germany's economic aid to Israel and its reparation programs for Jews are undermining the nation's position in the Arab countries and the "third world."

The traditional rightist press in France, once pro-Israel because of its anti-Arabism during the war with Algeria, has recently changed its tune and is ferociously anti-Israel on the ground that French interests require the development of good relations with the Arab world.

Communism and the Jews

Of much greater significance than obsessive old-style anti-Semitism are the basic positions on Jews taken by the Moscow-oriented Communist movement and the New Left.

Anti-Semitism was taboo in the early Soviet period, but it was overtly revived after the Moscow trials of the 1930s and became official policy after the war, particularly after 1949. Communism saw Zionism in particular as a hostile ideology. (The Soviet support for the establishment of the State of Israel was an aberration for political purposes, a move to force the British out of the Middle East.)

The Communist parties in Western Europe fully supported the extreme Soviet anti-Semitism during the last years of the Stalin regime, as manifested in the "Doctors' Plot" in Russia * and the Slánský trial in Czechoslovakia.** Western Communists insisted on the authenticity of accusations that "world" Jewish organizations were involved in a conspiracy to destroy the Soviet regime and its leaders.

In later years the Italian, French, and other Communist parties tried to defend the Soviet regime against charges of anti-Jewish discrimination; more recently, however, some Western Communist leaders have begun to take a critical view of Soviet policy. Outstanding among the critics is Umberto Terracini, a Jew and president of the Communist faction in the Italian senate, who publicly demanded that the Soviets fully restore to the Jews their fundamental rights as a distinct ethnic and religious group.

After the Six Day War, the Soviet Union's political campaign against Israel was marked by violent propaganda in all news media. The Western European Communist parties adopted the official Soviet line that Israel is the aggressor; that it is in the forefront of Western neo-imperialism; that it victimizes the Arabs in occupied

---

* Abortive blatantly anti-Semitic 1953 trial of prominent Moscow physicians, the majority Jews, accused of having plotted medical murder of Soviet leaders.

** Most important of series of purge trials aimed at consolidating power in Czech Communist party in hands of Moscow-controlled group. Rudolf Slánský, postwar Secretary General of Party, and group of others, mostly Jews, were tried in 1952 and executed on a charge of conspiracy against the State. The defendants, including Slánský, were subsequently exonerated by the Czech Supreme Court.

territories; and that the Palestine liberation movement speaks for the oppressed peoples in that region.

Going beyond the specific issues of the Middle East conflict, the Communists have also—as in classical anti-Semitism—presented Israel as a bastion of world Jewry which is powerful enough to influence political forces in the West. Judaism and Israel thus become fused as the conspirator in a plot to influence world politics, this hoary party line having its antecedent in the infamous, and utterly discredited, "Protocols of the Elders of Zion," the purported "master plan" for Jewish hegemony first circulated in Russia in the early years of this century. However, their purpose is not the perpetuation of the myth, but the advancement of political ends.

The complete identification of the Western Jewish communities with Israel's cause has also aroused anti-Jewish feelings, particularly in countries with a mass Communist following, like France and Italy. Luciano Ascoli, another prominent Italian Jewish Communist, in a recently published book, *The Left and the Jewish Question,* calls leftist anti-Zionism "nothing but a modern variant of an old passion not yet extinguished—anti-Semitism."

A public opinion poll conducted in France in November 1969 illustrates this point. One question was designed to elicit views on whether various groups, including the Jews, had more, less, or just "normal" influence in society. With regard to Jews, 24 percent thought that they had more influence, 4 percent thought they had less, and 45 percent thought it was normal; 27 percent did not know. However, of those crediting the Jews with more than normal influence, 51 percent were either supporters of the Communist party or of the non-Communist left.

Another source of tension for European Jews has been the inflammatory propaganda of Arab groups in various Western European countries. There now is a substantial Arab student body in France, Britain, and especially Germany: 1,800 at the University of Berlin alone. These groups sometimes present the Arab cause not in political anti-Israel terms, but speak of a Jewish-Israel design to oppress the Arab peoples. Al Fatah, which has many contacts in Western Europe, officially claims that it is opposed to traditional anti-Semitism and that its ultimate aim is to establish a democratic Arab state, with equal status for all. Its propaganda, however, belies this pronouncement.

Since about 1968 Zionism has been a principal target also of the

New Left. The argument used is simplistic: Zionism is a product of
the West and therefore part of Western neo-imperialism; Israel re-
ceives its major support from the United States and is therefore
tied to American imperialism; Israel is supported by world Jewry,
therefore . . . The final conclusion is left to implication and innu-
endo, but New Left followers do not miss the point, although some
of their most articulate leaders are Jews.

A case in point was the World Conference of Christians for Palestine, which was arranged by a group associated with the Paris leftist Catholic weekly, *Témoignage Chrétien*, and held in Beirut in
May 1970. Attended by four hundred Catholics and Protestants, the
conference voiced violent opposition to Israel and complete support
of the Arab guerrilla movement. While being careful to begin its
appeal with a condemnation of anti-Semitism, it accused the "Zionist state" of being "opposed to the dignity and liberty of man"—a
statement which was repudiated by Christian groups in France and
Belgium.

Particularly vehement was the anti-Israel campaign conducted by
the New Left in Germany. Young Germans are less inhibited by a
sense of guilt than their parents, who witnessed the Nazi atrocities;
they feel that they are not responsible for these crimes. They are
also extremely anti-American because they believe current government policy to be primarily a result of Germany's alliance with the
United States. Another important reason is that the major targets
of New Left hostility—particularly political leaders like Franz Josef
Strauss and press magnate, Axel Springer, who controls 40 percent
of the German newspapers and whom the New Left considers a
main pillar of the present system—are also among the leading pro-
Israel elements in the country.

Of late there has been a general decline of the European New
Left. As an organized movement it has lost its influence on youth,
particularly the student population, perhaps because the classical
radical forces have remained opposed to the totally negative attitudes of the extreme leftist groups. More important, however, the
European New Left lost contact, as it were, with the cause of the
Palestinians when fratricidal conflict arose in their ranks and Jordan eliminated the guerrilla forces as a military power in the Middle East.

A recent poll of French students established that the moderate
leftists are sympathetic to Israel and that even the extreme leftists

are less hostile than before. Two-thirds of the respondents conceded that Israel is entitled to retain part of the territories occupied in 1967, and 44 percent of the extreme-left students agreed. One-half of the students thought Jerusalem should remain part of Israel; one-third of the extreme left agreed. One-third of all students thought that the best way to solve the refugee problem is to establish a Palestinian state bordering on Israel.

There is little doubt that the entire complex of attitudes on Israel among various leftist groups of Western society—the Moscow-oriented Communists, the New Left, and others of all shades—poses a fundamental problem with regard to relations between Jews and non-Jews in this part of the world. And since it may be assumed that a solution is not in view and that therefore tensions will continue for some time, the following questions must be considered:

Has Israel been shown to world public opinion in a proper way? Can influences be brought to bear, at least on Communist movements outside the Soviet bloc, that would change their attitudes toward Israel and their readiness to transform anti-Zionism into anti-Judaism? Can ways be found to make the New Left perceive the unreality of its simplistic approaches and recognize the aspiration of Jews with regard to Israel in the light of historical development?

Jews and Christians

A fundamental change in attitude toward the Jews has been taking place in the major Catholic and Protestant churches of the West. Its effects cannot be fully evaluated as yet, but it already seems certain that religious anti-Semitism as expressed throughout the ages is losing its hold over the masses and that a new chapter is beginning in Christian-Jewish relations.

The change has been recorded in official pronouncements by both churches and in an unprecedented outpouring of Christian thought on both historic and contemporary Judaism. The most significant declaration, promulgated by Vatican Council II in October 1965, proclaims that "the Jews should not be presented as repudiated or cursed by God"; calls for "mutual understanding and respect . . . and brotherly dialogue"; affirms "the common patrimony with the

Jews"; and "deplores the hatred, persecutions and displays of anti-Semitism directed against the Jews at any time and from any source." Similar statements have been issued by the World Council of Churches, beginning with the New Delhi declaration, and by representative bodies of the Council's member churches.

No doubt, the negative aspects of Christian attitudes about the Jews will be eliminated. Of special importance is the examination of catechisms and other religious textbooks in Western Europe with a view to eliminating hostile references to the Jews. A team of scholars at Pro Deo University in Rome worked on Italian and Spanish textbooks; French-language material was thoroughly scrutinized by the Research Center at Louvain University.* In all, it is not unreasonable to expect that in time Christian teaching will cease to be a source of anti-Jewish prejudice. (A recent example of reaction to religious anti-Semitism was the universal condemnation of the Oberammergau passion play.)

Much work remains to be done, however, in the formulation and development of positive relationships between Christianity and Judaism. Thus far, implementation of the Vatican declaration has come primarily from churches in specific countries at their own initiative. Neither the Catholic nor the Protestant leadership has gone far in rethinking theological fundamentals, which is necessary for creating new attitudes toward Judaism. Christian theology in the past regarded Judaism as a relic, a witness to the denial of Christianity, and Jews as an entity whose designation "people of God" had been transferred to the Christian community. The need for rethinking is clearly understood by creative minds within the churches.

Another obstacle to further development in Christian-Jewish relations is the reemergence of a Jewish state on the soil of the Old Testament. It found Christian thinking totally unprepared; it simply does not fit into the old scheme. Also, both the Catholic and Protestant churches, having vested interests and affiliated religious communities in Arab countries, are shying away from considerations that might lead to acceptance of Israel's existence.

The ambivalent attitude of the Christian leadership to the State of Israel may be illustrated by two statements made after the hijacking of four planes in September 1970 by Arab guerrillas. Jean

* Both projects were co-sponsored by the American Jewish Committee.

Cardinal Danielou, a prominent member of the Vatican hierarchy, called for a reaction of "international conscience" to the violent acts, but added: "It is often difficult to know which side is on the right; perhaps both sides." Reverend Eugene Carson Blake, head of the World Council of Churches, condemned the acts of piracy, but added: "We comprehend the sentiment of frustration by the Palestinian Arabs." It is too much to expect that this vacillation will cease before a settlement of the Middle East conflict. What one can hope and work for is that the churches will not, on principle, identify themselves with an anti-Israel stand.

Future of the European Jewish Communities

In Western Europe, Jews are formally classified as a religious group and the status of the Jewish community in each country depends on the established relationship between church and state. In Italy, Germany, Austria, and Belgium the central Jewish religious bodies have the right to tax their members for the maintenance of religious institutions. In France, except for Alsace-Lorraine, there is separation of church and state. The Jewish Consistory is, in fact, a private organization, which the government unofficially recognizes as the spokesman for Jewish religious and social interests. In Great Britain the Board of Deputies of British Jews is the quasi-official lay body representing the Jewish community. It must be stressed, however, that these are only formal classifications: the Holocaust and the State of Israel have made the peoples and governments of Western Europe realize that Jews are more than a religious denomination.

Since World War II there has been a radical change in the attitudes of Western European Jews. Deliberate assimilation in the sense of denying or hiding one's Jewish origins has disappeared almost entirely. The young Jews of today, in Paris or London, Rome or Brussels, frankly and without self-consciousness say, "I am a Jew." The birth of Israel and especially the Six Day War, moreover, have evoked in many a sense of pride and a determination to aid Israel's struggle for existence. One can safely assert that Israel is dominant in the consciousness of the European Jew.

Jean Paul Sartre's recent criterion, "A Jew is authentic when he is aware of his condition as a Jew and has a sense of solidarity with all other Jews," is met by the majority of Jews in Europe today. (This, incidentally, is in contrast to Sartre's earlier definition, in *Reflections on the Jewish Question*, that a Jew is "one who is identified as such by non-Jews.")

The fear that manifestations of solidarity with other Jews, and particularly with Israel, would provoke charges of dual loyalty has been discarded by almost all Jewish leaders in Europe. The government and people of France are quite aware that Jews as a bloc are opposed to their government's Israel policies, but they take this Jewish attitude for granted; and the Jewish leadership, for its part, does not seek to hide its commitment to Israel.

This psychological association with Israel, however, has not been sufficient to give content to Jewish living outside of Israel, particularly for those who are not sustained by religious belief and observance. Not long ago a leading young rabbi of France, Josy Eisenberg, put it succinctly:

> The existence of Israel plays a role of catharsis for the Jew in the Diaspora . . . it purges . . . [him] of various charges (parasitism, noncreativity, laxity) and alters . . . [his] image . . . in Western consciousness. In this sense, Israel represents a factor which not only does not force the Jew to leave the Diaspora but, on the contrary, facilitates his integration here and now. . . . Israel gives psychological security and moral comfort to the Jews of the Diaspora. . . . The function of Israel is not to preserve and secure [them] . . . but to be a stimulating and creative factor. . . . The establishment of peace in the Middle East will have as a consequence . . . the profound modification of the content of the relationship which unites Israel to the Jews of the world. The problem of the nature of this content will arise within the framework of a crisis of identity. What does it mean to be a Jew? Nationality, culture, religion? . . . The most obvious definition of a Jew is that he is a man in search of his identity.

Tasks for the Future

This search for identity probably will continue everywhere. But West European Jewry is faced with special problems related to its demographic situation and the decline of its resources. In some countries—e.g., Switzerland, Sweden, Denmark, Italy—there has been a decrease in the Jewish population owing to a drop in the birth rate and a rise in mixed marriages.

Elsewhere the Jewish population has been and will probably remain stable during the coming decade. The Jews are now more determined than ever to survive as an entity, religiously, culturally, and in their attachment to Israel. Such determination, intangible and immeasurable, is, as we know from the past, sometimes decisive in assuring Jewish continuity. But the future of West European Jewry, its character and strength in a free and liberal society, will depend largely on three internal developments:

The first is the establishment of permanent links among the Jewish communities in the region for the purpose of developing central institutions and resources for various purposes. Many of the smaller communities cannot sustain themselves as distinctively Jewish; nor can a community of 10,000 or fewer Jews plan long-range programs to educate the general public regarding the significance of the Jewish historical experience, Jewish religious thought and practice, Jewish culture, and ties with Israel.

There has never been greater willingness on the part of secular educational institutions and information media in Western Europe to deal seriously with Jewish subjects. A number of universities have established chairs on various aspects of Judaism; others would embark on Jewish studies if properly stimulated. Newspapers, radio and television, and publishers are more willing than ever before to present to Western society all facets of Jewish life and culture; but they do not have the necessary resources.

A promising beginning was made toward linking the communities with the creation of the European Council of Jewish Community Services, which embraces the central Jewish communal bodies of Western Europe. Still in the process of formation, it has already demonstrated its potential by organizing common action for Jewish victims of natural and social disasters in the region and by establishing institutions for the study of Judaism in key centers (Paris, Brussels) where young Jews can familiarize themselves with the basic tenets and problems of Judaism. The Council also plans to provide guidance for maintaining welfare institutions and distributing cultural materials. With proper support and leadership, it may provide central coordination as well as creative stimulation for the European Jewish communities.

A second important condition for the viability of Western European Jewish communities is the strengthening of their relations with organized Jewish life in the United States and Israel. The re-

covery of the European Jewish communities after the war would
have been impossible without gigantic efforts by American Jews.
The Joint Distribution Committee has done heroic work in helping hundreds of thousands of survivors to reach a state of relative
normalcy and preparing them for resettlement. United Hias Service
has carried on ceaselessly the work of migration overseas. The Organization for Rehabilitation Through Training (ORT) has helped
train large numbers of youths and adults for useful occupations.
And the Jewish Agency has been the primary instrument in moving
large masses of Jews to Israel for resettlement.

West German restitution and reparation payments helped pay
for the daily needs of many survivors; they were also used by the
Conference on Jewish Material Claims Against Germany, and later
by the Memorial Foundation for Jewish Culture, to build and finance religious and communal institutions throughout Europe.

Other Jewish organizations, such as the World Jewish Congress
and the American Jewish Committee, have watched for signs of re-
surgent anti-Semitism in postwar Europe and have helped lay the
groundwork for reviving Jewish cultural life. They have been particularly active in promoting interreligious dialogue, which culminated in the radically new Catholic and Protestant positions on
Jews and Judaism.

The model of American communal institutions is perhaps another kind of contribution by American Jewry to the reconstruc-
tion of the European Jewish communities. The concept of the
Community Council is partially derived from the idea behind the
Council of Jewish Federations and Welfare Funds in the United
States; the concept of the United Jewish Appeal, the fund-raising
agency for local welfare and cultural needs and for channeling funds
to Israel, has been successfully applied in France and elsewhere;
and the native American institution for promoting Jewish social
and cultural life, the community center, has been used in Europe
with great success. There are now some 100 community centers in
eleven countries, where the new generation of Jews, dispersed in the
general population, can gather and express in creative fashion its
Jewish yearnings, customs, and needs. But these centers need com-
petent and imaginative guidance, and this too will have to be supplied on an all-European scale. To accomplish it there will have to
be intensive collaboration between the American and European
Jewish communities for some time to come.

Of utmost importance for the future of European Jewery is its relationship with Israel. One cannot overestimate the impact of Israel on the position and self-understanding of the European Jews. The contacts have been numerous and intensive; one may question, however, whether the resources of Israel have been fully utilized for the revival and strengthening of Jewish life in Europe.

European Jewry has undergone historic transformation and suffered unprecedented catastrophes since the beginning of the century, when it occupied the central position on the world Jewish scene. Mass migrations, social revolutions, and the Nazi Holocaust have extinguished ancient Jewish communities and decimated many others; and the relatively large Jewish population in the Soviet Union has been isolated and paralyzed. The center of gravity of world Jewry left the Old World as Jews fled to the Americas and Israel.

And yet, Western Europe remains central to Jewish concerns, for it lies in the heart of Western civilization and Christianity. It is the transit road from East to West; it is close to the Mediterranean world and to Israel; it still has vital roots which are capable of nourishing new life.

The problems facing European Jews immediately after the war were dramatic, striking—and specifically European. American Jews could identify with the goals of European Jews, the survivors of the Holocaust, as they sought to pick up the pieces of their individual and collective lives and rebuild Jewish communities, as they claimed indemnification and restitution, as they appealed for help to emigrate overseas or to begin life anew in European lands; but the problems of the Jews in America and of the Jews in Europe were tremendously different at the time.

Today's situation stands in sharp contrast. The Jews in the United States and in Western Europe face common problems and have common objectives. Eradicating the remnants of religious and traditional forms of anti-Semitism and planning a strategy for relations with Christian churches are as much a need and concern on one side of the ocean as on the other. And, regardless of differences in numbers and institutional strength, the fundamental issues in the search for Jewish identity are as pertinent in America as in Europe. The same is true of the effort to support Israel in its struggle for security and peace; to counteract Arab, New Left, and Communist themes; and to aid the Jews in the Soviet Union.

It is no accident, then, that even in the political sphere there is a quest for more extensive cooperation between American and Western European Jews, like that which has long existed in the area of welfare and was later extended to the cultural sphere. Nor is it surprising that the character of cooperation between the two Jewish communities has been shifting from a giver-receiver relationship to one of partnership, with both sides gaining in the exchange.

American-European interaction of the future must reflect these changes if it is to be truly relevant.

Chapter 6
Eastern Europe
Zvi Gitelman

Few dare to predict with confidence about world affairs generally, and to anticipate developments in the Communist world is particularly hazardous. The Communist world is secretive and does not provide data commonly available in Western societies. Because the Communist system has not evolved stable political institutions to keep pace with its modernized society and to provide for orderly political change, it tends to mask change as continuity and to cover it in Communist mythology, and it is difficult for the Western observer to penetrate that mythology to glimpse reality. The Western observer is also hampered by his own preconceptions. He sees the coercive nature of Communist regimes but tends to ignore their sources of genuine support. Unsympathetic to their authoritarianism, he tends to play down their genuine economic development. Constructing static models for analyzing the system, he sometimes fails to recognize its dynamic character or to understand the causes and mechanisms and consequences of social, economic, and political change.

In this paper I risk an attempt to identify some of the larger forces which will provide the context and shape the options in Eastern Europe in the next decade, and to anticipate the prospects for Jews in the various countries.

Internal Pressures for Political Change

For some time now, modernization in Eastern Europe has generated pressures for political change. In the beginning Communist leaders, engaged in establishing Communist power and mobilizing their societies for modernization, paid little attention to the foreseeable consequences of the economic, cultural, social, and political transformations which they were bringing about. Communist strat-

207

egies of modernization, developed mainly by Stalin in the 1930s, were applied with great zeal and achieved impressive results (though at high human costs), but Communist doctrine did not indicate how the consequences of modernization were to be dealt with, nor did it provide any guide for post-modernization development.

The need to plan for Communist development after initial modernization was brought home to the political elites by the very success of modernization. Because economic growth was impressive, the failure to maintain the high rates of growth, so important to claims of superiority of the Communist system, led to a shift from "extensive" to "intensive" economic development,[1] a new strategy emphasizing efficiency, technological expertise, and specialization. Economic reform meant also decentralization of decision making and, in most cases, opening the economy to foreign goods and technology while trying to penetrate foreign markets.[2]

Modernization also increased the functional differentiation of society as new job categories were created, the size and importance of the peasantry were reduced, and the urban sector grew rapidly. More individuals were given access to all levels of education and were exposed to mass media. A greater proportion of the population related to the political system, and more support for it as well as greater demands on it were generated, especially as coercion declined, encouraging political and social expression. A more complex and differentiated society required more information about the society; eliciting better information consistently is not merely a technical problem, but depends on an acceptable relationship between state and society, and the need for information has pressed political elites to improve that relationship.[3]

Generational changes have also called forth pressures for political change. When the gap between Communist mythology and socialist reality impinges on the consciousness of East Europeans,

---

[1] The terms are those of the Czech economist Ota Šik.

[2] The causes and resolutions of the economic crises in Eastern Europe are examined in Michael Gamarnikow, *Economic Reforms in Eastern Europe* (Detroit, Wayne State University Press, 1968).

[3] The Soviet dissenter Andrei Amalrik has said: "It is . . . paradoxical that the regime should devote enormous effort to keep everyone from talking and then waste further effort to learn what people are talking about and what they want." Andrei Amalrik, *Will the Soviet Union Survive Until 1984?* (New York, Harper & Row, 1970), p. 32.

some retreat into a cynical indifference to political and civic life, but others agitate for closing the gap between promise and performance.

A major impetus to political change has been the abandonment of terror as a common instrument for the mobilization, control, and integration of society, with profound consequences not only for individuals but also for the organizational patterns and political dynamics of the Communist system. Under Stalinism coercion was the cement holding state and society together throughout Eastern Europe and to a lesser extent in the Soviet Union; the abandonment of terror has compelled the regimes to establish new compliance structures which will achieve the same or better results at lower cost.

Finally, the disintegration of the imperial system, under which East European states had been satrapies of Moscow, has meant that those states, not yet fully autonomous but no longer mere extensions of Soviet power, have had to produce from within themselves forces which would integrate their populations with their political regimes. Post-invasion Czechoslovakia demonstrates the marginal utility of rule by coercion alone and dramatizes the necessity for systemic legitimacy if economic, cultural, and social progress is to continue.

The various post-modernization strains described above have combined to produce an "authority crisis" in Eastern Europe, especially outside the Soviet Union.[4] It has been most visible in Poland, Hungary, and Czechoslovakia, but we may expect similar tendencies in Rumania and Bulgaria as they complete their drives toward modernization. This authority crisis has pressed the regimes to seek a stable formula for successful political integration, for developing loyalty to the system on the basis of shared norms and values. Political integration is an ongoing effort, never completed, but substantial success would establish the legitimacy of the system, permitting government by authority rather than by coercion, and would enhance the stability of the system and of the regime. Political integration is also a prerequisite to further political development.

Political integration, we can expect, will be a primary concern of

---

[4] Zvi Gitelman, "Power and Authority in Eastern Europe," in Chalmers Johnson, ed., *Change in Communist Systems* (Stanford, 1970).

East European leaders in the next decade. Although most Communist governments maintain a stance of uneasy caution toward their populations, they are already experimenting with different integration strategies. One, tried with success in Yugoslavia but suppressed in Czechoslovakia, sought to democratize socialism, to guarantee genuine participation in decision making and some civil liberties. The abolition of censorship, judicial reforms, formation of workers' councils, revival of non-Communist parties, and legitimation of interest groups as participants in the political process were institutionalized expressions of the intention of the Dubček regime to democratize the Czechoslovak political system. While such a strategy may have great appeal for elements of the intelligentsia everywhere in Eastern Europe, political figures clearly will approach it with caution, in view of the Soviet reaction in Czechoslovakia.

Each in their own way, the Hungarians, East Germans, and Rumanians have followed an alternative strategy of political integration, aiming to reconcile the population to the system through unprecedented material benefits. In Hungary impressive economic reforms, coupled with Janos Kadar's minimalist philosophy of "he who is not against us is with us," has provided material benefits in return for less than ideological commitment, merely for abstention from active hostility. The hope is that as 1956 fades from memory genuine, active support for the system will be gradually accumulated. In East Germany astute political leadership has skillfully combined coercive methods, material rewards, and education to the realities of Europe. Since the construction of the Berlin wall it has turned the population's energies inward toward the economic development of the country and has achieved an impressive parallel to the West German *Wirtschaftswunder*. The Rumanians have also stressed the achievements of the socialist economy and have appealed as well to pride in their country's now playing an important and singular role on the world scene.

In Poland, on the other hand, Wladyslaw Gomulka's strategy was simply to hold on while all around him factions of the traditionally fragmented Polish party advanced their own formulae for political integration. (One may speculate that only Soviet insistence on stability elsewhere in Eastern Europe while the Czechoslovak issue was being settled prevented Gomulka from being replaced in the summer of 1968.) This situation of stagnation without stability fell apart with the ouster of Gomulka, but reintegration of state and society is a long way from achievement.

The Soviet Union is in a substantially different position. While, except in Yugoslavia and Albania, socialist regimes in Eastern Europe were installed largely by the might of a foreign power, the Soviet Union experienced an authentic revolution, and the new regime could count on more genuine, spontaneous support. Also, the Soviet population, more isolated from the rest of Europe than the peoples of the other socialist states, has been intensively socialized during more than fifty years, and pre-Communist mores, values, and even institutions have not survived as well as in other East European countries. The Soviet citizen, moreover, is impressed by consistent economic gains over the past half-century, whereas Czechoslovak, Polish, and perhaps Hungarian citizens can discern a less unilinear trend in their countries. Finally, the scientific and diplomatic gains of the USSR since World War II have strengthened "Soviet patriotism" as a bond between the masses and the political elite.

As a result, there is greater slack in the Soviet system, and the leadership enjoys wide support and can feel relatively secure. It is unlikely that within the next decade the system will undergo a profound transformation, although there might be serious dislocations which will force the regime either to revert to Stalinist coercion, make piecemeal changes in limited areas of policy, or reluctantly live with carefully controlled and delimited heterodoxy. The regime sometimes seriously misjudges the sources and nature of discontent, as it has with regard to Jewish nationalist manifestations, and may deal with it in a contradictory, bumbling, and ultimately ineffective fashion. But the Soviet system's ability to withstand foreign and domestic setbacks—whether in the Cuba missile crisis, the Arab-Israeli war of 1967, the trauma of de-Stalinization, or intellectual and nationality discontent—is impressive.

Still, the Soviet elite is not one to denigrate popular backing, witness the decision of the Twenty-fourth Party Congress, impressed by Polish consumer discontent, to spur the growth of the consumer sector of the economy. Albeit to a substantially lesser degree than in other Communist countries, then, authority crises will also trouble the Soviet leadership and influence Soviet policy in the years ahead.

The Impact of External Developments

Although the problems here identified are common to all countries in Eastern Europe, there are important differences in culture, styles of leadership, levels of development, geography, and policy, making the political situation unique in each country. Especially since the loosening of the Soviet bloc there have been important divergences among the Communist states, in particular in the prospects for the Jews of the different countries. But the Jewish situation in all countries is likely to be affected by external developments and by probable trends in Soviet foreign policy.

Soviet relations with other socialist countries in Europe are not likely to change dramatically. Although the USSR tolerated Rumanian and Hungarian heterodoxies, its invasion of Czechoslovakia indicates that whereas it no longer maintains monolithic control or insists on uniformity, it has not abandoned its role as the guide and regulator of the foreign, and to a lesser extent domestic, affairs of the East European countries. The policies of the East European governments toward their indigenous Jewish populations, then, will largely be determined by those governments themselves, though if the USSR becomes intensively involved in a nation's affairs, as in an "emergency," it may do what it sees fit in regard to local Jews and Jewish issues.

At least four factors external to Eastern Europe will doubtless have differential effects in different parts of Eastern Europe and potentially significant impact on the Jewish populations of the area: the Middle East conflict; East-West relations; the Vatican and other international religious bodies; Communist parties and radical movements.

Israel and the Middle East

Especially since the 1967 Arab-Israeli war, the states of Eastern Europe have generally followed Soviet policy in the Middle East, supporting the Arab cause and avoiding diplomatic and commercial relations with Israel. Yugoslavia too has associated itself politically with the Arab states, but has maintained visible economic relations with Israel. Less influenced by the Soviet Union, Yugoslav policy has been governed by the special relationship Tito had with Nasser, by Tito's idea of an Afro-Asian "third force" which would include suitable European and perhaps Latin American elements, as well as by the existence of a significant Moslem population in the country. Rumania, of course, has been a socialist maverick on the Middle East question as in other respects. Its careful neutrality and continued diplomatic and commercial ties with Israel are neither irrational nor sentimental, but another manifestation of Rumania's general policy of maintaining relations with as many countries as possible in order to strengthen its international position and prestige.

In some Eastern European countries policy toward Israel has had domestic consequences for the local Jewish population. In Poland the connection has been direct and open, in the USSR less open but perhaps no less direct. In Czechoslovakia, Israel became both a symbolic and a real domestic issue: those in favor of democratization pointed to Czechoslovakia's hostility to Israel as an example of the moral degeneration of the Novotny regime and of its exaggerated subordination to the Soviet Union, especially in foreign policy. In other countries, on the other hand, there seems to have been a clear and effective distinction between the official position on the Middle East issue and the treatment of the local Jewish population. That has been the case even in Hungary and Bulgaria, both following a hard anti-Israel line, and the latter having close commercial and diplomatic ties with several Arab states.

The impact of the Middle East situation on Soviet domestic policy is more complex. The Soviet regime has inundated the general population and especially the Jews with anti-Israeli propaganda so that no sympathy could develop for the Israelis as an underdog, as a progressive force, or as the enemy of states which receive unpopular Soviet aid. Although the authorities sometimes seek to show that Soviet Jews have no use for Israel, their failure to differentiate effectively between Israel and Jews, especially Diaspora Jews, has created a hostile atmosphere for Soviet Jews, discouraging them from expressing Zionist or Jewish feelings which might invite government repression as well as social hostility.

It is not clear why, like Hungary or Bulgaria, the USSR could not take pains to differentiate between anti-Israel policies and anti-Semitism. Perhaps the Soviet Jewish population is so large, visible, and strategically located in society that Soviet leaders fear lest it be swayed by Zionist sympathies, with dangerous domestic and for-

eign consequences. Of course, one cannot discount the possibility
that Soviet decision makers, even at the very highest level, are themselves receptive to anti-Semitic sentiments. Furthermore, given the
unsubtle, generally crude quality of Soviet propaganda—apparently
well suited to a nationalistic, unsophisticated population which
knows very little about the outside world—it would be unrealistic
to expect that as subtle a differentiation as that between Jew and
Israeli could be made consistently and effectively.

These trends will continue as long as the Arab-Israeli conflict
remains fundamentally unresolved. As long as there is Soviet involvement in the Middle East—and that involvement is likely to
grow rather than decrease—Israel will be a domestic issue in socialist countries: a symbol of "imperialism" to supporters of official
policy, but also an affirmative symbol to the proponents of internal
democratization and the realignment of foreign policy consistent
with professed socialist ideals. Official attitudes to Israel, with unhappy effects for local Jews, may even grow more hostile, perhaps
under pressure of competition with China for the favor of the
Moslem world and its sympathizers in the United Nations. If Israel
is forced to identify more and more closely with the West, and
with the United States in particular, its image as a "lackey of imperialism" will be reinforced throughout Eastern Europe, and not
only among non-Jews. Time would also further erode the original
sympathy for Israel as a new social experiment, a nation in the
making which arose out of the ashes of the Holocaust.

On the other hand, increased Chinese activity in the Middle East
might polarize "moderate" and "radical" Arabs and moderate and
radical Palestinians, with China sponsoring a more uncompromising and militantly anti-Israel grouping. The USSR may then be
forced to stand behind a moderate coalition, led perhaps by the
UAR, seeking some accommodation with Israel. Such differentiation of the Arab and Communist worlds would inevitably modify
Soviet and East European propaganda and probably soften the
image of Israel and the impact on East European Jews. Even a
limited Arab-Israeli accommodation would render Soviet hostility
to Israel no longer politically necessary, removing one source of
discomfort for Jews in socialist countries and perhaps opening the
way to greater emigration to Israel. However, in the Soviet Union
in particular, domestic obstacles to large-scale Jewish emigration
might well remain.

East-West Relations

Underlying the Middle East issues are East-West relations generally. By and large, improved relations between the superpowers should redound to the benefit of the Jewish communities in socialist countries, since those communities are perceived as having effective cultural and family ties to the large Jewish communities of the West. On the other hand, as the events of the early 1950s demonstrated, high levels of tension between East and West and campaigns promoting hostility toward the "capitalist" world are likely to engender suspicion and attacks on Jews as potential fifth columnists with divided loyalties.

One cannot speak with assurance of the future of East-West relations and their implications for the Jews of Eastern Europe. For fifteen years the Soviet Union has pursued a policy of "peaceful competition," rather than merely "peaceful coexistence," with the West. Ironically, Khrushchev's successors may prove more successful in that policy than was its chief formulator and advocate.

Often accused in the West of mediocrity, conservatism, and lack of imagination, the present team of Soviet leaders has skillfully exploited the military, international, and domestic consequences of the Vietnam debacle to pursue new initiatives in foreign policy which have succeeded at very little cost. Following the United States' clear, if tacit, indication that it would not interfere in Czechoslovakia, the Soviet leadership has pushed ahead with bold initiatives in Western Europe and the Middle East. With little attention to the United States, the USSR seems to have achieved a stabilization of "the German question" and gained badly needed technological and economic aid from West European powers. It has effectively closed the military gap, not only through rapid advances in technology, but also by imitating the American doctrine of "flexible response" to the point where it has established itself as a Mediterranean power at least equal to the United States and has a presence in other oceans and other parts of the world.

While future changes of leadership in the Soviet Union are unpredictable, there is no indication that basic Soviet foreign policy would be significantly altered by any of the potential successors now on the horizon. Furthermore, as West Germany, France, and Britain continue along an uneven path toward economic, and perhaps political, rapprochement with the USSR, the United States might well find itself increasingly distant from Europe. Given the diminished support for Israel among Western European governments and populations, the continued success of Soviet policy in Western Europe may increase Israel's isolation as well. These results can have only ill effects on the Jewish community of the USSR and, to a lesser extent, of other socialist countries.

Transnational Religious Influences

Jewish welfare in socialist countries will be only marginally affected by domestic or transnational religious influences. Local religious authorities are generally subservient to the regimes, and none is likely to oppose the government on behalf of the Jews. In the Soviet Union the predominant church has no links to any center abroad which might exert influence on Soviet religious or other policy. Some countries of Eastern Europe have large numbers of adherents of churches with international connections, for example the Catholic Church, but the Vatican has not effectively intervened, and is not likely to intervene in the future, except perhaps in regard to dramatic, gross manifestations of anti-Semitism. (The general philo-Semitic attitudes of Vatican II have had little real consequences in Eastern Europe.)

Neither general Jewish welfare nor Jewish religious life and institutions, then, would be significantly modified by changes in regime-Church relations in various Eastern European countries. The Soviet Union, surely, will be free to determine religious policy without regard to such external influences. The pressure exerted on Judaism in the USSR has been much greater than that in other socialist countries, and there is no reason to suppose that that will change much. (The influence of world Jewry on the situation of Jews is discussed below.)

International Communism

It remains a moot point as to how much influence the "world Communist movement," or more accurately the nonruling Communist parties which associate themselves with Moscow, exert on Soviet policy. As on most other questions, the Soviet leadership is probably not of one mind on the proper role of these nonruling parties, and their political significance probably changes with their own domestic fortunes and with politics within the Soviet leadership. (Not surprisingly, leaders like Mikhail Suslov who deal directly with the world movement tend to pay more attention to that constituency.) Clearly, where the Soviet leadership judges that vital issues are at stake, as in regard to reformist Czechoslovakia, it disregards the advice of nonruling parties and accepts even mass defections from their ranks. The influence of such parties would doubtless grow if the Chinese continue to make inroads on Soviet domination of the movement or if the USSR found other reasons to increase its interest in the world movement and its constituent parts. The influence of the Italian Communist party would grow if, as is not unlikely, it became at least a partner in a ruling coalition.

Although there is little hard evidence for their view, many observers believe that Western Communist parties succeeded in moderating Soviet policy toward Russian Jews. Even if so, and even if Soviet interest in these parties grew in the next decade, there is little reason to assume that the parties will earnestly concern themselves with the welfare of Jews in socialist countries: they are unlikely to argue, say, for the right of Jews to emigrate or for Jewish cultural rights or other measures advocated by "bourgeois" Jewish circles in opposition to official policy. The Canadian, British, and American parties, in particular, will have a declining proportion of Jews in their membership and will be less fearful of alienating their own members or the local Jewish communities. In general, if leftist circles in the West continue to display hostility toward Israel, and a more subtle, but perhaps more basic distaste for domestic Jews as the incarnation of all that is repugnant in a degenerate bourgeois society, there is little hope that they will act in behalf of Jews in socialist countries: having gone from underdog to "establishment" in some countries, Jews everywhere, apparently, can no longer expect empathy from some who claim to speak in the name of justice for the downtrodden.

In sum, external forces impinging on the general political atmosphere in socialist countries and on policies and attitudes toward Israel and toward local Jewish populations do not seem favorable to the Jews of Eastern Europe. The most important determinant of the Jewish future in particular socialist countries, of course, will be the internal political forces and trends.

Jews in the USSR

The collective leadership which succeeded Khrushchev has surprised many foreign observers by its longevity and seeming ability to avoid serious fractionization. This success has been achieved at a price: a conservatism in domestic policy that has left major problems unsolved. Fundamental decisions on the future of the system have been postponed or seriously hedged. Economic reforms, once heralded as the long-range solution to the USSR's post-modernization problems, have been withdrawn or watered down to such an extent that many features (and consequences) of the command economy survive. The Soviet economy continues to muddle through from year to year, lurching from campaign to campaign to campaign, though not nearly as frequently or as hard as in Khrushchev's reign.

A new Soviet constitution, promised since 1963, has not been promulgated, indicating that there has been no agreement on reforms and changes in basic political institutions and goals. Questions of succession, civil liberties, and cultural policy have not been settled. No consistent policy has been applied to the intelligentsia, and nationality policy continues to be a contradictory mixture of encouragement and suppression of nationality cultures. No agreement with the Chinese has been reached, and other issues in the world Communist movement also await solution.

The stagnation of Soviet policy is substantially a consequence of the structure of the leadership: the need to achieve consensus among several individuals or interests who can bring impressive countervailing power to bear on each other means that often what emerges as policy is the lowest common denominator of agreement. When no hedged or partial solution is possible, as on the invasion of Czechoslovakia, the divisions within the leadership, based not only on personal preferences but on bureaucratic interests and political philosophies, emerge more clearly. We can then observe contradictory turns in policy and, when the final decision is taken, less than enthusiastic support for it by some members of the ruling coalition.

The structure of the leadership is only one of the sources of the regime's conservatism. Perhaps the system itself inspires conservative policies. The enshrinement of Marxist-Leninist doctrine, once a powerful formula for change, serves as a brake on innovative thought and action. The myth of the proletariat and the myth of the withering away of the state tempt Communist theoreticians to deny problems of social differentiation and the need to revise political institutions. The consequences of development are not easily faced because they do not always accord with the vision of a classless society of virtuous proletarians, a society whose political institutions will begin to fade away as the need declines for repressive instruments to deal with social conflict, itself only the result of class conflict.

True, Soviet ideologists have not gone as far as the Chinese in denying the end of the revolutionary period and refusing to reconcile themselves to consequences of the institutionalization of a revolutionary movement, but neither have they come as far as the Czechoslovaks, Yugoslavs, and others in Eastern Europe in acknowledging the need to face up to changing circumstances. They have resisted political and ideological innovations originating in other socialist countries,[5] and have been even more resistant, of course, to nonsocialist political ideas.

The role of the USSR as the leader of a regional grouping of states as well as of an ideological movement diminishes its ability to experiment and innovate, for it must always calculate the effect of innovations, and even of noninstitutionalized changes in policy and personnel, on its various constituents. For example, Soviet politicians may reason that while their own population is "politically mature" enough to adjust gracefully to a political innovation, the populations of certain East European countries would seize upon such innovations and turn them into weapons against an unpopular system.

These impressive barriers to innovation and experimentation in the Soviet system can doubtless be surmounted. The absence of change-making institutions, however, means that change depends to a very great degree on subjective factors. In the absence of a competitive party system or even legitimate public discussion of alternatives, the personal desires of the politically powerful become very important. Assuming that the present leadership will not bring about systemic change, it can come about in the next decade by strong one-man rule, or less likely, by a new collective leadership

[5] Zvi Gitelman, "The Diffusion of Political Innovation from Eastern Europe to the USSR," Sage Professional Papers in Comparative Politics, Vol. 3, 1972.

with such a high degree of consensus that it could undertake major policy departures without fear of alienating any group powerful enough to overthrow it. Personal or collective courage, ideological authoritativeness, and a great deal of political power would be required of the individual or group that could achieve a fundamental revision of the Soviet system, or even in the general direction of policy.

The present leadership has been tested in a number of difficult situations and has weathered all the storms, making only minor adjustments. Despite the slow emergence of Brezhnev as the *primus inter pares*, it is tempting to forecast the continuance of the present type of leadership as long as no major catastrophe, internally or externally generated, befalls the USSR. Minor adjustments in policy and personnel will obviously be made from time to time, but the basic strategy of muddling through will be maintained. Both the routine problems and the by now routinized successes of the system will be dealt with in routine ways. Changes will not be made unless extremely heavy pressure, with prohibitive costs for ignoring it, forces the leadership to move away from the status quo. There will be a renewal of the agreement not to rock the boat, because if the boat overturns all its passengers might end up overboard.

As regards the Jews, government by consensus purchased at the price of conservatism means that separate Jewish identity is maintained and even buttressed by formal regulations, such as the official identification system, and by informal means, such as propaganda on foreign and domestic matters. These inevitably heighten Jewish consciousness, and make non-Jews aware that Jews exist in the USSR and elsewhere and that they present certain "problems." On the other hand, Russia's two and a half million Jews are denied the means by which Jewish identity could be positively preserved and given some content—schools, social and cultural organizations, mass media, theaters, etc.

Continuation of the present political arrangements in the Soviet Union is likely to mean continuation of the present policy toward the Jews. For while the Jewish question may be intrinsically trivial from the leadership's point of view, the international attention it has received and the close scrutiny with which "Jewish policy" is observed within the USSR make it a highly visible and somewhat sensitive issue. Changes in Jewish policy, moreover, would undoubtedly have immediate and marked effects on Soviet intellectuals who make the "Jewish question" a proxy issue in the liberal-conservative struggle, and on the other non-Russian nationalities. Increased exposure of Jewish national consciousness, then, would probably be countered by repression, by allowing Jewish malcontents to emigrate, or by allowing some Jewish expression and channeling it into the least objectionable and most manipulative forms.

Demographic Trends

As one of the more responsible students of demographic trends among Soviet Jews has pointed out, "the rate of increase for Jews is almost certainly below that of the population as a whole." [6] Preliminary figures from the 1970 census show the number of those declaring themselves Jews to be 2.15 million, a decline from 2.27 million in 1959. (Of course, some Jews might have preferred not to identify themselves as such to an official questioner.) In the USSR urban European groups generally have lower birth rates than rural Asian ones, and the Jews are among the most urbanized and modernized. As the birth rate among Asian Soviet citizens continues to outstrip that among Europeans, the proportion of Jews in the total population may be expected to decline.

The dramatic "overrepresentation" of Jews in higher education, the sciences, and the intelligentsia will also be reduced, and not necessarily as a result of conscious governmental discrimination. As education and economic development open new opportunities for the less-developed nationalities, they begin to enter where for long Jews, Armenians, and some other nationalities were represented far above their proportion in the total population. This "spontaneous" trend is helped along by the official policy of promoting the less modernized nationalities into "scientific work." Anti-Semitic officials at all levels also take advantage of that trend to discriminate against qualified Jews. At the same time the absolute number of Jewish students increased in the mid-1960s: "We may well suppose that the recent rise in the number of Jewish students in higher education will be reflected within a few years by a significant rise in the number of Jewish graduate specialists." [7]

---

[6] J. A. Newth, "Jews in the Soviet Intelligentsia—Some Recent Developments," *Bulletin on Soviet Jewish Affairs*, No. 2 (July 1968), p. VII/3. Institute of Jewish Affairs, Ltd., London.

[7] *Ibid.*, p. VII/2.

Even within those elites in which Jews are either proportionately represented or overrepresented, however, they are likely to be underrepresented in high positions, as on editorial boards, in directorships of institutes, and in party and governmental leadership posts. They are almost wholly absent from sensitive posts such as the diplomatic corps and the party Politburo and Central Committee.[8] These exclusions are due to the fact that the Jew is regarded as somewhat of an alien; he is suspected of having dual political loyalties and foreign psychological identifications. The recent dramatic manifestation on the part of some Soviet Jews of an attachment to the State of Israel has reinforced and confirmed that suspicion.[9] The process of "nativization" of elites, to which Khrushchev made explicit reference in connection with the decline of the number of Jews in elite positions, can be expected to continue. Only in the arts and in some sectors of the sciences where political loyalties are not so crucial can Jews expect admission to the very highest levels.

While we have statistics about the increasing rates of intermarriage in the late 1920s and early 1930s, reliable and complete data for the postwar era are scarce. In the RSFSR as early as 1926, 21 percent of the marriages involving Jews were mixed, and that proportion rose considerably in the 1930s.[10] At the present time in the RSFSR "at least one Jewish husband in seven has a non-Jewish wife. . . . In the other republics considered (Belorussia, Moldavia, Ukraine) the extent of mixed marriages is very considerably less."[11] In the Ukraine 10.3 percent of the Jewish urban population and 9.8 percent of the rural Jewish population are in "mixed families" (families of several generations in which at least one member is married to a non-Jew); the number of mixed marriages is therefore lower than the number of "mixed families."[12] Fragmentary data

---

[8] See Yaroslav Bilinsky, "The Rulers and the Ruled," *Problems of Communism*, XVI, 5 (September–October 1967); U.S. Superintendent of Documents and Alec Nove and J. A. Newth, "The Jewish Population: Demographic Trends and Occupational Patterns," in Lionel Kochan, ed., *The Jews in Soviet Russia Since 1917* (London, 1970).

[9] On this point see Zvi Gitelman, "The Jews," *Problems of Communism*, XVI, 5 (September–October 1967), p. 98.

[10] See I. I. Veitsblit, *Di dinamik fun der yidisher bafelkerung in Ukraine* (Kharkov, 1930).

[11] Nove and Newth, *op. cit.*, p. 143.

[12] V. I. Naulko, *Etnicheskii sostav naseleniia SSR: Ukrainskoi SSR* (Kiev, 1956), p. 109.

from other areas is insufficient for broad generalizations, especially since rates of Jewish intermarriage seem to vary widely in the different regions of the USSR.[13]

In the absence of survey research, or even an unfettered gathering of impressions, it is very difficult to ascertain the attitudes of Soviet Jews, their hopes, aspirations, and beliefs. Information is so fragmentary and impressionistic that it is possible to deal only in tentative generalizations. On the other hand, it is misleading to generalize broadly about "Soviet Jewry." The Soviet Jewish population is heterogeneous, displaying a wide variety of attitudes, life styles, and aspirations. There are assimilationists and Zionists, religious believers and militant atheists, Communists and anti-Communists among them. The Jewish communities in different regions differ markedly from one another. By and large, for example, Georgian Jews are less assimilated, more religious, more nationalistic, and more militant than Jews in the Ukraine. The Jews in the Western territories acquired by the USSR in 1939–40 tend to be more closely attached to tradition and to Yiddish-Hebrew culture than those who have been Soviet citizens for over fifty years. The Jews of Belorussia, Moldavia, and the Ukraine are probably less assimilated than the Jews of the RSFSR.

Contrary to popular belief, only a minority of Soviet Jews are assimilated, if assimilation is understood as the adoption of a new culture to such an extent that one no longer bears characteristics identifying him with his former culture. Official—and in many strata of society, unofficial, but no less effective—identification of the Jew prevents him from assimilating even if he wished to. On the other hand, almost every Soviet Jew is "acculturated" into a non-Jewish culture, usually the Russian. (By acculturation we mean adopting the culture of another social group.) To be acculturated without being assimilated, and with only limited possibilities of assimilating, means that most Jews are in a perpetual identity crisis. Their options are few, and the tensions ensuing from simply being a Jew are relatively great. The possibilities of resolving such tensions are limited, though they are greater now than they have been at any time since the mid-1930s.

---

[13] See Mordechai Altshuler, "Netunim Akhadim al Nesuei Taarovet Bekerev Yehudai Brit Hamoetzot," *Behinot*, No. 1, 1970. Israeli Executive of The World Jewish Congress, Tel Aviv, Israel.

The majority of Soviet Jews may well be content to be carried along letting events and developments beyond their control determine their fate as Jews. Many, however, will see choices confronting them in the 1970s: to attempt to assimilate, to struggle for equal rights, to create a viable Soviet Jewish community, to emigrate to Israel, or to oppose the system as a whole (whether by "internal emigration," passivity, or active opposition). The question is under what circumstances will one option or another be favored by large numbers. Given the great variety in local conditions, attitudes, age groups, and social position, generalizations are impossible, but it is possible to specify conditions under which certain options might be more likely to be exercised. The most important condition, of course, will be the general political climate. If past history is any guide, a very repressive atmosphere will be conducive to attempts to "hide" by assimilating or by simply maintaining a low profile. Mild repression might also encourage some assimilation but will also force an awareness of identity and might induce some militancy and a struggle for emigration. Political liberalization might encourage the exercise of all the options. Since continuation of the present climate with minor modifications is most likely, will the Jewish population remain heterogeneous, with roughly the same distribution of attitudes as presently exist?

In recent years we have witnessed the emergence of two relatively new trends: increasing militancy and closer identification with the State of Israel. There is little doubt, for instance, that perhaps the majority of youth conscious of their Jewishness became more Zionistic after the 1967 Arab-Israeli war. Whereas a good number of them had been concerned with the fight against anti-Semitism and with the revival of Jewish culture in their homeland, many became more concerned with Hebrew culture and with the State of Israel (and emigration to it). The struggle to be an aware, identified Jew, fought against strong political, social, and even parental pressures, can continue only if more emigration is permitted and if the environment remains hostile enough to breed discontent but not so hostile as to make the cost of dissent prohibitive: militancy which goes totally unrewarded will soon be transformed into apathy; absolute frustration will breed resignation and passivity.

We come, then, to dissident movements in the USSR and Jewish protest and dissent. It must be realized that while political and cultural dissent in the USSR has deeply impressed Western information media, the "Democratic Movement" (Andrei Amalrik's term) thus far has been concentrated in the Russian intelligentsia and has had limited impact on Soviet society and politics. Because of official control of Soviet media, the vast majority of the Soviet population either has no knowledge of the dissenters and their ideas or is hostile to them.

Jews seem to be very much involved in the movement: of 486 names signed to petitions and letters in connection with the Ginzburg-Galanskov trial and other literary and political issues, at least 125, or 26 percent, of the signatories have distinctly Jewish names.[14] Yet only one of these people, the scholar Mikhail Zand, can be identified as active in the Jewish civil rights or Zionist movements. Similarly, with the exception of the famous speech by the Ukrainian intellectual Ivan Dzyuba at Babyi Yar in 1966, one finds little reference to Jewish problems in the literature of Ukrainian or Baltic dissidents, just as dissenting Jews rarely make reference to the problems of other nationalities.

There are historical and political reasons for this. It is clear that some militant Jews have given up on Soviet society, that they see no real prospect for its reform and therefore do not concern themselves with attempts to improve or transform the Soviet system; their solution is to leave it altogether. There is evidence of cooperation between Soviet political dissidents and Zionist Jews, especially in Moscow, but thus far this cooperation seems largely tactical and may not be permanent. In any case, it cannot be denied that for the foreseeable future Jews can only harm their immediate interests by supporting political dissent, since their fate rests firmly in the hands of the establishment.

Another important, though less obvious, factor conditioning the future of Soviet Jewry is the interest of the non-Soviet Jewish world in the Soviet situation. The recent tactic of petitions and appeals, used by some Soviet Jews who want to protest conditions in the USSR or leave it altogether, is made possible only by the attention that Jews and non-Jews in other countries have focused on the Soviet Jewish community. If that attention should wane, not only will the options of the Soviet Jews be more limited but a growing feel-

---

[14] For the petitions on which this analysis is based, see Abraham Brumberg, ed., *In Quest of Justice* (New York, Praeger, 1970), pp. 101–178 *passim*.

ing of isolation will cause them to risk less and be less assertive.

Whatever else happens, Jewish religious institutions and observances will probably decline even further in the coming decade. Indeed, since the vast majority of synagogue worshippers are in their sixties, seventies, and eighties, there will probably be a precipitous decline in synagogue attendance with a concomitant closing of houses of worship. Even nationally-conscious young Jews, with rare exceptions, are confirmed atheists and cannot be counted on to maintain religious observances. (Some survey data indicate that the attrition of religious belief and practice is greater among Jews than among other faith communities in the USSR.[15])

Nevertheless, as the only functioning Jewish organization in Soviet society, the synagogue will continue to serve as the "Jewish address," the locale for socializing with other Jews and for expressing one's Jewish identity positively, as in the Simkhat Torah celebrations which have become a tradition for Jewish youth. The synagogue is also the last visible symbol of Jewish civilization and culture, and, unlike some of their elders, few atheistic young Jews regard the synagogue with hostility. Thus, while it would be a gross exaggeration to say that the synagogue for Jews in the Soviet Union is analogous to the Church for the people of Poland, it may be regarded as performing a similar function even though it is incomparably weaker than the Polish Church and cannot perform its national-cultural function actively.

The prospects are equally dim for a revival of Yiddish culture or for any Hebrew cultural development. Though *Sovetish haimland* has been carrying a "Teach Yourself Yiddish" column for Russian-speakers, this is no meaningful substitute for formal Yiddish education. There is little prospect that Yiddish schools will be introduced, and it seems that that issue has declined in the list of priorities of Soviet Jews.

In sum, it is not possible to say whether Jewish national consciousness, having grown in recent years, will continue to increase, will level off, or will decline. Much depends on the response of Soviet society, and also of elements beyond the borders of the USSR, to the attempts by Soviet Jews to resolve their identity crisis. Whether or not Soviet immigrants integrate successfully into Israeli society will have a great impact on the aspirations and plans of Jews

---

[15] See Gitelman, "The Jews," *op. cit.*, p. 93.

in the USSR. There are no foreseeable dislocations—population shifts or massive social change—which would profoundly influence the outlook of Soviet Jews. The general political climate and their perception of the world and of their place in it remain the two most important determinants of the immediate future of Soviet Jewry. Clearly, a change in Soviet Middle Eastern policy, which would be reflected in domestic propaganda, would have some impact on the attitudes of Soviet Jews, perhaps stimulating a more assertive expression of sympathy with Israel.

It would seem, then, that the USSR will retain the political loyalty of the majority of Soviet Jews, and that only a minority will be driven into generalized opposition to the system. Most Soviet Jews, like other Soviet citizens, have been effectively socialized into the system.

Poland

By the mid-1960s it became apparent that there would have to be an important change of regime in Poland. The question was not whether Gomulka would be replaced, but who would replace him. The liberal and "revisionist" elements that had played a decisive role in the Polish October (1956) anti-Stalinist and anti-Soviet revolt continued in disarray, without leadership and without a cohesive program. The much publicized "Partisan" faction, an authoritarian, nationalistic grouping, was apparently not regarded with favor in the USSR, and its leader, General Mieczyslaw Moczar, was successfully fought off by Gomulka and appears to have been checked by the present party leader, Edward Gierek, as well. A team of economic experts and "technocrats" now stands at the head of a broadly based coalition, not unlike the collective leadership in Moscow. Such a leadership is likely to emphasize the most rational use of national resources, including personnel, and would not be distracted into irrational campaigns against Jews, especially as it would now serve little political purpose.

The fact is that after the purges of Jews from government positions in 1968 and the subsequent Jewish emigration, Polish Jewry has lost even its symbolic political significance. Anti-Semitism was used as a weapon by Moczar and the Partisans to discredit the Gomulka regime as one not truly representative of the Polish nation, as Gomulka had himself inaugurated and exploited anti-Semitism earlier. Correctly judging that a wide gulf separated state and society, and that this made it impossible for the regime to mobilize the population for political and economic efforts, Moczar proposed to achieve political integration by Polonizing the regime so that the 98.8 percent of the population which is ethnically Polish could identify with it and, eventually, with the values and aspirations of the system. This resulted in the wholesale purge of Jews from official posts and a mass emigration in 1968–69 which reduced the Jewish population from about 16,000 to half that number. But political integration has not been achieved, and the *pays légal* and the *pays réel* (which some say is represented by the Church) will have to be made more congruent. Whatever formula Gomulka's successors adopt in pursuit of political integration, the "Jewish question" will have little part in it.

There are quite a few Communists among the 8,000 Jews left in Poland, but they are mainly older people who have already been retired or are being phased out of party life. Among younger cadres there are perhaps some of Jewish origin, but most of them have "passed" as Poles for many years. Because of the small size of the Jewish population and its peculiar age structure and political makeup, there is no future for organized or communal Jewish life in Poland. The Yiddish theater, the Jewish Historical Institute, and the Jewish Social-Cultural Society may be propped up for some time to come, and indeed the regime has been at pains to give the impression of an organized Jewish life in Poland, but these are vestigial organs, small collectivities of lonely individuals rather than manifestations of a living and active community. The "Jewish question" in Poland, no matter what it might be in the minds of some anti-Semitic fanatics, has been reduced to a question of individuals. And the only solution to that question for Jews who are interested in preserving their Jewishness is emigration: whatever the future holds for Poland, it holds nothing for its few remaining Jews as Jews. By the same token, once the "Jewish question" has passed from the scene it will be easier for those who cannot or will not leave to disappear into Polish society.

Czechoslovakia

As in the Soviet Union, Jews and Jewry have played a symbolic role in recent Czechoslovak politics. A Czechoslovak's attitude on the "Jewish question" is usually a clue to his general political stance: liberal reformers and more radical proponents of change make equality for Jews their own cause, while reactionaries and some conservatives identify Jews with excessive liberalism. In 1968 the reformers raised the issues of anti-Semitism and the official attitude toward Israel and condemned both. Hostility toward Israel was seen as a symbol of Czechoslovak degradation: it showed how subservient Czechoslovakia was to the Soviet Union and how the leadership was prepared to sacrifice morality on the altar of expediency. With the arrestation of the "Prague spring" by a massive Soviet invasion, the conservatives made the predictable counterattack, pointing to the Jewish origins of some prominent reformers (Šik, Goldstucker, Kriegel), using anti-Semitism in attempts to mobilize antiliberal sentiment, and returning to the previous hostile line on Israel.

Among the Communist nations the need for political integration, for establishing the authority of the regime and the legitimacy of the system, is nowhere as obvious as it is in Czechoslovakia. The present regime rules largely by power—foreign power—and not by authority. Even if the present leadership succeeds in staving off still more reactionary elements, the best the population can hope for is a situation not unlike that prevailing in Poland, where the promise of a reconciliation between state and society was also disappointed. At present, widespread demoralization, reflected in abysmally low labor productivity, is much more acute than in Poland, and though the economic situation may improve somewhat there is little prospect that public morale will rise greatly in the near future. General demoralization and instability are certainly not propitious for Jewish security, though the absence of a native tradition of anti-Semitism, at least in the Czech lands, probably insures against a repetition of the events in Poland. The Soviets and their Czechoslovak supporters have tried to introduce anti-Semitism—in the guise of anti-Zionism—but there has been no concerted campaign against Czechoslovak Jews.

The events of 1968–69 caused some Jews to leave the country, and it has been estimated that the Jewish population is now about 10,000. Many of the Jews in Bohemia and Moravia are both acculturated and assimilated—Czechoslovakia had one of the highest rates of Jewish intermarriage in Europe even before World War II—while Jewish identity and organized Jewish life are stronger in

Slovakia. With the departure of Rabbi Elias Katz of Bratislava and the death of Dr. Richard Feder of Brno, there is not a single rabbi in the entire country, although it is reported that a young man is being trained in England to assume rabbinical duties in Prague.

A tiny handful of religious Jews in the Czech lands and a larger number in Slovakia attempt to keep up religious life and they are not harassed by the government. Jewish cultural and historical treasures, particularly in Prague, are maintained as part of the national heritage, especially since they earn much needed foreign currency as tourist attractions. (The fact that all but two of the guides in the Prague Jewish museum are not Jewish is revealing.) Jews remain prominent in the arts and in intellectual life in general, and some writers even write about Jewish themes.

But Czechoslovak Jewry, insofar as it is interested in things Jewish, focuses its attention on the Jewish past in Czechoslovakia, and for good reason. Czechoslovak Jewry does not have the internal resources to permit a flourishing Jewish cultural and religious life. Intermarriage and assimilation continue high, and while even highly acculturated Czechoslovak Jews seem to be less concerned with denying their ethnic origins than acculturated Polish Jews—reflecting the difference between Polish anti-Semitism and Czech toleration—an identity with purely historical associations and without dynamic and behavioral content cannot be counted as a basis for organized Jewish life. The prospects for Czechoslovak Jewry are not bright, though religious and cultural activities will probably last longer in Slovakia than in the Czech lands. The possibility of emigration should not be excluded, since for economic as well as political reasons the Czechoslovak government may find it in its interest to permit some Jewish emigration, as the Rumanians and Poles have done.

Rumania

In Rumania the governing authorities have been successfully integrating state with society and demonstrating virtuosity and independence in domestic and foreign affairs. The fundamental premise of Rumanian foreign policy is that ideological considerations should not interfere with the pursuit of the national interest, defined as what benefits Rumania most economically and politically. The regime also seeks to enhance Rumania's international role. For these related reasons, Rumania maintains relations with as many countries as possible, including both China and the Soviet Union, and both Israel and the Arab states. In the Sino-Soviet dispute Rumania has sought to play the role of mediator, thereby elevating its status in the Communist world. It has led the way in attracting Western investment and trade, simultaneously decreasing its dependence on the USSR and deriving important technological and economic benefits, particularly from West European countries.

At the same time, the Rumanian regime has remained internally rather conservative. The excesses of the Stalinist period have been decisively rejected, especially following the 1968 purge of Alexander Draghici, former Minister of Interior, and his secret police, but strict controls are maintained over political, economic, and cultural life. A combination of nationalism and authoritarianism is often associated with difficulties for Jews, especially in a country with a strong tradition of anti-Semitism; nevertheless, despite the purge of such leaders as Ana Pauker who was Jewish by birth—which was due to the "nativization of elites" and the replacement of the "Muscovite" faction by "native" or "underground" Communists— the Rumanian leadership has refrained from making political use of anti-Semitism. Jewish religious and cultural life is allowed relatively wide scope, and such symbolic gestures as the election of the chief rabbi to the parliament affrm the legitimacy of organized Jewish life. Substantial emigration to Israel has been allowed at various times, and trade relations between Israel and Rumania are well developed.

These policies have not been flowing from humanitarian sentiments, but are manifestations of an overall strategy serving perceived national interest. Emigration to Israel brought considerable financial and economic benefits to the regime, and since the categories of emigrants were carefully specified, it was also a form of social engineering. The policy enhanced Rumania's public relations abroad, though the regime had to be careful not to alienate Arab states and others opposed to further Jewish emigration to Israel.

However, since 1967 emigration has been drastically curtailed, though it has picked up since Golda Meir's visit to Rumania in May, 1972. At the same time, the government seems not to have foreclosed the possibility of large-scale emigration: for example, Jewish students have been forbidden to do doctoral and other research in certain areas of nuclear physics on the grounds that they have relatives abroad and might eventually emigrate themselves, taking with them knowledge of fields which are under security regulations. Some might agree that this is a legitimate restraint, the price for the potential freedom to change one's political allegiance, but it suggests that the regime considers Jews, as a class, more likely than others to wish to end their allegiance to Rumania.

Future emigration from Rumania, then, will depend heavily on the leadership's assessments of its internal needs and of the possible gains which Jewish emigration might bring. A favorable economic situation, a larger supply of Rumanian professionals and skilled workers, an easing of tensions in the Middle East, the continuation of an independent foreign policy, are some factors which might lead to a resumption of emigration.

With a population of about 100,000, the Rumanian Jewish community is the largest and most active in Eastern Europe outside the USSR. The vitality and resources of the Rumanian Jewish community have been somewhat exaggerated in the West. There are only two rabbis in the entire country, both in Bucharest. Chief Rabbi Moses David Rosen's function is political as well as religious: he serves as a leader of the Jewish community and as its representative both to the regime and to the outside world. External assistance, notably by the Joint Distribution Committee, helps maintain much-needed institutions. The kosher cafeteria in Bucharest, for example, serves about four hundred people a day, including a substantial number unable to pay even the minimal fees and who are served without charge. Jewish schools exist, but are plagued with a shortage of qualified teachers. Other religious institutions, such as kosher butcher shops and ritual baths, are in serious decline, and there is no reason to expect a reversal.

In Rumania a larger proportion of Jewish youth than in other socialist countries seem to be seriously committed to maintaining their Jewish identity and infusing it with religious and cultural content. Weekly lectures by Chief Rabbi Rosen and others for the benefit of university students in Bucharest, where the majority of Jews reside, are attended by over a hundred students. There are formal and powerful informal associations of Jewish students, a minority of whom conscientiously study Hebrew and do not hide their hope to emigrate to Israel. If emigration is permitted, the Jewishly-conscious young Jews might well choose that path, leaving only the more acculturated and assimilated Jewish youth in Rumania.

Despite the seemingly favorable environment for organized Jewish life, precisely those who are interested in that kind of life are uninterested in perpetuating it in Rumania in the long run. This may be largely due to the widely expressed perception, even among university students, that whatever government policy may be, the Rumanian population has not abandoned its anti-Jewish prejudices. Unlike most Soviet Jews, a good proportion of young Rumanian Jews seem critical of the political system as a whole, so there is little to arouse their allegiance to their native country.

The prognosis for Rumanian Jewry, then, is roughly similar to, though less complicated than, that for Soviet Jewry: Jewishly-conscious elements seem to prefer emigration to attempts to maintain and expand domestic Jewish life, while the more acculturated Jews are not motivated to seek emigration on ethnic grounds. In both the USSR and Rumania, however, many acculturated Jews are driven to seek emigration by general political-social alienation or by purely materialistic considerations. These Jews, if given the chance, are less likely to go to Israel and would prefer the United States, France, Scandinavia, England, Latin America, or even West Germany.

Hungary

Hungary has enjoyed the most successful economic reform and the most impressive economic growth (aside from East Germany's) in Eastern Europe. That and a gradualist policy demanding little active political support from the population have helped the state achieve a limited détente and even rapprochement with the previously alienated and embittered population and it has moved far toward healing the wounds of 1956. There is every reason to believe that since Soviet reaction to Hungarian policies has been generally favorable, Kadar will continue to make incremental progress in politics as well as in economics.

One of the costs Hungary bears for Soviet toleration of its domestic experimentation is subservience to the USSR in foreign policy. Taking extreme care not to offend the Soviets, as the Czechoslovaks had done, is one of the cardinal principles of the Hungarian regime. Therefore, Hungary can be expected to follow the Soviet lead on such matters as policy toward Israel and the emigration of Hungarian Jews. It is unlikely, however, that the Hungarians will feel impelled to follow the Soviet Union as regards treatment of its own Jewish population and institutions. Even in foreign policy matters Hungary is not obligated to imitate every detail of Soviet policy: for example, some commercial relations with Israel have continued even since the June 1967 war. No spectacular departure from the Soviet pattern can be expected, but in small ways the Hungarians can be more flexible than the Soviet Union, which has the responsibility of being the chief sponsor of the Arab states, the primary opponent of Western policy, and cue giver to other socialist states.

While it is difficult to obtain reliable demographic information about Hungary's 75,000 Jews, it is widely believed in Budapest that the proportion of Jews above the age of fifty is very high. Religious life is still very much in evidence, with a small but vigorous Orthodox community located mainly in Budapest, and a larger group of "Neolog" Jews whose center is the famous Dohanyi Street synagogue (Tabak Temple). Several hundred attend Sabbath services and several thousand attend High Holy Day services in the Dohanyi synagogue, the largest synagogue in the world. A rabbinical seminary and Jewish high school still exist, though the former is reported to have but one student. An official, well-organized community looks after Jewish affairs, and, as in Rumania, there is a widely read Jewish weekly. Even among youth there has been developing a lively interest in things Jewish.

Nevertheless, the fact that the great majority of the community's constituents are elderly dims the prospects for organized Jewish life. As in past generations, many Hungarian Jews, particularly among the intelligentsia, where they are still well represented, are thoroughly assimilated into Hungarian culture and society. There is little doubt that as time goes on whatever Jewish consciousness they possess will diminish further, especially since popular anti-Semitism, which flared up in 1956–57, seems to be declining.

Bulgaria and Yugoslavia

While the Jewish communities of these two Balkan countries are somewhat similar, the governing political systems are very different. Bulgaria is one of the more orthodox socialist states and is very closely allied to the Soviet Union on international questions; for example, it probably has more highly developed relations with the Arab world than any socialist country except the USSR. Yugoslavia too has good relations with the Arab states, though it is not as militantly opposed to Israeli policy as is Bulgaria, and despite the rupture in diplomatic relations it continues its commercial relations with Israel. Yugoslavia's friendship with the Arab world derives from independent calculations, not from alliance with the USSR.

Both countries have small Jewish communities, each numbering less than 10,000. Both are organized communities with significant annual publications (*Jevrejski Almanah* in Yugoslavia and *Godishnik* in Bulgaria), with some communal institutions, such as old-age homes and cultural centers, and with quite good relations with the government and the party. In neither country is there a serious problem of anti-Semitism.

Jewish religious life is practically nonexistent in the Yugoslav republics of Slovenia and Croatia (the capital of Slovenia has only seventy-seven Jews). The 1,800 Jews of Zagreb are mainly old people, some of them immigrants from other parts of Central and Eastern Europe, and the outstanding Jewish institution in the city is, symbolically, an old-age home. Belgrade's 1,500 Jews do maintain a synagogue, but only in the tourist season is attendance sufficient for conducting a service. The Jewish community of Bosnia, largely Sephardic, is a bit more vigorous. In the Voivodina areas (especially in the city of Novi Sad) there remain pockets of Orthodoxy, largely of Hungarian origin. There is quite a bit of social and cultural activity in Belgrade, the headquarters of the Yugoslav Jewish community. As members of the World Jewish Congress, Yugoslav Jews maintain contact with other communities. Yugoslav Jews seem to have warm feelings for Israel. Relative freedom to travel enables Yugoslav Jews to visit Israel, and there is a small annual flow of Yugoslav Jewish youth working for a summer on Israeli kibbutzim. As a scattered and quite variegated community, Yugoslav Jewry does not seem to have the numbers or the will to sustain itself as a vigorous entity indefinitely, though it is not unreasonable to assume its continued existence through this decade.

Bulgarian Jewry, diminished by large-scale emigration to Israel, is politically well integrated. Even Jewishly-conscious Jews seem to follow the party line on Israel, and in contrast to their Yugoslav counterparts, the official leadership of the Bulgarian Jewish community openly supports the government's anti-Israel policy. Jews are to be found in the professions and academic fields, and there is at least one Jew on the party's Central Committee. The official community publishes a Jewish newspaper (in Bulgarian) and maintains an impressive building in downtown Sofia. Religious life is weakening, a few old Sephardim carrying on the tradition, but some Jewish scholarship continues. Again, the majority of those active in Jewish life are elderly. The general impression is that intermarriage is very widespread among the postwar generation. Here too, the Bulgarian Jewish population seems to consist of the more highly acculturated elements who did not exercise the option to emigrate to Israel, together with small numbers of Jewishly-conscious, elderly people. There is no reason to expect a nationalist or religious upsurge in Bulgarian Jewry.

Conclusion

In view of undeniable demographic facts, one is forced to conclude that the Jewish communities of Poland, Czechoslovakia, and Bulgaria are in the last stages of their existence as organized entities, with Yugoslavia's Jews displaying somewhat more vigor. The Rumanian and Hungarian communities are considerably larger and certainly more active, but in the long run they too will decline to the point where it will no longer be possible to speak of a future for Jewish life in these countries. In America's future-oriented and youth-centered value system it is sometimes assumed that only that which has possibilities of future development is worthy of interest and support. But surely dying men are entitled to at least as much care as healthy ones.

East European Jewish communities require both support for Jewish life and aid in emigration. At first glance these may appear to be self-contradictory: by abetting emigration one weakens the Jewish community quantitatively and qualitatively; but realism requires that Jews in other parts of the world regard East European Jewry from two perspectives at the same time. From the perspective of the continuity of the Jewish people and of Jewish civilization it is clear that emigration remains, sadly, the greatest contribution that East European Jewry can make. On the other hand, regarding Jews in Eastern Europe not only as components of a greater whole but as individual human beings to whom the option of emigration is not always available or desirable, the chance to live a Jewish life should be afforded to them even though they may be the last to live such a life.

Although there are demographic reasons for uncertainty about Soviet Jewry as well, the primary problem there is political. Soviet Jews are deprived of the ability to lead a legitimate communal life. While the experience of the 1920s and 1930s casts some doubt on the possibility of creating a radically different, Communist Jewish existence, it is legitimate, realistic, and necessary to press for the removal of political and social obstacles to the revival of Jewish institutions. At the same time, recognizing that certain authentic forms of Jewish existence, including its most fundamental and defining characteristic—religion—cannot be legitimized in any foreseeable Soviet society, there must be a strong and continuing effort to extend the option of emigration to Soviet Jews, especially in light of the recent dramatic evidence that significant numbers would exercise that option. To borrow a phrase, there must be a "struggle on two fronts." Those Soviet Jews, probably a majority, desirous of staying in their homeland should not be denied the rights and protections spelled out in the Soviet constitution and other authoritative pronouncements on nationality policy. Jews who no longer consider the USSR their legitimate motherland should be allowed to exercise the right of emigration, recognized in international charters to which the USSR is a signatory.

Not only the small but important gains made by Soviet Jews in the last decade, but also attitudinal and psychological changes among them are in substantial measure due to the concern and activities of Jews abroad. It is the responsibility of the Soviet government and party to rectify the wrongs that have been done to Soviet Jews. But it is equally the responsibility of non-Soviet Jews constantly to remind the Soviet government of its obligations and at the same time reaffirm to Soviet Jews their membership in the Jewish people. For the time, Soviet Jews are not fully free to act for themselves or even to express themselves as Jews; other Jews will have to act for them until that time when they are restored to active membership in the nation of Israel.

The next decade may well be decisive: despite their greater numbers, Soviet Jews may suffer the same fate as their brethren in other parts of Eastern Europe; but they may also emerge to a new creativity and dynamism, in familiar ways or in new ones, in their present homeland or in others. The outcome will not be determined by impersonal historical forces alone. It will be shaped by the decisions and activities of men—inside and outside the Soviet Union.

Chapter 7

Latin America

Chaim Avni

A Continent in Turmoil

Twenty-four independent states and several colonial territories lie south of the Rio Grande and Florida.[1] In eighteen of the states the official language is Spanish; in one, equal in size to six or seven large states, Portuguese is the principal tongue; French is the language of one state; and in four new small states English is spoken. In large areas the local populations are of Indian origin and speak various Indian dialects. Many have questioned, therefore, the appropriateness of the term "Latin America" to describe the whole region. On the other hand, the attempt by some historians and scholars to describe the area as "Indo-America" has particular ideological connotations and disregards large concentrations of blacks of African origin in certain parts of Brazil, the Caribbean islands, and the west coast of South America.

The problem of finding a suitable appellation for the area results, of course, from the ethnic and cultural diversity in its great expanses. Because of that mighty natural geographical barrier, the Andes Mountains, which hinder contact between the inhabitants of the Atlantic and Pacific coasts of South America, and the great climatic and ecological differences between the Amazon region in the northeast and the endless pampas of the south, the pre-Columbian cultures of the region developed in distinct and diverse ways. Spanish and Portuguese culture was imposed on these early civilizations

---

[1] See table, pp. 270–271.

when the Iberian representatives arrived on a mission of conquest, but the two continued to clash.

Nevertheless, the people of Latin America have a deep sense of kinship. Even when the policies of the various governments are effectively separatist, their ideological statements still reflect a belief in the need to create Latin American unity. While some of this is lip service, masking narrow, nationalistic tendencies, it nevertheless demonstrates that the vision of José de San Martín and Simón Bolívar, liberators of South America, who envisaged the establishment of a "United States" of Latin America, or at least of large blocs within it, has not disappeared without trace.

The sense of regional identity and the aspiration to unity appear frequently and in various forms. At the United Nations the Latin American countries endeavor to coordinate their policies and appear as a united bloc. Economic organizations in Central America (the Central American Common Market, which includes seven countries) and Latin America (the Latin American Free Trade Association, with eight members, including Mexico) have as their declared objective the creation of a kind of regional common market. But achievements have been limited. During the 1960s trade between Latin American states constituted only a small percentage of the region's total international trade figures. In 1958 the countries of the continent were exporting only 9.3 percent of their total exports to one another, and twelve years later, in 1969, after protracted efforts aimed at expanding mutual trade, the figure had reached only 11.9 percent of the total.[2]

Though no significant steps toward unification have been made, contemporary Latin America has a certain sense of shared destiny; a feeling of deprivation pervades the entire continent. This sense of common fate was clearly expressed at two very different conferences in recent years. The first was convened in 1966 in Havana and was attended by representatives of "revolutionary" governments and of left-wing underground liberation movements from the "third world." With the exception of the Cuban government, which played host, the Latin American delegates represented only left-wing underground movements, and many of them were wanted at

---

[2] Calculations according to the *United Nations Statistical Yearbook, 1970* (New York, 1971), p. 412, Table 146.

the time by the police of their countries. After several days of discussion, not lacking in tension and excitement, the conference drafted a number of resolutions which constituted a challenge from the developing to the developed and prosperous nations.

The second conference, held in November 1971 in Lima, Peru, was attended by ministers from ninety-six developing countries and aimed to create a common front to safeguard the future economic development of the third world, particularly in light of the fluctuations in trade and in currency rates which had occurred in the previous year. This gathering, too, tried in its own way to find methods of strengthening ties with the developed countries and, as at the Cuban gathering, the Latin American delegates expressed their awareness that underdevelopment was the common factor uniting their countries.

Despite the vast gulf dividing the Havana delegates from those who met in Lima, both groups representing Latin America shared the feeling that economic and social backwardness constitutes the central problem of their continent. And this fact is one of vital importance to the situation and future of the Jewish communities of the region.

"Developing" Nations

Two indicators, one economic, one social, illustrate the nature and causes of underdevelopment in the countries of Latin America.

Economics

There is an enormous gulf between the per capita income of the Latin American countries and that of the developed nations.[3] If we disregard the special case of Venezuela (whose income comes mainly from oil), we find that the average income in even the most developed nation of the region, Argentina, is only a little more than

---

[3] In 1969 the per capita income in representative developed countries was as follows: Japan, $1,288; Italy, $1,254; France, $2,106; Sweden,* $2,905; and the United States, $3,814. In Latin America, representative figures for the same year were: Venezuela, $803; Argentina, $682; Uruguay, $552*; Mexico, $511*; Chile, $493; Colombia, $299; Brazil, $263*; Paraguay, $202; Peru, $246*; Ecuador, $214; Bolivia, $167. *Ibid.*, p. 598, Table 184. Asterisked figures relate to 1968.

half that of the poorest of the developed nations. The gap between Argentina and the other Latin American countries only highlights the backwardness of the region as a whole. In 1967 the average income for the whole of Latin America was $370 a year as against $1,400 for the European countries outside the Soviet bloc.

In comparison to their counterparts in other developing continents, the peoples of Latin America may seem fortunate, in some cases appearing closer to the developed than to the underdeveloped nations. There was only one country (Haiti) with a per capita income of less than $100, while in Africa there were four, and four also in Asia—including such vast and heavily populated countries as India and Indonesia. The visitor to Buenos Aires, São Paulo, Mexico City, and some other Latin American capitals will certainly find signs of advanced industrial development; light and mechanical industry; and television sets, Western-style luxury buildings, and other appurtenances and comforts which are to be found in New York, Paris, and London. But a trip through the rural interiors of these countries will reveal the tremendous gap in development and standard of living between these areas and the capital regions.

One reason for this terrible gap in national income is the high birth rate. In 1963–70 the population of the continent increased at an annual rate of 2.9 percent, the highest in the world. In the same period the population of Asia grew by 2.3 percent a year and that of Africa by 2.5 percent, while the United States grew an annual rate of only 1.2 percent, Japan by 1.1 percent, and Western Europe by 0.8 percent. As a result of their population explosion, the Latin American countries had to keep increasing production just to stay where they were, and it took great effort for them to make any advance.[4]

If Latin America is to extricate itself from its plight, even in a distant future, the economies of most of the countries must change. Although most of them were liberated from colonial rule more than 150 years ago, the economies of the majority have not changed basically since then; they continue to be suppliers of raw materials and foodstuffs to the developed countries, and many of the countries export one commodity in particular.[5] This inevitably leads to dan-

---

[4] Figures on the natural increase rate are taken from *United Nations Demographic Yearbook* (New York, 1970), pp. 105–18, Tables 1, 2.

[5] In the late-1960's oil accounted for 93% of Venezuela's exports, tin and some other ores for 72% of Bolivia's exports, sugar for 90% of Cuba's,

gerous dependence on market conditions and other fluctuating circumstances. The development of synthetic production methods during World War I and the world economic crisis of the early 1930s destroyed the market for sodium nitrate, which for some fifty years had been Chile's main, almost sole, source of income. When it broke relations with Cuba, the United States cancelled the import quotas for sugar, Cuba's main export, severely damaging its economy. In several Central American countries bananas are the sole export.

In 1958 two-thirds of the total industrial exports of Latin American states emanated from enterprises established for export purposes alone, and almost all of it was controlled by foreign concerns.[6] In the following decade exports expanded but foreign ownership was not reduced. The Latin American economies have also been gravely affected by a general drop in the price of the goods they export and the steep rise in the prices of those products—mainly industrial—which they import.

The backwardness of several of the countries can be blamed in large part on irrational and primitive methods of production. Efforts to improve production are sometimes blocked by vested interests, for example, the landowners, who prefer the present situation and the high prices for their produce on the local market to a drastic change in methods of land utilization, which would increase output considerably.

The existence of masses who live at the minimum substance level and who because of their poverty cannot be regarded as consumers of even the most basic products, and small numbers of fabulously

---

and copper for 78% of Chile's. Some 57% of Colombia's exports consisted of coffee, in competition with Brazil, where the corresponding figure was 41%. Coffee was also the main export of El Salvador, Guatemala, and Costa Rica (44%, 33%, and 29% respectively), while bananas were the main export of Ecuador, Panama, and Honduras (53%, 59%, and 47%). Even such a relatively developed country as Argentina relied mainly on its oldest established export products—meat and cereals—from which it derived some half of its foreign trade income. (Kenneth Biddle and Mukhtar Hamour (editors): *Statistical Abstract of Latin America 1969* (Latin American Center, UCLA, December 1970), pp. 272–73.

[6] Data from *Tercera Reunión Interamericana de Ministros de Educación* in Bogotá, Colombia, 4–10 de Agosto, 1963), Anexo 111 al acta final: "Perspectivas del desarrollo de la Educación en América Latina" (Washington, D.C., 1964), p. 10.

rich individuals—is a distinguishing feature of every Latin American country. The local oligarchy, part of it representing privileged classes in the semifeudal social structure preserved from colonial times and the beginnings of the era of indepenednce and part consisting of industrial and commercial interests, is anxious to maintain the existing economic system, even when it means dependence on foreign production and continued underdevelopment at home. This "internal colonialism" constitutes one of the greatest obstacles to political solutions for economic backwardness.

Education

A second indicator of underdevelopment in Latin America is the state of education. The close connection between education and economic progress in Latin America was recognized by the conference convened in 1961 at Punta del Este in Uruguay under the initiative of President Kennedy, at which the Alliance for Progress was established. A special committee was then appointed by the Organization of American States to study the problems of education in Latin America and to put forward practical proposals for their amelioration. After the committee completed its work, Latin American ministers of education convened in 1963 to discuss its recommendations and adopt resolutions.

The picture which emerged from the committee's report was extremely gloomy: large numbers of children without any elementary education whatsoever; teachers, particularly in rural areas, without even a secondary school education; a lack of school buildings and equipment; and a failure to tackle the problem of multicultural education, so vital in populations with Indian traditions and among migrants from backward areas. Even in the more developed countries—Argentina, Chile, Uruguay, Venezuela—the committee found that of every hundred children entering elementary school, 33 percent dropped out after one year, another 11 percent quit after two years, and only 30 percent reached the sixth grade; in the less-developed countries the dropout rate reached as high as 95 percent.[7]

---

[7] *Ibid.*, p. 73ff. Data refer to 1960. The countries were divided into three categories, the classifications being based on a combination of data, such as per capita income, percentage of economically active population engaged

These figures shed light on the statistics on literacy published by official sources. According to these figures (for 1960), 91.4 percent of the population of Argentina, 83.6 percent in Chile, 90.3 percent in Uruguay, and 76.2 percent in Venezuela could read and write.[8] But it is doubtful whether the knowledge of reading and writing acquired by the lower classes during only two or three years of elementary schooling is sufficient for the complex skills necessary for industrial development and can contribute much to the modernization of Latin America.

Economists, in particular, stress the vital need for improvement of the educational system as the first step toward emergence from a state of backwardness. The conference of ministers of education, taking into account the resources they could muster, set themselves the aim of reducing the elementary-school dropout rate by 1975 to 30 percent in the more developed countries, 40 percent in the second group, and 50 percent in the third. Since most of the population of Latin America is concentrated in the latter two groups of countries, it means that the 1963 plan envisaged that even in 1975 at most only 60 percent of their youth would be completing six grades of elementary schooling.

Since the early 1960s considerable efforts have been concentrated on improving educational standards, and according to figures for 1967–68, the various countries are close to attaining the goals laid down by the conference of ministers as regards the number of pupils registered in elementary schools.[9] But quality education, so essential for guiding large population groups toward modern patterns of thought and behavior and social mobility, remains the privilege of relatively small groups in most of the countries. This precludes the training of sufficient manpower for modern tasks and condemns to economic backwardness even those countries that could find the necessary capital.

---

in industry, per capita energy consumption, percentage of rural population in general population, etc. Argentina, Chile, Uruguay, and Venezuela were included in the first group, i.e., relatively developed countries; Guatemala, Honduras, and Haiti were classified in the third, least developed group; the twelve other countries (all the Ibero-American countries, excluding Cuba, and the four English-speaking countries) were included in the second group.

[8] See data on each of the countries in *Socio-Economic Progress in Latin America*, Social Progress Trust Fund, 8th Annual Report (Inter-American Development Bank, 1968).

[9] *Ibid.*

Political Changes

The Alliance for Progress was established in August 1961. The conference which launched it was preceded by some ten months of preparations and the public announcement made it clear that the practical intention was social reform and politically significant structural changes in all the participating countries. Under the alliance, each nation was to carry out, with the aid of the United States, what President Kennedy termed "a peaceful revolution." They would undertake agrarian reform, which would, at the least, reduce the size of large land holdings and achieve a more balanced distribution of land; improve local administration by eliminating corruption; introduce a progressive and rational tax system; and bridge the social gap through improving education, housing, etc.

Unfortunately, no real political backing could be found for these projects. The ruling forces were against most of the proposed changes out of fear for their own status, and other, nonrevolutionary forces were too weak. Nor were the necessary supporting institutions developed in the United States. The Alliance for Progress became just one more aid organization; the decade which was supposed to usher in the era of "the great leap forward" saw only limited gains.[10] It is true that between 1963 and 1969 the economies of many Latin American countries progressed considerably, but the developed countries advanced even more and the gap between rich and poor increased.[11]

---

[10] See the stimulating discussion by Peter Nehemkis, *Latin America: Myth and Reality* (New York, 1966). His relevant chapter is entitled "Death of an Alliance." He was a member of the team which in December 1960 drafted for President Kennedy the first proposal for the Alliance for Progress and later served as a member of the Committee for the Alliance for Progress of the U.S. Department of Commerce.

[11] Argentina increased per capita income from $485 to $682. In Chile per capita income rose from $260 to $493, in Colombia from $227 to $299; other countries displayed similar achievements. The United States increased its per capita income from $2,562 to $3,814, and the European countries, which had made the leap from devastation and ruin to economic development during the 1950s, also expanded their growth (Belgium from $1,186 to $1,873, France from $1,323 to $2,106, and Italy from $797 to $1,254). Dollars according to value in these years and not by fixed value. *United Nations Statistical Yearbook, op. cit.*

Economic and social advancement in Latin America will depend, above all, on finding appropriate political solutions. In most of the countries the political struggle is no longer confined to the upper class, the Church, and the army; the middle class, the urban proletariat, and sometimes even the peasant class now play a more or less active role. The wide-scale internal migration, which has transferred masses of landless peasants from traditional societies to the larger cities, has created on the outskirts of every capital concentrations of poverty and frustration. Through modern means of communication, particularly radio, news of local and world events reach even the remotest regions, and the lower classes have gained a new political awareness.

Politics in Latin America are changing. In several countries, the trade unions are important forces and students and intellectuals are active in left-wing movements. All these elements regard economic and social underdevelopment as the crux of the national problem, and for all of them nationalism is a driving force. Both left and right, each with its own emphasis, regard national homogeneity as the ideal and the borders of the state as the framework for realization of their dreams. There is, at this writing, no political movement in Latin America with a cosmopolitan outlook.

In the early 1970s Latin America displays a range of regimes, each developing under its own special circumstances, though repercussions are felt far beyond national borders. It would appear that all that any nation in search of a new political system needs do is to adapt to its own tastes one of the regimes already tried out elsewhere on the continent.

Brazil and Argentina now represent the right-wing military solution to the problems of the continent. Although military dictatorship is a long-established and accepted form of government in Latin America, the coups d'état in the two largest countries of the continent occurred after a relatively long period of constitutional government, to prevent possible left-wing revolt. In both countries, the revolution won the support of the middle and upper classes and the military authorities undertook major economic tasks as the sole chance of overcoming underdevelopment.

In Brazil the revolution led to an amelioration of the economic situation. The galloping inflation of the last decade, which reached 80 percent in 1964, decreased in 1970 to 20 percent. Production increased, as did exports and per capita income. Foreign investments flowed into the country under the explicit encouragement of the United States. Tax collection was improved and treasury income rose. But the Brazilian army found it necessary to employ brutal methods of suppression: mass arrests of student activists, torturing of political and other detainees, denial of political rights for ten years to a large number of prominent personalities, suppression of freedom of speech and the press by stringent "voluntary" censorship. These measures were slightly mitigated after the November 1970 elections and the restoration of the Congress. But after seven years of military rule, the atmosphere of economic stability is enjoyed mainly by the middle and upper classes. The real wages of the workers lagged far behind the increase in cost of living and inflation. The educational situation has improved only slightly, and the economic and social gap has not grown smaller.

In Argentina the military revolution involved less political suppression. The trade unions were allowed to carry on their usual activities. The press, as a rule, was not hindered, and the authorities even tolerated unofficial activities by previous political groups. In 1971 Argentina's president, General Alexandro Lanusse, promised that democratic elections would be held in March 1973 and parliamentary government restored.

But the economic goals of the revolution have not been achieved. Inflation continues at a rate higher than when the army seized power, exports remain stagnant, and among the workers—whose real wages have been reduced—unrest is increasing. Argentina, like Brazil, has attempted to attract capital investments, and even the oil industry, nationalized in 1963, has been again opened up to American concerns. However, the results so far have been limited.

Chile, under President Eduardo Frei Montalva (1964–70), sought to escape its economic torpor through a progressive democratic regime. Other constitutional regimes existed in the 1960s in a number of Latin American countries and some have endured— Costa Rica, Venezuela, and Uruguay. But the 1964 Chilean presidential elections offered a clear-cut choice between two alternatives: liberal, progressive capitalism, and socialism. The victory of Eduardo Frei's Christian-Democratic party appeared, at the time, to offer Western democracy a last chance of demonstrating its ability to bring development to Chile. The Chilean experiment then seemed particularly important in the light of the existence of similar regimes in Argentina and Venezuela, and Frei's election therefore aroused great hopes outside Chile as well.

In Chile itself the event aroused a readiness to cast off routine methods and tackle enormous tasks. New schools were established all over the country, a popular housing scheme was introduced, and these and other progressive plans aroused considerable public response. The agrarian reform, aimed at correcting a situation in which 75 percent of the agricultural land was owned by 3,000 people, won the explicit support of the Church, which even began to introduce such reform into its own economic holdings. But the alliance with the conservative forces in the country, which had enabled Frei to win the election in the first place, and the unwillingness of many members of the middle class to accept basic changes soon led to a split in the ruling party. Left-wing elements in Frei's party began to move closer to the leftist opposition in Congress, and the ship of reform ran aground.

The great, and probably somewhat exaggerated, hopes which had accompanied the birth of the new regime now bred a sense of frustration in the lower classes. The split in Frei's party and the appearance of two candidates for the presidency within the center-to-right bloc in the 1970 elections made things easier for the Socialist candidate, Salvador Allende. His Popular Front, a wide coalition ranging from the Communists through his own Socialist party to the left-wing section of Frei's party, won 1.3 percent more votes than either of his rivals. Although this figure represented only a minority of the voters, Allende became the constitutional president of Chile.

The platform of this diverse alliance of political forces has been aimed mainly at the confiscation of privately owned companies and their transfer to state ownership. In his first year of office Allende nationalized foreign-owned copper companies and private banks, and widely confiscated land. Politically, he has aimed at changing the structure of the Congress, to convert it into a unicameral body so as to weaken the opposition, which constitutes a majority in both houses.

The Socialist victory naturally aroused great immediate hopes among the lower classes, but implementation of campaign promises was less than immediate, and frustrations mounted. President Allende was obliged to prevent violent takeover of private land and to grant mining and industrial workers smaller wage increases than had been anticipated. It is almost certain that these will not be the sole, or the gravest, problems he encounters, but other Latin American regimes are watching with great interest the Chilean experiment in socialism.

Peru represents yet another type of regime: the left-wing military government. Here too the move to the left resulted from disillusionment with a progressive democratic regime; here too it occurred after that regime had done much to extricate the country from its state of backwardness. When he came to power in 1963, President Fernando Belaúnde Terry promised to carry out "the work of twelve years in six years of presidency." He began to improve the education network, construct new roads in the Andes area, and expand agricultural areas and rural cooperative movements. But this impetus, though it raised the national income, was not as revolutionary as many of the voters had anticipated. And when the president, despite his promises, refrained from nationalizing the foreign oil companies and when corruption became rife in his "reformed" administration, a military revolt took place.

In October 1968 a group of officers deposed Belaúnde and exiled him to Argentina. When he arrived in Buenos Aires, he announced that this had been a routine barracks revolt (*cuartelazo*). But in the following few months Latin America came to realize that the military regime of the new president, General Velasco Alvarado, did not resemble the right-wing military governments of Argentina or Brazil. His first action on coming to power was to nationalize the great American oil company, International Petroleum Company (an affiliate of Standard Oil of New Jersey), and to exercise Peru's oft-declared sovereignty over waters to a distance of 200 miles from its coast, thus depriving American vessels of rich fishing areas. Shortly afterward, vigorous agrarian reform was introduced, as well as progressive social legislation and the restriction of foreign and private bank ownership. The consequences of these measures for the economic betterment of the masses are as yet unclear, but the new regime has, at least temporarily, satisfied those elements in the population which were demanding drastic and revolutionary change.

Despite the strengthening of diplomatic and economic ties with the Soviet Union and a change in Peru's attitude toward Cuba, the military government does not regard itself as Communist. The convening of the ninety-six developing nations in Lima in November

1971 and the appointment of the Peruvian UN representative as chairman of the "third world" bloc illustrate the special place of the Peruvian military regime in the gamut of political solutions in Latin America today.

The other political solutions in Latin America are older. The first is Mexico's revolutionary regime, which, like the Soviet regime, is celebrating its fifty-fifth anniversary in 1972. The national revolution, which began with agrarian reform and which confiscated the American oil industry in the 1930s, never achieved general nationalization of the economy. It concentrated on increasing state participation in the economy and implementing extensive social legislation, while preserving the capitalist system. The Mexican revolution brought profound economic changes and also transformed cultural orientation and national identity. The secular trends and the violent struggle against the Catholic Church, the desire to base society on the autochthonous culture, with its Aztec, Mayan, and other elements as a central component, integrated with the Conquistadores' culture, created a national entity such as does not exist in other countries with similar population compositions.

In the last two decades Mexico has displayed tremendous economic progress, and despite the high rate of population increase (3.5 percent) the per capita income leaped from $272 in 1958 to $511 in 1968. During the fifty years of rule of the Partido Revolucionario Institucional, there have been many rebellions, inspired mainly by the failure to implement fully the promised agrarian reform. But since it encompasses all political forces, including the army, this party has succeeded in maintaining power with a firm hand. Furthermore, it has not needed to resort to explicitly dictatorial powers; elections are conducted regularly, and although restricted, there are two opposition parties. For these reasons, Mexico would appear to serve as an example to other Latin American countries. But as in other countries on the continent, there are extreme contrasts beneath the appearance of stability and progress. The economic gulf between rich and poor is very wide, and large sections of the population have not had even elementary education. Criticism of the existing situation was reflected in the vehement student protest in 1968, which was suppressed with bloodshed.

Another outstanding and more flamboyant alternative, of course, is the Communist regime in Cuba. The conditions leading to Fidel Castro's revolt in the second half of the 1950s would appear to be present in many other states on the continent. An economy based on one product (sugar) under the decisive influence of a foreign country (the United States); a tremendous gap in standard of living between property owners and workers; widespread illiteracy; and great frustration resulting from the physical proximity of the "have-nots" to the modern commodities and those who enjoy them; a dictator (Fulgencio Batista) employing oppressive security measures—these are not unknown in other Latin American countries, and there was good reason to believe that Castro's political experiment might be repeated elsewhere. In fact, the 1960s witnessed Castro-type rural guerrilla struggles in several states, the best-known being that led by Ché Guevara in Bolivia. All these attempts met the same fate as Guevara himself. What is more, Castro's dependence on the Soviet Union compromised the chances of the Cuban experiment (he himself felt the need in 1968 to demonstrate his independence of Moscow). Nonetheless, Cuba continues to serve as an example of a desirable solution, at least in the eyes of Latin American Communist parties.

The Prospects

The political struggle in Latin America is basically between those whose prosperity depends on maintaining the status quo, and those whose plight results from the status quo. The former include great landowners, industrialists enjoying the protection of the government, and leaders of commerce and service. That includes the great majority of the middle class, which unlike that in the developed countries, is not a militant force for democracy in itself. Many of those in industry and services have a proclivity to upper-class behavior and conventions, and they fear that their future might be endangered by entrusting political power to the lower classes. Legality is not sacrosanct in Latin America; constitutional "illegitimacy" rather is the political norm, and the middle class is unwilling to make sacrifices for democracy if that entails accepting basic changes in the social structure.[12] The Catholic Church is a permanent ally of this camp—and was for a time one of its central

---

[12] I. L. Horowitz, "The Norm of Illegitimacy—The Political Sociology of Latin America," in I. L. Horowitz and others, eds., *Latin American Radicalism* (New York, 1969); and Frank Tannenbaum, *Ten Keys to Latin America* (New York, Vintage Books, 1962), pp. 145–52.

pillars—and the entire alignment rests on the support of the armed forces, which hold senior positions and enjoy esteem and material rewards in the present social and economic structure.

In the other camp are ranged the trade unions and the amorphous and unorganized masses. Their political struggle is not impelled by ideology, and their loyalty is generally not to a political program but to a leader. They are impelled by their daily plight, and their objective is mainly amelioration of their living conditions. Their strength lies in their massive presence in urban centers and—at election time—in their numbers. With them, or rather, beneath them, stands the peasant class. The peasants are less aggressive when agrarian problems are not the issue and, because of the tremendous cultural gap between town and village which characterizes most countries of Latin America, of lesser political significance. Ché Guevara's failure to arouse the Bolivian peasants and the lack of success of rural guerrilla warfare in Venezuela and Colombia bear witness to their weakness.

But what the lower class lacks in leaders and ideology is supplied abundantly by left-wing intellectual circles. It has always been the declared task of university students and teachers in Latin America to involve themselves in political struggles. For generations future politicians were educated in law faculties and commenced their political activities during their student days. This tradition has endured to the present day; Latin American universities hum with political activity, which is not confined to the university campus.

In the fifties and sixties some of these leftist intellectuals engaged in direct action, both within and outside the existing party framework. They became increasingly militant and struggled to establish common cause with the trade unions. This effort was not always successful and, instead, rural terror became a means of winning popular support and undermining confidence in the existing regime. When such rural activities were suppressed at the end of the 1960s, urban guerrilla tactics replaced them. The kidnapping of diplomats in Guatemala and Brazil, armed takeovers of suburbs and small towns in Argentina, and even direct confrontation with the army in Córdoba—in which workers also took part—were the milestones in this terrorist campaign. It culminated in the exploits of the Tupamaros in Uruguay, who as a result of a series of robberies, kidnappings, and assassination attempts and their ability to evade the law, have won the admiration of youth throughout Latin America.

Acts of terrorism, however, cannot overthrow the existing regimes, and it is also doubtful whether they can win the support of the majority of the population. In the November 1971 elections in Uruguay, the Popular Front, which the underground forces supported, met with failure. But terrorism can sometimes undermine confidence in the regime and confuse government supporters. Above all, it succeeds in highlighting the country's social ills.

Throughout the 1960s the upper classes relied on military rule against this left-wing subversion. But the army's success in furthering economic stability in Brazil has only reinforced the left's demand for progress toward solving the country's social problems. This demand may be supported by part of the middle class, which will come to recognize what the Alliance for Progress tried to make clear: that economic advancement will be crippled so long as a wide social gulf divides the society. The army itself may yet recognize that. In any event, right-wing military intervention cannot constitute the last stage of development even in Brazil. In Argentina, where the military regime has failed to carry out its economic objectives, this is even more valid.

Latin America's social and economic underdevelopment, and the left-wing militancy which will not permit it to be ignored, are causing some erosion in the ruling oligarchic camp. This is evident in several countries in the changing attitude of one of the central forces in this camp, the Catholic Church. In Brazil and Chile high Church officials have begun to support demands for solution of social problems. In Argentina, Colombia, and other countries, identification of novice priests with the militant leftists has overstepped accepted bounds, and although this movement now includes only a few individuals its significance may increase in years to come.

In the 1960s the status quo was further undermined from an even more threatening and unexpected direction—the army itself. The enduring left-wing military regime in Peru and the short-lived military regime which followed it in Bolivia show that there is no guarantee that sections of the army will remain immune to the challenge of the "leftward leap."

What is likely to be the reaction of the upper and middle classes in future years? The initial response of many to the atmosphere of political instability has been to attempt to safeguard their capital. The flight of capital has undercut the economy in Argentina and Uruguay in the past few years, and also in Chile in the uncertain period which preceded the 1964 elections and again after the 1970 elections. A similar reaction is evident elsewhere under similar circumstances. But it is possible, too, that, being aware of the imminence of social change, these circles might attempt to implement and shape it by legitimate political activity within a constitutional framework. In Chile during Frei's regime the middle class was not up to it; at least they were not ready to draw far-reaching conclusions from the revolutionary situation in which they were embroiled. Has the victory of the left in Chile opened the eyes of the middle class in Argentina, leading them to carry out basic reforms on their own initiative? Most observers doubt the readiness of property owners to bring about real reforms in the structure of land ownership and the distribution of wealth, and there is pessimism in this great and rich country with regard to the political and economic future.

Nor are the horizons of the left-wing regimes—the constitutional, the military, and the Communist—free of heavy shadows. The ability of these regimes to bring about drastic changes in society and land ownership is not doubted. The question is whether they are capable of keeping their promises as regards economic progress. In Chile the exaggerated hopes pinned on the victory of the left have already produced the first problems, and the central question now is whether the electorate will be patient and allow the government to persevere in the implementation of reforms the fruits of which will only appear at a much later date. The second great question is whether a left-wing democratic regime can change the structure of society without simultaneously affecting its economic stability and without annihilating democracy itself. To the extent that this can be appraised after only one year of rule, it is likely that there will be an increase in the influence of extremist forces in the coalition in the event of a grave economic debacle or if the opposition provides the pretext. Such a shift in mood could lead to an attempt to introduce a left-wing totalitarian regime. In this case the grave possibility of civil war cannot be disregarded.

Although it is not dependent on the will of the electorate, the military regime in Peru faces similar problems. But its leaders are well acquainted with the economic problems of Cuba and despite evident strain in their relations with the United States, it is very doubtful that they are anxious for a confrontation with the United States, which might put them in a position like that of Cuba. Their ability to persist in social and economic reforms without endangering economic ties with the United States naturally depends in large measure on American reactions.

Of the three left-wing regimes, Cuba's would seem now, at the beginning of the 1970s, to be entering a better era. Fidel Castro's first trip abroad in twelve years symbolizes the end of the total isolation he endured throughout the 1960s. Thanks to his new comrades in Chile and Peru, there may even be a revision of the Latin American resolutions against him.

But that, like much else in the future of Latin America, depends to a large extent on United States policy. The fact that in 1969 it hesitated to impose sanctions against Peru in reaction to the nationalization of American property may mark the commencement of a certain flexibility in its relations with these regimes and an attempt to find a modus vivendi which will facilitate social and economic changes without undermining the Pan American Union. Governor Nelson Rockefeller undertook a tour on behalf of President Nixon in 1969 for the purpose of studying the problems of the economic, social, and political future of Latin America. The basic conclusion of the report he submitted was the inevitability of social changes on the continent and the need to cooperate with them. The vital question is whether the United States will agree to regard left-wing solutions as legitimate frameworks for social change. Will it attempt, through a constructive attitude toward them, to persuade its traditional oligarchic allies in these countries to be more receptive and even to take initiatives toward social reform? Is the United States willing and able, for its own reasons, to help attain the social objectives of the Alliance for Progress?

Relations with Israel

Political developments in various countries in Latin America raise questions about the future of their relations with the State of Israel.

It was the support of thirteeen Latin American nations in 1947 that made possible the adoption of the UN resolution leading to the establishment of Israel. During the following two decades Latin America and Israel established extremely close cultural ties as well as economic and political cooperation. On political issues with the Arab states, Israel could usually rely on the support of the Latin American nations. Israel assisted Latin America in development and training projects in irrigation, agricultural settlement, and the use of the army for peaceful purposes. The Arab states did everything in their power to disrupt these relations but, until the Six Day War, without success.

In 1967 the Latin American states still formed part of the bloc at the UN which prevented the passing of one-sided anti-Israel resolutions. But as the danger of an Israel-USSR confrontation increased and as the influence of revolutionary forces grew in Latin America, this support diminished. In a debate on Middle Eastern problems at the General Assembly in 1970, Israel found only eight Latin American countries on its side; in 1971 only six Latin American countries supported Israel at the UN; in both years the largest and most important states were not among Israel's supporters.

It is incumbent upon Israel in the 1970s to make every effort to restore and maintain the political support of this region. The task will not be made easier by the entry of the People's Republic of China into the United Nations.

Jewish Communities in Latin America

The wide differences that belie any suggestion that Latin America is a single homogeneous area extend as well to the Jewish communities of the continent. Are dozens of communities, dispersed over thousands of miles and remote from one another, identical?

The table on pages 270–271 reveals two basic facts. The first is that the communities are young and of recent growth. In Argentina and Peru the first manifestations of organization appeared more than one hundred years ago, and in Venezuela the Jews can mark the one hundred-fortieth anniversary of Jewish settlement (the oldest Jewish cemetery in continental Latin America is in the old colonial town of Coro, where one of the headstones bears the date 1832); however at the end of World War II the Jewish communities other than in Argentina were very small. The great majority of Latin American Jewry today, then, consists of an immigrant generation, the first native-born generation, and their children.

The second basic fact is a tremendous disproportion in the size of the communities.[13] Argentina has some 450,000 Jews, more than half the estimated Jewish population of the entire continent; at the other extreme are the small communities of Paraguay, Costa Rica, and Jamaica, and even smaller ones in the Dominican Republic, Nicaragua, and Haiti. There are some growing communities. (Uruguay, Venezuela, Mexico), and some have shrunk considerably in the past two decades (Bolivia, Ecuador, Cuba).

On the face of it, these communities have no common denominator. But an examination of the ratio between the size of the Jewish community and the percentage of "white" or "European" elements in the general population will explain the disproportionate Jewish dispersal as well as provide a basic principle for classifying the various communities. It is evident from the table that the larger Jewish communities are to be found in countries where the European element is of great demographic importance. With one exception, Costa Rica, this element reflects the open immigration policy of these countries since their independence. The southern states, particularly Argentina, explicitly encouraged immigration in the last quarter of the nineteenth century. (Argentina was so anxious to attract immigrants that in the 1880s and again at the beginning of the twentieth century it even paid the passage of immigrants.) Chile also followed the same policy for short periods, deliberately encouraging immigration.[14] Uruguay did the same somewhat later, and in Brazil the state of Rio Grande do Sul outdid all the others. When slavery was abolished in Brazil, the state of São Paulo began inviting immigrants from Europe and elsewhere and for decades this state and other southern Brazilian states were a common destination for immigrants.

In contrast, other Latin American countries, particularly the Andine states (e.g., Peru, Ecuador, and Bolivia) and the Central American states, had a closed-gates policy, except for isolated cases in which small groups of immigrants were permitted to settle. Typical is Venezuela, which has only partially changed its attitude even in recent decades. According to the 1936 census, there were only 47,026 foreign-born persons residing in Venezuela; only 8,620 more had been added by 1941. The rate of immigration did increase con-

---

[13] The figures in the table are based on estimates, generally the lowest figures from various estimates.

[14] Carl Solberg, *Immigration and Nationalism: Argentina and Chile, 1890–1914* (Austin and London, 1970).

siderably in the 1940s and 1950s; in 1961 the 7,524,900 inhabitants of Venezuela included 526,188 persons born abroad, i.e., some 7 percent. This rise accompanied the development of oil production and the industrial and commercial expansion and general invigoration of economic life which followed.[15]

The larger Jewish communities, then, were created by large waves of immigration which influenced considerably the composition of the general population. In these countries immigrants and their offspring, Jews along with non-Jews, enjoy a sense of belonging and have roots. This is not the case in those countries where the immigrant is regarded as an alien. There, he and even his native-born children may enjoy rights and assume civic obligations but they are still not regarded as "one of us."

There are, therefore, two kinds of Jewish communities in Latin America: those in relatively young societies of a diversified origin and those in relatively old societies in which the mestizos, descendants of the Indians and of the Iberian rulers, constitute relatively homogeneous and closed societies. The communities of the first type are also the largest; the others are smaller and less stable. Mexico is an exception in the latter group. Many Jews came there, particularly in the 1920s, hoping vainly to be able to continue their wanderings northward to the United States. For similar reasons, a relatively large number of Jews came to Cuba in the same period, although in their case there was the additional factor of the special economic ties between Cuba and the United States.

The differing demographic background in the two types of countries naturally creates considerable differences as regards Jewish identity and the long-range prospects of Jewish survival.

Economic Concentration and Stratification

A further study of the table on pages 270–71 will reveal a clear correlation between the size of the Jewish community and the economic condition in the various countries. The higher the per capita income, the larger, relatively speaking, the Jewish population. In part this reflects that the countries which welcomed immigration had an impetus for development and reached a level of industrialization which most of the other countries have not attained. But there has also been a deliberate migration movement among the Jews from

---

[15] Chi Yi Chen, *Movimientos Migratorios en Venezuela* (Caracas, 1968).

the less developed countries to their more developed neighbors. This has occurred not only in those communities which have not developed educational and cultural opportunities for the young generation (for example, Ecuador), but also in those which have (like Bolivia). It obviously reflects the lack of stability in these countries and, perhaps, a stronger sense of alienation there. Brazil is no exception, only a special situation. Despite the low per capita income, this country takes second place only to Argentina in the extent of Jewish settlement. But 50 percent of Brazil's national income originates in the southern states, and Brazilian Jewry is almost entirely concentrated there—in São Paulo, Rio de Janeiro, and Pôrto Alegre.

In addition to its concentration in the relatively developed countries, Latin American Jewry has two additional characteristics. One is geographical: urban concentration; in all the countries the great majority of Jews live in the capital. In several countries up to 80 percent of the Jews live in the capital, and in others virtually all of them do. Jewish concentration in the capital becomes particularly striking because of the second factor, professional concentration. Most of the Jews of Latin America are employed in a few, similar occupations, and therefore, even within the cities, they are clustered in certain quarters and totally absent in others. This and the economic and social stratification of the Jews has given the Jewish presence a visibility disproportionate to their actual numbers in the general population or even the metropolitan population, and the non-Jewish public is often led to exaggerate the number and strength of the Jews.

There has been little systematic study of the social and economic stratification of the Jews, but several facts provide a basic impression. An attempt to conduct a census of the Jewish population in São Paulo was made in 1969 by the local federation of Jewish organizations. Its study showed that 15 percent of the employable Jews were in the liberal professions, 15 percent in administrative tasks, and 27 percent were employers. Those figures, together with data on ownership of apartments, cars, and other property and on employment of domestic help, showed that the great majority of São Paulo Jewry could be classified in the middle and upper sections of the middle class or the lower ranks of the upper class.[16]

---

[16] *American Jewish Year Book*, Vol. 71 (1970), p. 382, and an unpublished lecture of Henrique Rattner at the Congress on Jewish Studies, Jerusalem, August 1969.

A similar picture emerges from a few surveys conducted in Argentina in the last decade. One of these, on the Sephardic community of Buenos Aires, carried out by the American Jewish Committee, revealed that between 95 percent and 99 percent belonged to the middle class and the majority of these to its upper echelons. This parallels earlier findings concerning a large group within the Ashkenazi community.[17] In Chile a survey of Jewish students interviewed in Santiago in 1966 indicated that 77 percent of their families owned cars; 89 percent of the families were classified as belonging to the middle and upper sections of the middle class.[18]

These scattered surveys cannot provide a complete picture, but they leave little doubt that Latin American Jews belong to the prosperous sections of the societies in which they live. There are various explanations for this. When the opportunities for industrialization were created in the various Latin American countries (just before or during World War II), many Jews were in a position to take advantage of them. Many made the transition from commerce and brokerage to local production of consumer goods, thus joining the former artisans who were expanding their workshops into small factories. The relatively high number of university graduates among the Jews aided this process. There was, then, a general movement upward both in the quality of occupation and in income level. The Jews who reached some of the Andes countries as refugees in that period brought basic capital and, particularly, modern know-how, and soon became entrepreneurs in activities which had not existed in those countries. Their economic weight as consumers and soon as manufacturers and merchants in cities as underdeveloped as, for example, La Paz, Bolivia, far exceeded their numerical importance. This trend continued in the 1950s and 1960s despite political crises, and was interrupted only when the political instability became acute.

There is also poverty among Latin American Jews. A glance at the situation of poor Jews in Buenos Aires throws light on a forgotten corner of Argentinian Jewry. Under the outer layer of prosperity, in

---

[17] For a summary of information on this field in Argentina, see Haim Avni, "Argentine Jewry: Its Socio-Political Status and Organisational Patterns," in *Dispersion and Unity*, No. 12 (1971).

[18] *Estudio de Opiniones—Estudiantes Universitarios*. An unpublished survey directed by E. Rogovsky and carried out by the American Jewish Committee.

proximity with it and sometimes within the same family, there is great poverty and suffering. According to the records of the welfare department of the Ashkenazi community in Buenos Aires, no less than 6,211 persons sought aid in the first six months of 1970.[19] The Sephardic community has its own welfare institutions, and there are other bodies also providing assistance to the poor. In São Paulo, Montevideo, and even Caracas there are Jews who need charity. But although poor Jews include some young people of working age, they are mainly the elderly. Thus Jewish presence among the proletariat in Latin America particularly among the "blue collar" workers is insignificant.

Since throughout the continent the Jews are largely in the middle class, their response to economic and political developments is like that of other elements in this class. For a considerable number of the Jews this essentially conservative reaction may clash with the socialist beliefs of their youth, and others find themselves in conflict not only with themselves but with their children, particularly university students. But whether they like it or not, economic and social realities seem to impose on them the need for political identification with the status quo.

This was particularly evident in the 1960s. The change of regime in Cuba, though it was not accompanied by any particular threat to the Jews, nevertheless led to the virtual end of the Jewish community. Although there are no precise data, there is evidence that among the approximately 1,500 Jews remaining in Cuba there is a conspicuous absence of the younger age group. In Chile the Jews, like the middle- and upper-class non-Jews, were gripped with panic by the election in 1970 of a Socialist president and many left the country. (There are no sound data on the extent of the Jewish exodus and, even less, on how many returned and on how the situation has crystallized in the past two years.) In Argentina, as a result of the prolonged political and economic crisis, there is confusion and lack of confidence in the future, among the Jews as among other members of the middle class. The Jews are particularly vulnerable to the economic regression, not because they are Jews but because of their high concentration in particularly vulnerable parts of the economy. The same is true in Uruguay. By contrast, in Brazil and Mexico there is a sense of optimism about the economy and it is shared by

[19] Report of meeting of the Ashkenazi Community Council in Buenos Aires, July 28, 1970, *Yiddishe Zeitung* and *Die Presse*, July 7, 1970.

many members of the Jewish community, although in Brazil it has been accompanied by unease because of the political suppression.

Although the unease and uncertainty in Latin America have not found expression in any hosility toward Jews, the economic, social, and political problems besetting the continent warrant profound apprehension with regard to the future of the Jews.

Legal Status and Security

When the first Jewish immigrants arrived in Latin America they found that emancipation had been granted and safeguarded by law. Inspired by the ideals of the French Enlightenment and the constitutional example of the United States, the Latin American countries adopted constitutions guaranteeing religious freedom and individual rights for all. But these constitutional principles did not alter the total identification of the citizens of these states with Catholicism, just as it did not eradicate other aspects of colonial life, and in most Latin American states there is an explicit, close, official connection between Church and State. The custody of Church affairs which the Latin American republics inherited from the Spanish and Portuguese regimes was reflected in the constitutions. The formal entrusting of the *Patronato* over the Church to the president of the republic, which appears in many constitutions, precludes the election of a non-Catholic to the office of president or vice-president.

In the countries that welcomed immigration (unlike the others), the struggle between liberals and conservatives occurred long before the Jewish immigrants arrived. The liberal triumph toward the end of the nineteenth century established religious freedom and equal rights, so that Jewish communities emerged in a context of full equality. But even these states did not wish to increase their Jewish population, and when, after the waves of immigration, they introduced selective immigration policies, Jewish immigrants were among the first groups rejected, not by legislation but by discriminatory administrative directives. The history of Jewish migration to Latin America in the 1930s is a saga of unceasing struggle, by all possible means, against such restrictive and discriminatory regulations. In Argentina such discrimination continued even after World War II, although that country then absorbed tens of thousands of immigrants, including a large number of German Nazis and other fascists, driven to emigrate by the downfall of Germany.

In the countries that had not welcomed immigration liberal constitutional processes did not develop until the twentieth century. In some of these countries a small Jewish community had already been established by then. In many cases the acceptance of Jewish immigrants in the 1930s and 1940s was accompanied by restrictions on employment and sometimes on place of residence. Although these restrictions were not strictly observed, they had, along with the official Catholicism of the regime, a detrimental effect on the Jews' sense of equality and their self-image as citizens.

Nevertheless, in the 1960s the Jews enjoyed full equality as regards individual and communal liberties in all countries of Latin America. Restrictions which affected some of them as aliens or naturalized citizens did not apply to their native-born children, and for them the processes of integration could operate without hindrance. Yet the decade also witnessed an increase and diversification of anti-Semitic phenomena.

In several of the communities, above all in the largest, Argentina, anti-Semitic outbursts accompanied the beginnings of Jewish presence at the end of the nineteenth century. In the 1930s hostility reached a peak, fed by local nationalism and explicitly supported by the Nazi propaganda machine with funds from Germany. Several Latin American states later became centers for anti-Semitic publications, and this activity has continued to this day. The veteran anti-Semites have recently found a new ally in the Arab League, which has done its best to recruit the loyalties of Arab immigrants to Latin America for the struggle against Israel and against Latin American Jewry, an effort which apparently has met with only partial success. Traditional anti-Semites now use "anti-Zionist" slogans, even when the content of their literature is "classically" anti-Semitic, and despite their small number their propaganda is apparently winning wider response than in the past, particularly in Argentina, where they are most active. Many non-Jews are increasingly identifying *Israelitas* (Jews) with Israelis.

Anti-Semitic propaganda has been particularly successful recently in left-wing political circles, which in the 1930s were generally free of hostility toward the Jews. Israel's confrontation with the Soviet Union and its satellites, of which many Latin Americans were unaware before the Six Day War, has become so prominent in recent years that positive identification with Communism has, in most cases, entailed a negative attitude toward Israel and its supporters. Israel's ties with the United States, its dependence on American support and arms, have intensified this hostility and it is now quite frequent in leftist circles to regard Israel as an enemy of the "third world." Representatives of the Palestinian military organizations attended the tricontinental conference in Havana in 1966 and the Latin American conference of Castro's supporters in 1968, and both conferences passed resolutions attacking Israel. And the sympathy toward Israel displayed during and after the Six Day War by military and right-wing circles in several Latin American countries did nothing to improve Israel's image with leftist groups. This unhappy and deteriorating situation also poses a threat to Latin American Jewry, which has close ties with the State of Israel.

The economic and social stratification of Latin American Jews is not, of course, conducive to lessening left-wing hostility. The absence of Jews from the trade unions makes it difficult to check the spread of dangerous moods there. In the past, militant anti-Semitism was concentrated mainly in the extreme right and never succeeded in igniting the latent anti-Semitic spark in a wider public. Now there is increasing danger that hostile attitudes, rooted in the Catholic background of the lower classes, will be activated by aggressive left-wing propaganda.

In their confrontation with anti-Semitism, the Jews cannot find adequate security in democratic constitutions and processes. Despite their concentration in metropolitan areas, the limited size of the Latin American Jewish communities makes it impossible to create a "Jewish vote" which would carry weight at election time, and, at any rate, elections do not mean that much on the Latin American political scene. In Argentina right-wing anti-Semitism reached its height under democratic presidents (Arturo Frondizi and Arturo Illia); despite sympathetic declarations of the authorities and despite legislation which outlawed anti-Semitic organizations, the onslaughts did not cease. Indeed, in the country with possibly the healthiest democratic tradition, Costa Rica, the authorities themselves in 1941 and again in 1948 undertook legal initiatives which were mainly directed against the Jews.

A method of influencing the authorities to which various Jewish groups have had recourse—inviting intervention of American official agencies—has become extremely hazardous in the past few years and, in view of mounting anti-American feeling, may be even more so in the future. Even if such intervention could bring some immediate relief, public knowledge of it could strengthen the view, already prevalent as a result of anti-Semitic propaganda, that local Jews have special ties with the United States.

Thus the methods of safeguarding Jewish security are extremely limited in Latin America. In each country this task is entrusted to a central Jewish institution within which all the important organizations are united, generally on a confederative basis. These organizations attempt forceful counterpropaganda to appeal to those sections of public opinion likely to agree that anti-Semitism constitutes a threat to basic values of the society, notably the liberal and democratic elements and the trade union leaders.

A special role is being played by the "Christian-Jewish Friendship" leagues in Argentina, Brazil, Uruguay, Chile, and Costa Rica, which have been established not by official representatives of the Jewish community but upon the initiative of individuals and small groups. But these organizations for Christian-Jewish dialogue have had only limited influence on the Catholic Church, and even on the Jewish public. Their activity has been confined to meetings with a small number of philo-Semites within the Church; but they have not succeeded, for example, in altering the stubborn opposition of several heads of the local clergy in Argentina to the Vatican's "Jewish document." In Chile and Brazil, however, several leading Church figures have been demonstratively sympathetic.

All these measures, and even the determination of certain young Jews to resort to self-defense in extreme cases, may prove effective against traditional right-wing anti-Semitism, but they would be totally insignificant if violent left-wing revolution should acquire an anti-Semitic flavor. This has not happened. The Cuban revolution occurred in a country in which there was no anti-Semitic tension at the time, and it has not become anti-Semitic since. In Chile the upheaval took place without anti-Semitism playing any part; on the contrary, both right and left endeavored by special gestures to emphasize their positive attitude toward the Jews. Nor was left-wing activity in Uruguay, despite its violence, directed against the Jews. These are certainly encouraging signs, and give reason to hope that left-wing revolution elsewhere will avoid racist and other reactionary trends. But these precedents do not preclude the possibility of a conjunction of grave anti-Semitic outbursts and a sharp turn to the left, in which anti-Semitic activists might succeed in joining the ranks of the revolution and marking out the Jews as a special target. In this respect there is no difference between typical immigration countries, such as Argentina, and a country with a very small European element in its population, such as Guatemala.

Jewish Identity and Organization

In contrast to some other countries, where it is the religious aspect of Jewish identity that is emphasized, Jewish identity in Latin America is based largely on national and cultural elements, i.e., the secular heritage which most immigrants to Latin America, members of the first generation to rebel against their ultrareligious background, brought with them. This antireligious rebellion received support from the attitude of the general society in Latin America toward religious and ethnic minorities. Because there was a majority religion, even an "official" religion, the consciousness of the majority society could not allocate equal room to other religions, even though their constitutional rights to operate freely had been recognized. Adherence to the Jewish religion, therefore, made the Jew a little less than equal.

Another factor operated to reinforce cultural identity. In the countries that welcomed immigration the great waves of newcomers created an ethnic and cultural heterogeneity, which flourished in a context of freedom of voluntary organization and in a period in which nationalism as a militant ideology had only few advocates. The definition of these immigrant groups on an ethnic basis, therefore, was natural, and it was reinforced by the principle that a man's nationality was determined by his place of birth. The Jews, therefore, were classified as Russians, Poles, Turks, or whatever; such official identification by country of origin extended legitimacy to ethnic organization. In the countries which did not have a policy of welcoming immigration, all immigrants—and their descendants as well—were marked as aliens, giving impetus there, too, for national identification and organization.

By force of the heritage they brought with them and the close ties they maintained with their countries of origin, the Jews of Latin America constructed for themselves institutions and organizations resembling those they had left behind. Jewish culture—in its Yiddish manifestations—was brought to Latin America and nurtured there. Daily newspapers, weekly journals, and novels were published in Yiddish and were widely read even in the smallest communities. To this day, the Jewish community as it existed before the Holocaust in Europe still serves the generation of immigrants as a source of emulation and identification, and in some places—Buenos Aires and other Argentinian cities, Montevideo, Santiago, Mexico City, Caracas—that is the basic organizational form of Ashkenazic public life. The situation is the same among the Sephardim, but with less nostalgic emphasis on the community patterns destroyed by the Holocaust.

With their strong sense of Jewish national identity, Latin American Jews naturally support the State of Israel. The Zionist parties continued to exist even after the establishment of the state, and many of the larger communities are run by leaders elected in general elections on a Zionist party basis. Left-wing parties, such as the Bund or the Jewish Communists, also participate, though the latter are generally ostracized and do not take part in community administration.

The various elements of the organized Jewish community have devoted great effort to developing ways to preserve their Jewish character and to transmit their ideology to the younger generation. Jewish schools have been established in most communities, and each allocates a large percentage of its income to Jewish education. The declared aims of the educational effort, in which the Jewish Agency helps by training teachers and dispatching advisers, are to hand down to the younger generation their Jewish heritage, to reaffirm their Jewish consciousness, and to strengthen their ties with the State of Israel. It is also hoped that education of this generation will assure the continuance of Jewish community life in Latin America.

The educational effort is particularly remarkable in the smaller communities of the "nonimmigration" countries. Thus in the most recent figures we find that there were 5,240 children (from kindergarten through high school) in the Jewish educational network in Mexico, as against 2,442 in Uruguay and only 1,520 in Chile, although the Jewish communities of all three countries are about the same size. The Caracas community, with some 10,000 members, maintained an educational network for more than 1,800 children in 1970. In Lima, with an estimated Jewish population of 4,500, there is a Jewish school with 850 pupils. The smaller communities—in Costa Rica, Paraguay, Panama, and Curaçao—also maintained Jewish schools despite the limited funds at their disposal. In many of these countries, comprehensive Jewish day schools were being set up, covering all educational age-groups. In contrast, until 1967 Jewish education in the largest Latin American Jewish community, Argentina, was mainly part-time (generally two and a half hours each afternoon, five times a week), reaching only a small percentage of school-age children.[20]

These differences may, of course, reflect the state of available government education in the smaller countries, but they may also result from the greater sense of alienation of the Jews there, encouraging them to more vigorous efforts to ensure their children's Jewish education. Whatever the reason, the fact is that in these smaller countries the great majority of Jewish children attend Jewish schools, while in the veteran immigration countries Jewish education is given only to a small minority of the young.

As against these forces to preserve and maintain Jewish life, opposing, often stronger forces are operating on the younger generation. Spanish or Portuguese is spoken in the street and in school and is gradually breaking down the linguistic barrier which the advocates of Jewish cultural nationalism had hoped to erect around their younger generation. A desperate struggle to preserve the Yiddish language is still being conducted in Argentina, Mexico, and Uruguay, but these communities are not producing new consumers of Yiddish literature or audiences for any other form of Yiddish culture. Even the Hebrew language, which is gradually taking over in all the educational institutions, is not becoming a vital cultural factor, inspiring local cultural creativity or greatly increasing the demand for imported Hebrew works. In light of the rich and variegated general culture around them, many of the young generation regard secular Jewish culture as meager and empty, and even affinity to Zionism and the State of Israel does not override this feeling. What is more, under pressure of local nationalism and the challenges presented by activity for local social reform, many believe loyalty to the State of Israel to be in conflict with their civic loyalties. Such beliefs are particularly strong among Jewish university students, who have become an increasingly significant section of the young generation in the past ten years. As a result, Jews are now

---

[20] With the exception of Venezuela, see *World Census on Jewish Education, 1968* (World Council on Jewish Education), which gives figures for 1967–68 and 1968–69.

conspicuous in left-wing movements, while many others have preferred to retreat into private lives without any Jewish content.

This wide retreat from organized Jewish life is particularly troubling because, despite the decades of organized Jewish life and the rise of a Jewish intellectual class, the Jewish communities have not succeeded in producing a young Jewish intelligentsia that can tackle the uncertainties and confusions of the young generation. Because of this lack of a young leadership providing a spiritual focus meriting esteem and capable of supplying an answer to the cultural and ideological challenges posed by the majority society, most young people in Latin America regard Judaism as lacking such an answer. The appeal to remain within the Jewish fold, therefore, seems to them an anachronistic demand for parochial, sectarian isolationism.

This problem is particularly severe at the beginning of the 1970s because most of the communities are undergoing a transition crisis. The founder generation is seeking its heirs, and in many cases is not finding them. Questions are being asked about the efforts invested in education, and there is a frantic search for ways to stimulate the emergence of a new leadership. It is clear that the intergenerational crisis is not only a matter of language (Yiddish as against Spanish), but revolves around the importance of Jewish institutions in the lives of the younger generation. In the 1969 elections to the leadership of the Jewish community in Buenos Aires, only one-third of the electorate exercised their right to vote and a statistical examination, based on a limited sample, revealed that only a very small percentage of young people participated.[21] A similar picture emerges from the elections in São Paulo.

The unwillingness of young people to take over communal leadership is not, however, universal. Both the Ashkenazic and Sephardic communities of Caracas, for example, have found a way of bringing young members of the liberal professions into the community leadership. Elsewhere, too, many members of the younger generation are attracted to new forms of communal activity, as directors of the sports and recreation centers which have sprung up in all Latin American communities in the past twenty years, in the

---

[21] Teresa Kaplanski de Caryevschi, *Características de los Socios de la AMIA* (Buenos Aires, 1970, stencil).

Jewish Communities in Latin American Countries

	Estimated Number of Jews			General Population 1970[5] (in thousands)	General Population[7] % White or European	General Population[5] Annual Increase Rate	Per Capita Income, 1969[8]	Literacy Rate[6]
	1917–18[1]	1950[2]	1970[4]					
South America								
Argentina	123,000	385,000	450,000	23,364	90	1.5	$682	91.5 (1960)
Chile	500	32,000	30,000	8,835	majority	2.4	$493	89.6 (1968)
Uruguay	1,700	38,000	50,000	2,886	95	1.2	$552 (1968)	90.5 (1963)
Brazil	5,000	125,000	140,000	92,238	60	3.2	$263 (1968)	71.0 (1969)
Paraguay	600	4,000	1,200	2,386	minority	3.2	$202	74.4 (1962)
Bolivia	25	5,000	1,700	4,931	small minority	2.6	$167	39.8 (1968)
Peru	300	4,000	5,000	13,586	15	3.1	$246 (1968)	61.1 (1961)
Ecuador	?	5,000	1,100	6,093	15	3.4	$214	69.7 (1969)
Colombia	80	9,000	11,000	21,117	10–15	3.2	$299	72.9 (1964)
Venezuela	500	5,000	12,000	10,399	20	3.6	$803	73.9 (1969)
Guyana	?	1,500	40	714[4]	2	3.0	$244 (1968)	?
Central America								
Panama	500	1,500	1,807 (1961)	1,425	11 (1940)	3.3	$507	76.7 (1960)
Costa Rica	?	2,000[3]	1,000	1,649[6]	majority	3.5 (1960–68)	$412	84.4 (1963)

Nicaragua	50	450–600 [3]	130	1,848 [6]	20	3.4	$333	49.8 (1963)
Honduras	1	150 [3]	100	2,582	1	3.4	$226	47.3 (1961)
El Salvador	60	600–800 [3]	300	3,534	10–15	3.8	$245	49.0 (1961)
Guatemala	75	2,000	1,100	5,111	(approx) 5	2.9	$276 (1968)	37.9 (1964)
Mexico	(?)500	20,000	35,000	48,377	10	3.5	$511 (1968)	83.7 (1969)
Caribbean States								
Trinidad-Tobago	?	?	150	945	2.5	2.8 (1960–68)	$633 (1968)	88.6 (1960)
Jamaica	1,500	2,000	600 (1960)	1,865	1.1	2.3	$444	81.9 (1960)
Dominican Republic	35	1,500	280	4,012	28.1 (1950)	3.6	$238 (1968)	53.1 (1968)
Haiti	50	?	50	4,867		2.0	$81 (1968)	22.0 (1967)
Cuba	1,000	11,000	1,500	8,553	75	2.1		78 [9]
Barbados	?	?	75	238	1.1		$417 (1967)	97.4 (1960)

[1] On Argentina: Simon Weill, *Población Israelita en la República Argentina* (Buenos Aires, 1963); on other countries: Harry O. Sandberg, "The Jews of Latin America," *American Jewish Yearbook 5678*, 1917–18.

[2] Y. Lestschinsky, "America," in *Hebrew Encyclopedia*.

[3] Jacob Schatz, *Comunidades Judías en Latinoamérica* (Buenos Aires, 1952).

[4] See *Encyclopaedia Judaica* on Latin America.

[5] *United Nations Demographic Yearbook, 1970*, 22nd issue (New York, 1971).

[6] Inter-American Development Bank, *Socio-Economic Progress in Latin America*, Social Progress Trust Fund, Tenth Annual Report, 1970.

[7] See *Encyclopedia Britannica* on Latin America, 1968 edition.

[8] *United Nations Statistical Yearbook, 1970* (New York, 1971), Table 184, p. 597.

[9] *Intercom*, Vol. VIII, No. 5 (Sept.–Oct. 1966), p. 44.

Conservative and Reform congregations organized in the same period, and in the various aid organizations connected with Jewish education. Do these phenomena suggest new outlets for public activity, more suited to the values of the younger generation? It seems vital to find an answer to that question, for surely the needs and aspirations which inspired the founder generation no longer seem valid to their children.

A more decisive question, with far-reaching implications, is whether it is at all possible to lead a full Jewish life, including the national aspects of Jewish identity, on a continent where underdevelopment is intensifying nationalistic and even xenophobic emotions. According to the basic concepts of the right-wing nationalists, nationalism is anchored in each country in the cultural heritage of the nation, of which the Catholic Church, or at least the Christian religion, is an inseparable part. This argument fits well with the thinking of the common people, particularly in those countries not having large immigrant populations. While left-wing nationalism does not generally rely on these traditions, the people, even in the "countries of immigration," hardly share the secular ideologies of the leftist intellectuals.

Will the tendency to regard the cross as one of the symbols of nationality increase in the various nationalist movements? Will these nationalistic emotions engender pressure on nonconforming elements in the population? Will this pressure grow to the point of denying the rights of minority groups to national and ethnic identifications of their own?

Above and beyond the economic and social problems, and even the problem of legal status and physical security—though closely involved with them—there loom these basic questions, an awesome challenge to Jewish leadership.

Latin American Jewry at the Crossroads

Latin American Jewry is today unique in that it is the only section of the Jewish people located in a developing continent. With the exception of the remnants of the Jewish communities in the Arab countries and in Turkey and Iran, all Jews now reside in developed countries. Despite the considerable similarity to other Jewish communities (in geographical origin, occupation, and social stratification), the fate of Latin American Jewry differs because of the condition of the societies within which they live. This Jewry, then, is in the long tradition of diasporas, for the entire history of the Jewish people can be seen as a process of wandering to and fro from underdeveloped regions, and this movement certainly characterized nineteenth-century Jewish history. But in contrast to other periods and other areas, where the Jews were themselves an underdeveloped group, the Jews of Latin America presently enjoy full equality and considerable economic prosperity. Yet now, at the beginning of the 1970s, they stand at a fateful crossroads.

One way in which the majority society in Latin America may disintegrate is through violent revolution. If this should occur—and particularly if the process is protracted—the Jewish population, which is conspicuous among the middle classes, might find itself the target of special hostility. In that event, the Jews might see only one choice: to escape the landslide as fast and as well as they can. That may never happen, but it should not be regarded as impossible.

Alternatively, there may be change, even leftist change, but without major violence, or at least none directed against the Jews. In this eventuality, too, a large section of the Jewish population might feel obliged to emigrate, since a leftist regime would be likely, inter alia, to affect adversely those occupations in which Jews are concentrated. Because most of the Jewish communities are young and many of their members have already been immigrants once in their lives, they might feel a stronger desire to leave than would non-Jewish members of the same class.

Some percentage of the Jews, however, would doubtless prefer to stay and attempt to integrate in the new regime. For unlike the members of the first generation, most of whom are in commerce and industry and might see their property and function virtually destroyed by nationalization, second-generation members generally belong to the liberal professions and although they might have their rewards limited by nationalization, they could still maintain their functions and tasks. What is more, if the new regimes attempt to combat underdevelopment they will need these professional skills (this was explicitly reflected in the platform of Chile's socialist president). For many Jewish professionals, then, and particularly those with left-wing leanings, the political change may constitute a special challenge—and possibly even an opportunity for gaining access to administrative posts which they could not have attained under the previous regime.

But in 1972, with the exception of Cuba, Chile, and to a much lesser extent, Peru, most of the Latin American countries are on two different roads: that of constitutional government based on the center and the right, and that of authoritarian government based on the army and enjoying the support of the upper and middle classes. They have in common the hope that despite past failures the ruling classes will still find a way to carry out basic social reforms by evolutionary methods and the conviction that in the absence of such changes the status quo can be regarded as only a temporary solution.

In both cases the problems now facing the Jewish community will become more acute: the need to ensure the continuation of organized Jewish life, while adapting it to changing conditions within the community; the need to counteract the alienating factors which are drawing the young away from Jewish identity; the need to prepare for the long-range implications of the problems of underdevelopment for the majority societies, how to meet the upsurge of nationalism that characterizes these societies and the threat of open or veiled anti-Semitism. As minority groups residing within open societies, the Jewish communities can plan and act only on the basis of moral persuasion and a volunteering spirit. Even the success of pressure on their own members depends on their willingness to respond to these pressures.

Latin American Jewry can confront the great tasks which it faces only if there is basic improvement in two vital spheres. Each of the communities must find a political leadership and spiritual elite which, through moral authority, can influence the decisions and actions of individual Jews. Equally important, the instruments for transmitting the Jewish heritage, above all, the Jewish educational network, must be improved and adapted in scope and content to the need of creating a new generation proud of its Judaism, aware of its special position on a developing continent, and capable of acting on the inevitable consequences of that position.

The continuation of the status quo in most of the Latin American countries provides the Jewish communities with an unknown but almost certainly all-too-brief span of time to create these basic conditions. If they use that time wisely, the 1970s may prove to be a decade of well-exploited opportunity.

Part V

Jewish Rights As Human Rights

Chapter 8
International Protection of Human Rights
Sidney Liskofsky

Jews had sought and secured some international recognition and protection of their rights in the nineteenth century (at the Congresses of Vienna, 1815, and Berlin, 1878) and in the peace settlement that ended World War I (the Minorities Treaties).[1] These limited and special guarantees, however, were frequently violated, and lapsed with the collapse of the international arrangements to which they were tied. The advent of the United Nations promised protection for Jewish rights within the framework of a universal system applicable to all nations and peoples.

In substantial part, this promise owed its inspiration to the Jewish experience. The fate of the Jews at Hitler's hands was a major impetus for the decision to make the protection of human rights a principal purpose of the UN. Jews were prominent among those who, even before the UN founding conference in San Francisco, joined in publishing (in December 1944) a "Declaration of Human Rights" asserting that "an International Bill of Human Rights must be promulgated" and that "no plea of sovereignty shall ever again be allowed to permit any nation to deprive those within its borders

---

[1] C. Adler and A. M. Margalith, *With Firmness in the Right: American Diplomatic Activity Affecting Jews* (New York, 1946), pp. 115, 138–39, 165–67; M. L. Margolis and A. Marx, *A History of the Jewish People* (Philadelphia, 1941), p. 633; Hersh Lauterpacht, *An International Bill of the Rights of Man* (New York, 1945), pp. 215–24; Jacob Robinson and others, *Were the Minorities Treaties a Failure?* (New York, 1943); Rodolfo de Nova, "Human Rights and the Protection of Minorities," *Howard Law Journal*, Vol. II, No. 2 (Spring 1965), pp. 275–90.

of those fundamental rights." [2] They affirmed their belief in "the equal and inalienable rights of all members of the human family," and they assumed that the human rights of Jews would be respected and secured in the degree that the rights of all men were honored and safeguarded.

The twenty-five years since the adoption of the United Nations Charter have witnessed a vast amount of international human rights activity. Apart from the attacks on the racial policies of southern Africa, a great part of this activity has been devoted to general objectives rather than to specific situations: to the effort to formulate and achieve agreement on norms and principles and to establish institutions and processes to help realize them.

During most of this period Jews stood in the vanguard of those advocating additional human rights laws of general applicability and stronger measures of enforcement. In addition, they invoked international norms and protections in behalf of Jews suffering discrimination and persecution, chiefly in the Soviet Union and in Arab lands, and, as in the Nazi period and earlier, questions of Jewish security and rights became a constant and dramatic area of contention. Recently, however, the Jews of one country, Israel, and Jews in general by association, have found themselves in the unfamiliar role of defendant in respect to the human rights claims of another group, the Palestinians.

As the human rights activities of the United Nations proliferated, as new states were admitted and new claims asserted, a disquiet began to enter the minds of committed supporters, including Jews. Many international declarations and treaties had been adopted and a vast amount of other human rights activity had been carried on for a quarter-century, but who had been tangibly helped? The doubling and more of the UN membership had radically altered the character, program, and priorities of the organization, but how had the Charter's human rights purposes fared in the process? How had these changes affected the human rights concerns of different nations, races, and peoples, including Jews? What ought to be the goals and what are the portents for the 1970s, in the UN and international organizations generally?

---

[2] American Jewish Committee, "Protection of Human Rights," in *To the Counsellors of Peace* (New York, 1945), pp. 21–22.

The present paper cites highlights in the development of the field of international human rights since 1945, and reviews the accomplishments, difficulties, and prospects from both a general and a Jewish perspective.

International Protection Since 1945

The Political Context

International protection of human rights [3] is a political activity which cannot be isolated from the manifold other activities of international society. The authority of international norms, and the receptivity of governments to international institutions and procedures for enforcing or promoting them, depend on forces in the UN and in other international organizations that reflect to a large extent the international "system" of which they are part; the system, in turn, depends on internal developments within countries and on political, economic, and other relations among them.

The UN began as a Europe-centered organization of fifty-one members, of which only two were black African and only eight Asian. It rested on various assumptions—for example, that the member states were and would continue to be relatively stable and more or less democratic (in the Western political tradition); that they had acceptable boundaries and were content to live at peace; that any aggression would be deterred by a system of collective security; and that interstate disputes would be settled by a system cooperatively administered by the big powers.

With regard to human rights, it was assumed—or at least this was the rhetoric used—that never again would states be permitted, behind the shield of national sovereignty, to violate the fundamental rights and dignity of their people; an international bill of rights would be adopted which, as prophesied in President Harry S. Truman's closing address at the San Francisco conference, "will be as

---

[3] Human rights have not been precisely defined, and might surely include some matters often put into other categories, e.g., the laws of war, the treatment of criminal offenders, various economic and social questions. The emphasis in this review will be on activities and issues identified as human rights matters, principally in the United Nations. Even here, there are important omissions, e.g., women's rights.

much part of international life as our own Bill of Rights is part of our Constitution." [4] Human rights were conceived largely in Western terms, as in norms and principles to preserve individual liberties against governmental tyranny and to eliminate racial [5] and religious discrimination. Economic rights too were seen in terms more relevant to the developed West than to the underdeveloped regions. There was also emphasis on the right of "self-determination of peoples," though without any clear notion of its meaning or awareness of its revolutionary implications. As to implementation, there were proposals for a world court of human rights, an international criminal court, a right of individual petition, and an attorney general for human rights.

To this general ideal Jews, also chiefly in the West, gave their enthusiastic support, on the premise that "the best protection for Jews is the security of all human beings and the enforcement of their fundamental rights." [6] Apart from their plea for a Jewish national homeland in Palestine, they sought special treatment for Jews only temporarily, in the special situations of former Nazi-dominated countries. They saw no inconsistency between belief in international human rights and a Jewish homeland, though for some, commitment to the latter reflected a skepticism as to whether Jews could find security elsewhere, even in liberal Western societies.

The UN and the political world which it mirrored, as all know, changed quickly and radically. Cold war came early, then nuclear stalemate between the superpowers, and proxy conflicts and competing interventions. The Western Europe- and American-centered character of the UN was on the way out by the early 1960s. By 1970 the membership was two and one-half times as large as in 1945, and the organization differed in other fundamental respects from its original conception. Most members were located in the southern half of the globe. Ranging from primitive to moderately developed, these states were generally politically unstable and militarily weak. They comprised a large part of the world's population but enjoyed

---

[4] *The New York Times*, June 27, 1945, p. 10.

[5] The notion of race was then more broadly conceived and not, as today, centered on color differences.

[6] *To the Counsellors of Peace: Recommendations of the American Jewish Committee* (New York, 1945); *Toward Peace and Equity: Recommendations of the American Jewish Committee* (New York, 1946).

only a small share of its total wealth. Afro-Asian grievances against their former colonial rulers and against the United States were endorsed by the Communist states, which were replaced by the West in minority status in the General Assembly and other UN bodies. Encouraged by the Soviet Union, the Afro-Asian members imposed their priorities: ending western colonialism in Asia and Africa, combating white racism, promoting economic development.

The transformation of the organization modified its human rights programs as well. Human rights activities have continued and indeed expanded, but with few exceptions the dominant members, like their Western predecessors, have viewed these efforts as an adjunct to their diplomacy for particular ends, rarely as an impartial means to benefit all mankind. Whereas in the early years the Western members energetically denounced denials of freedom in the Communist countries, they exhibited little readiness to translate their professions of belief in racial equality into commitments and they resisted seeing human rights issues in continued colonialism. On the other hand, while Afro-Asian states, abetted by the Communist governments, succeeded in bringing the "group" concept of self-determination, at least its colonial aspect, under the human rights umbrella (and even in giving a degree of legitimacy to the use of force in realizing it, notably in southern Africa), they have been less than eager to encourage the organization to deal seriously with questions of individual liberty, which they view very differently than do Western states.

In addition, the Communist, Arab, and most Afro-Asian states, while eager to establish ad hoc bodies to deal with selected situations that concerned them, chiefly in southern Africa and Israel, resisted efforts to establish an effective permanent system for dealing with human rights generally, including individual liberties within all nations. They also interposed obstacles to nongovernmental uses of UN channels to draw attention to human rights violations, pressing for restrictions on these activities because they mistrusted their broader human rights perspectives. But a good deal of the progress in international protection of human rights was also a byproduct of Afro-Asian attempts to use the machinery of the organization in the struggle against the colonial powers, Rhodesia and South Africa. To that end some of them reluctantly accepted more liberal international norms and procedures than they would have liked.

Norms and Principles

The UN Charter

The UN Charter declares as one of the organization's purposes "to achieve international cooperation" in promoting respect for human rights and for fundamental freedoms for all without distinction as to race, sex, language, or religion (Article 1 [3]). Similar language is included in the Charter definitions of the functions of the General Assembly, the Economic and Social Council, and the trusteeship system, and in the purposes for which "All Members pledge themselves to take joint and separate action in cooperation with the Organization" (Articles 55, 56). The Economic and Social Council is expressly required to establish a human rights commission (Article 68).

There has been endless discussion as to the import of these provisions—what obligations they impose on member states, and what powers they give to the organization. Debate has centered in particular on what limits on UN human rights activities are implied in the provision in Article 2(7) stating that nothing in the Charter "shall authorize the United Nations to intervene in matters which are essentially within the domestic jurisdiction of any state." The questions are unresolved in principle, but the UN's practice and world moral opinion confirm that states have some international obligation in human rights matters and that the UN, correspondingly, has some authority.

In the beginning, the major Western states—including the United States, which dominated the organization—shared the Soviet Union's reluctance to establish strong implementation machinery; today the Western states appear to be more willing, while the active opposition comes from the Communist and Afro-Asian (especially Arab) states. The failure of the Western states to act when they could perhaps deprived mankind of a historic opportunity that may not soon come again, for today the "political arithmetic" of the organization is not favorable for the expansion of international jurisdiction in the field of human rights.

Understandably, no state has welcomed criticism or investigation, but some that strongly resisted scrutiny, notably the Communist and Arab states, were not inhibited from urging inquiry into the policies of their political enemies: in resisting inquiry, they invoked Article 2(7); in urging action in regard to others, they invoked the human rights provisions of the Charter. Proposals to establish institutions or procedures to deal with specific human rights problems—an office of High Commissioner for Human Rights or a meaningful procedure for dealing with nongovernmental communications—met similar reactions: opponents cited Article 2(7) and insisted that such machinery could be established only by new treaties; supporters claimed such authority was contained in the Charter's human rights provisions, though they also favored additional conventions. But advocating conventions did not necessarily signify endorsement of additional means of implementation, for some of these advocates opposed forceful implementation, while some who favored it declined to ratify the conventions that provided them. Consistency was not a requirement for participation in the human rights process in the UN.

The Universal Declaration of Human Rights

At San Francisco, some urged that the UN Charter include a bill of rights, but it soon appeared that many participating states were reluctant to assume specific legal commitment. When, soon after the Charter was adopted, the Human Rights Commission set its hand to preparing such a bill, these states again opposed a legally binding undertaking. In compromise, the Commission decided (December 1947) on a three-part bill, consisting of a nonbinding declaration, a binding covenant, and a system of implementation for the latter. Because the Declaration was generally conceived to be without legal force, and perhaps because the cold war had not yet begun, it was completed with remarkable speed: on December 10, 1948, the General Assembly adopted the Universal Declaration of Human Rights as "a common standard of achievement for all peoples and nations," to be promoted "by teaching and education" by "every individual and every organ of society." Included in the Declaration are the rights of equality, liberty, and security commonly recognized in Western countries, as well as economic and social rights stressed in socialist countries, e.g., the right to work. Of special contemporary interest in relation to Soviet Jewry are the right of everyone "to leave any country, including his own" and the freedom of everyone, "alone or in community with others and in public or private, to manifest his religion or belief in teaching, practice, worship and observance."

Though the popular view, shared by most governments, is that the Declaration is not legally binding, scholars have advanced the thesis that it has derivative legal authority as an elucidation of the undertakings in the Charter and that the uses to which it has been put over the years have given it the status of customary international law.[7] Binding or not, its influence is obvious in the actions of UN bodies, the regional inter-governmental organizations, and non-governmental groups, in the constitutions of many new nations, in statutes and decisions of old nations. Without doubt the Declaration is the high mark of the UN's achievement in human rights to date. (It has been observed about the Declaration, as about the American Bill of Rights, that if presented for adoption today, it could not be approved, surely not in its present terms.)

The Covenants and the Protocol

The next and more difficult stage of the international bill of rights took more than eighteen years to complete. The General Assembly early decided on two separate instruments, one on economic, social, and cultural rights, the other on civil and political rights. The majority considered that while civil and political rights were suitable for enforcement by adversary procedures, economic, social, and cultural achievements could be only goals rather than "rights," to be implemented only gradually by governmental and community planning. But it was not until the end of 1966 that the Assembly approved the draft Covenants, and, largely because Communist nations as well as many new Afro-Asian states resisted intrusions on their "sovereignty," the implementation provisions were greatly weakened even in the Covenant on Civil and Political Rights.[8]

That Covenant provides for reporting of violations by governments to a committee empowered to review and comment on these reports in general terms, and establishes an ad hoc conciliation com-

---

[7] Hersh Lauterpacht, *International Law of Human Rights* (London, 1950); Egon Schwelb, *Human Rights and the International Community* (New York, 1964).

[8] Draft International Covenants on Human Rights, Report of the Third Committee of the General Assembly A/6546, December 13, 1966.

mission. States were given the option, but *not* obligated, to grant to other states the right to complain of violations against them to the committee, and a right of petition for individuals and private groups was also made optional and relegated to a separate protocol. (A provision in an earlier draft giving states limited rights to proceed against violators in the International Court of Justice was eliminated in the wake of the Court's unpopular decision in the South-West Africa case.)

The Covenant on Economic and Social Rights only requires parties to report on their compliance.

Substantively, too, the Covenants reflected many compromises and included provisions which some states found objectionable. There was added, for example, a right of self-determination for "peoples," which some Western states considered inappropriate in treaties concerned with individual rights; and "peoples" being undefined, that provision, they argued, would have an unsettling effect on world order. Other Western nations were unhappy over the omission of a right to property, and they objected to the double standard in the Economic and Social Covenant under which developing nations have the right to discriminate against non-nationals in the enjoyment of economic rights. Still others, especially the United States and the United Kingdom, were troubled by the infringement on free expression in the provision requiring states to prohibit "propaganda for war" and "advocacy of national, racial or religious hatred that constitutes incitement to discrimination, hostility or violence."

When they were approved by unanimous vote in the General Assembly, spokesmen for many states asserted that the adoption of the Covenants was an event of great historical significance. But indications are that, notwithstanding the right of states to adhere with reservations, much time may elapse before they receive the number of ratifications needed to bring them into force—and even if they should enter into force, their implementation measures are so weak that it is doubtful they would be effective.

As of September 1971 the Covenants had twelve ratifications each (four Arab states—Iraq, Libya, Syria, and Tunisia; four Latin-American—Colombia, Costa Rica, Ecuador, and Uruguay; one African—Madagascar; two Communist—Bulgaria and Yugoslavia; and Cyprus), and the Optional Protocol, five (the four Latin-American states named above and Madagascar). The identity of the twelve ratifying states suggests that professed adherence to the Covenants, as to other human rights conventions, does not necessarily assure respect for human rights in practice. The United States has not signed either of the Covenants, much less seriously considered ratification.

Specialized Instruments

Early pessimism about the prospects of the Covenants encouraged the belief that quicker progress would be achieved by accumulating more limited and specialized conventions. The earliest was the Genocide Convention, adopted in 1948 simultaneously with the Universal Declaration. Designed to complement the Nuremberg Charter for war-connected "crimes against humanity," it made planned destruction of racial or religious groups in peacetime also an international crime. The Convention has been ratified by seventy-five states, not including the United States, though President Truman recommended adherence as early as July 1949 and President Nixon has recently again asked for Senate consent to ratification. Other specialized conventions adopted by the UN deal with refugees and stateless persons, women's rights, slave practices, and the elimination of racial discrimination, but an early undertaking of the General Assembly, a convention on the freedom of information, has long languished. Though not adopted under UN auspices, the four 1949 Geneva "humanitarian" conventions, designed to protect the wounded, prisoners, civilians, and other vulnerable groups in wartime, now occupy a prominent place on the UN agenda.

The Convention on Racial Discrimination [9]

In December 1962 the General Assembly requested the Human Rights Commission to prepare two sets of parallel documents, each

---

[9] Text of the International Convention on the Elimination of All Forms of Racial Discrimination (Office of Publication Information/213, reprinted from *UN Monthly Chronicle*, January 1966); Egon Schwelb, "The International Convention on the Elimination of All Forms of Racial Discrimination," *International and Comparative Law Quarterly*, October 1966, pp. 966–1068; Howard D. Coleman, "The Problem of Anti-Semitism Under the International Convention on the Elimination of All Forms of Racial Discrimination," *Human Rights Journal*, René Cassin International Institute for Human Rights, Strasbourg, France (December 1969), pp. 609–31;

comprising a declaration and a convention, on racial discrimination and religious intolerance. (A proposal to deal with racial and religious discrimination in the same instrument, as had been traditional, was rejected on the insistence of the Communist and most Afro-Asian states.) Progress on racial discrimination was rapid: a declaration was adopted in November 1963; a convention was adopted two years later and entered into force in January 1969. As of September 1971 it had fifty-three ratifications: ten Communist (including Yugoslavia), ten Latin American, eight black African, seven Arab, eleven non-Communist European, Canada, Nationalist China, India, Iran, Nepal, Pakistan, and the Philippines.

The Convention is comprehensive in outlawing various manifestations of racial and ethnic discrimination. But an effort, led by the United States and Brazil, to include a specific condemnation of anti-Se⸴ iitism was met by a Soviet-Arab amendment to condemn also "Z onism, Nazism, neo-nazism, and all other forms of the policy and ideology of colonialism, national and racial hatred and exclusiveness, etc." The Assembly decided overwhelmingly not to mention any particular manifestation of racism, though it had already included such a reference in respect to apartheid.[10] This decision was especially ironic, in that the very incentive for the Convention owed a great deal to the question of anti-Semitism, notably the concern aroused by the world-wide swastika outbreak of 1959–60.

The Convention also provides for comprehensive implementation. A committee of independent experts oversees compliance by considering governmental reports, on which it may make "suggestions and general recommendations" to the General Assembly.[11] It

---

Natan Lerner, *The UN Convention on the Elimination of All Forms of Racial Discrimination: A Commentary* (Leyden, A. W. Sifthoff, 1970), p. 132.

[10] Natan Lerner, "Debate on Anti-Semitism and Zionism in Committee III of the UN General Assembly," *International Problems* (quarterly of Israeli Institute of International Affairs), Vol. 14, Nos. 1 & 2 (January–June 1966), pp. 52–64; Roberta Cohen, "United Nations—Stand on Anti-Semitism," *Patterns of Prejudice*, Vol. 2, No. 2 (March–April 1968), Institute of Jewish Affairs, London, pp. 21–24.

[11] Kamleshwar Das, "Measures of Implementation of the International Convention on the Elimination of All Forms of Racial Discrimination with Special Reference to Provisions Concerning Reports from States Parties to the Convention," in *Human Rights Journal* (Cassin Institute), Vol. IV, Nos. 2–3 (July 1971), pp. 213–62.

may receive and consider state-to-state complaints and, if it fails to settle the disputes within a given period, must appoint, with the consent of the Parties, a conciliation commission; that commission, in turn, is required to report back with findings of fact and recommendations for a friendly solution. The Convention also provides for an optional right of individual petition (binding only on accepting states), and (following a Saudi Arabian proposal) accepting states may establish or designate a national body to consider such petition before allowing the petitioner to have international recourse. States may also bring to the World Court questions of "interpretation or application" of the Convention.

The committee of experts, the first body established to oversee the implementation of a human rights convention adopted under UN auspices, is in operation; but it does not yet have authority to consider individual petitions; there have not yet been the ten adherences necessary to bring that optional procedure into effect.[12]

To date the committee has not received any state complaints, but its early handling of governmental reports has not escaped criticism. Though chosen as independent experts, some committee members were in fact members of permanent missions to the UN and behaved like official representatives. In the main, the reports were checked for compliance with formal requirements but not scrutinized for veracity. Seizing on a technicality, the Arab and Communist members persuaded the committee to dwell at length on alleged Israeli wrongs, even though Israel, like the United States, was not a party to the Convention. Some observers expect that the committee's performance will improve as its members are rotated and as it learns to navigate the uncertain waters of state sensitivity to "interference" in domestic affairs. Others are less hopeful.

Efforts to Deal with Religious Intolerance [13]

The Human Rights Commission began to work on a declaration on religious intolerance in 1964, but put it aside and began to draft

---

[12] As of December 1971 only Uruguay had agreed to give the committee this authority.

[13] E/8330, July 6, 1971, note by Secretary General to General Assembly (XXVI); Sidney Liskofsky, "Eliminating Intolerance and Discrimination Based on Religion or Belief," *Reports on the Foreign Scene* (published by the American Jewish Committee), February 1968.

a convention. By 1967 it had agreed on a preamble and twelve substantive articles, but due to lack of time and—the real reason—division of opinion, it could not complete the task. Considering the Commission's work in 1967, the General Assembly amended the title of the Convention to reflect the insistence of Communist and some other states (e.g., Mexico) that it equally protect nonreligious belief. Again, the Assembly eliminated mention of anti-Semitism as an example of prejudice leading to religious intolerance and discrimination when the Arabs proposed adding Nazism, Zionism, and fascism as other examples.

The Assembly has not returned to this agenda item, engendering the suspicion that it will languish indefinitely. Religious bodies and other original supporters are disinclined to press for resumption of work on the draft convention lest the resulting document contain an antireligious bias, as portended by the already approved preamble. They anticipate harsh treatment by the Communist states and their allies of other provisions in the Commission's draft, particularly Article 3, on which Jewish groups place high importance: that article requires states to insure to religious groups and adherents of other beliefs the freedom of worship and assembly and to protect their freedom to teach and learn sacred doctrine and languages, to publish religious books and train religious personnel, to maintain charitable and educational institutions, and to participate in local, national, and international associations. Some of the original supporters would prefer that the Assembly turn its attention to the as yet untainted declaration, while others prefer an altogether fresh start in dealing with the subject.

ILO and UNESCO Conventions

Specialized agencies of the UN have also adopted human rights instruments. The activities of the International Labor Organization indeed long antedate those of the UN. Since its birth after World War I it has promoted more than 130 conventions and recommendations, some on specific subjects (e.g., seafarers' pensions), others of broad human rights import (e.g., forced labor, the right of labor to organize, discrimination in employment).

The ILO constitution requires member states to report not only on their compliance with ILO conventions to which they are parties, but also on their conformity to those they have not ratified and even to "recommendations" of the ILO General Conference. Members (including the Soviet Union) generally report, and a committee of experts scrutinizes these reports and pursues evidence of inadequate performance. Private complaints and governmental replies are also reviewed by the committee of experts and cited in its public reports.

The constitution provides for a right of state-to-state complaint to the ILO's governing body and of any member of a state's tripartite delegation—government, labor, and employer representatives—to complain to this body that a member state (even a nonratifying one) is not conforming to a convention. The governing body may also initiate a complaint on its own motion and may designate a commission of inquiry to study complaints and make recommendations. If either party to a dispute rejects the body's recommendations, the other may bring the case to the World Court. The International Labor Conference (the ILO's plenary body) is authorized to take action to secure compliance with the inquiry commission's recommendations as well as with the court's judgment.

The ILO has special procedures for examining complaints in respect to trade union rights, employment discrimination, apartheid, and forced labor, and it has sent visiting missions to inquire into conditions in many countries, including South Africa, Spain, Greece, and the USSR.

Overall, other than recourse to the World Court, the ILO's highly sophisticated implementation machinery has been extensively and effectively used. However, one investigator has concluded from a case study of its record in the area of freedom of association that countries respond positively to adverse decisions inversely to their need for international supervision.[14]

The Educational, Scientific, and Cultural Organization (UNESCO) too has adopted human rights conventions, notably on discrimination in education. The UNESCO constitution provides measures for implementing conventions and recommendations adopted under its auspices. In the case of its Convention Against Discrimination in Education, a special protocol (1962) provides additional implementation, including a permanent good of-

---

[14] Ernest B. Haas, *Human Rights and International Action: The Case of Freedom of Association* (Stanford University Press, 1970).

fices commission of independent experts to receive complaints and try to settle interstate disputes.

Special Declarations and Developing Rights

The UN has also dealt with particular problems in nonbinding declarations, either because the subject was not considered suitable for a legal instrument, or to enable states unwilling to bind themselves legally to accept at least a "moral" obligation, or as a step toward a later convention. There are such declarations on the rights of children, discrimination against women, territorial asylum, independence for colonial countries and peoples, and permanent sovereignty over natural wealth and resources. But work on other principles stemming from studies of the Human Rights Commission and its Subcommission on Discrimination and Minorities—e.g., freedom of religion, freedom from unjust arrest and detention, and the right to emigrate—has been repeatedly postponed.

On the other hand, new draft principles on equality in the administration of justice and revision of the 1949 Geneva Conventions are under study. The 1968 General Assembly expressed concern over the potentially harmful effects on human rights of recent scientific and technological developments, citing as examples the impact of recording techniques on "respect for the privacy of individuals and the integrity and sovereignty of nations," the impact of advances in medicine and biochemistry on the "protection of the human personality and its physical and intellectual integrity," and the impact of electronics on the "rights of the people." The Assembly called on the Secretary General to study these with the help of other UN agencies, and considered that the subject required continuing interdisciplinary study "which may serve as a basis for drawing up appropriate standards." Though this resolution was adopted unanimously, ideological and political controversy has already appeared in debates on these subjects.

Implementation Under United Nations Protection Machinery

The Record to Date

Though the legal quality of the UN Charter's human rights provisions has never been agreed on, and members have resisted proposals that the UN establish general machinery to protect human rights in all countries, UN organs have frequently considered human rights conditions in particular countries.[15] In the UN's early days most of the cases, taken up mainly at the behest of Western members, involved political rights, including the right to representative government (e.g., Spain, 1946; Czechoslovakia, 1948; Hungary, 1956). With the growth of Communist and Afro-Asian influence, that type of case was no longer raised, and complaints focused principally on ending colonialism and combating racial discrimination.

The UN helped end Western colonialism in Asia and Africa but failed to consider Soviet and other domination of territorially contiguous peoples, or the claims of intrastate minorities—e.g., Kurds in Iraq, Nagas in India, Chinese in Indonesia, Ibos in Nigeria—or other human rights violations within the borders of those states. It dwelled on white discrimination in southern Africa and recently on alleged violations by Israel of Arab rights in the occupied territories, but attention to other alleged discriminations was only intermittent and fleeting. Racial and ethnic discrimination in the Communist countries or within the "third world" received minimal attention. Nor was there even much inclination to inquire into racial or other human rights conditions in the United States and other Western countries, though occasionally Communist or Arab representatives would indulge in hit-and-run charges, usually in retaliation for failure to vote as they wished or for critical pronouncements on their countries.

UN resolutions concerning particular situations have varied, some merely noting and expressing concern, others deploring or condemning. Some resolutions recommended that the situation be corrected, while others (relating mainly to southern Africa) called for punitive measures, such as ending diplomatic and commercial relations, expulsion from the UN and the specialized agencies, even the use of armed force. In some instances there were studies, investigations or reports by special committees or ad hoc expert groups.

Though there was not enough support for establishing permanent machinery to look into human rights violations, and though not taken up formally, violations in particular countries were frequently

---

[15] Evan Luard, "Promotion of Human Rights by the UN Political Bodies," pp. 133–59, in Evan Luard, ed., *The International Protection of Human Rights* (New York, Praeger, 1967).

spotlighted in the course of debates on other questions: Iran criticizing Iraqi maltreatment of its Iranian minority; the political situation in Haiti; Communist and some Western states commenting on political repression in Greece; Pakistanis alluding to anti-Moslem discrimination in India and Indians to genocide in Bangla Desh; and the Soviets attacking racism in the United States and the United Kingdom.

Efforts to Strengthen Human Rights Machinery [16]

Failure to develop adequate machinery for dealing with violations within the framework of conventions has spurred some governments and nongovernmental groups to seek to have machinery established under the UN Charter's authority.

The Charter expressly provides for a right of petition in relation to trust territories, and especially in the early years, the Trusteeship Council received many petitions from individuals and private groups, granted hearings, and sent visiting missions. These precedents were later extended to UN bodies concerned with other dependent territories, notably to the Assembly's Committee on Colonialism. They were extended also to a wholly independent country, South Africa, by the Assembly's newly established Special Committee on Apartheid. But despite the precedents they established, the Afro-Asian states, supported by the Communists, have opposed Western efforts to give the UN the capacity to deal with human rights violations everywhere by means of generally applicable procedures.[17]

After years of wrangling, however, there was agreement in the Economic and Social Council (ECOSOC) in May 1970 on a procedure for dealing with human rights complaints ("communications") from private individuals and groups. It authorized the Subcommission on Discrimination, on the recommendation of a five-

---

[16] John Carey, *UN Protection of Civil and Political Rights*, Vol. 8 in the Procedural Aspects of International Law Series (Syracuse University Press, 1970).

[17] E/4647, May 7, 1969; press release, ECOSOC/2628–73, May 15–June 3, 1969; E/SR 1580–1595, May 19–June 3, 1969; Sidney Liskofsky, "The UN Reviews Its NGO System," *Reports on the Foreign Scene* (published by the American Jewish Committee), January 1970; press release, ECOSOC/2801–2814, February 10–20, 1970; press release, ECOSOC/2902–2903, May 27, 1970; E/INF/117, July 28, 1971.

member working group, to bring to the attention of the Human Rights Commission those complaints which "appear to reveal a consistent pattern of gross and reliably attested violations," including racial discrimination and apartheid in colonial and dependent countries. The Commission would decide whether it should undertake a thorough study or, with the consent of the government concerned, arrange for an investigation and submit a report and recommendations to the Council.

After further challenges, chiefly from the Communist members, the Subcommission in August 1971 advanced the procedure another important step by agreeing on criteria for the admissibility of complaints. On their face, these criteria are not overly restrictive, though a majority on its working group wishing to block consideration of a particular case could render the procedure useless.

Proposal for a United Nations High Commissioner [18]

Since 1965 the United Nations has had before it a proposal for a UN High Commissioner for Human Rights, modeled partly on the highly regarded UN High Commissioner for Refugees. Over determined Soviet opposition, the Human Rights Commission recommended that the General Assembly establish the office within the UN framework, with the necessary independence and prestige; that the holder of the office maintain "close relations" with the relevant UN organs and specialized agencies and assist them, as well as member states, "upon their request"; that he have access to the communications addressed to the UN and be empowered to present appropriate ones to the Assembly on developments in human rights; and that he be assisted by a panel of expert advisers drawn from the several geographic regions and legal systems appointed by the Secretary General in consultation with him.

---

[18] A/8333, August 20, 1971, note by Secretary General to General Assembly (XXVI); R. St. J. MacDonald, "The United Nations High Commissioner for Human Rights," *Canadian Yearbook of International Law 84,* 1967; Roger S. Clark, "The Proposed High Commissioner for Human Rights" (Martinus Nyhoff, the Hague, 1972); A/8231 (1970), containing Report of General Assembly's Third Committee 1970 Debate on the High Commissioner; Report of the Working Group to Study the Proposal to Create the Institution of a United Nations High Commissioner for Human Rights (Salvador P. Lopez, chairman-rapporteur), E/CN4/934, February 8, 1967.

Supporters of the proposal for a High Commissioner, mainly Western states, a fair number of the "third world" countries, and most nongovernmental organizations (NGOs), view the job as mainly promotional. They envisage that the Commissioner would encourage states to ratify conventions and declarations, and in other ways serve as catalyst for the creation of conventional and customary international law on human rights. He would assist UN bodies in improving their procedures for dealing with reports and in conducting fact-finding or good office missions. He would bring significant communications received by UN bodies to the attention of the states concerned, and by "quiet persuasion"—and perhaps ultimately by publicity—bring about policy changes.

The Commission's recommendation was endorsed by ECOSOC in June 1967 and transmitted to the Assembly, but the effort to take it up in 1970 was prevented by a Soviet-led filibuster. In the brief Assembly debate on the subject in 1971 the Soviet Union reiterated its arguments that the proposal was illegal and that existing implementation machinery was adequate, and declared it would not cooperate with the office if it were established. Some delegates stated that they supported the proposal in principle but felt that it was impolitic to adopt it while so many countries were opposed. (Poland suggested that perhaps it should be tried first experimentally on the regional level.) In view of the vehement opposition of the Soviet Union and of Arab and other Afro-Asian states, and the lukewarm support of others, the portents for speedy approval are not favorable.[19] As with other proposals for implementation, some who support the proposal publicly express private doubts as to its feasibility or effectiveness in the present international climate.

Communications to the UN Information Centers

Over many years there has grown an informal procedure of private petition, as individuals increasingly sent complaints of human

---

[19] Action on the proposal was postponed again at the 1971 General Assembly. A procedural resolution intended to give "highest priority" to consideration of it in 1972, "with a view to the possibility of its conclusion," was amended to eliminate the expression of urgency and to postpone further consideration to 1973. Even this weakened resolution was adopted by a disappointing vote of 52–40–25. A/C.3/SR 1900–1901 (December 8–9, 1971); A/8594 (Third Committee Report, December 15, 1971); A/PV.2025, p. 62.

rights violations to the various UN Information Centers, which in turn transmitted them to the UN Headquarters. In 1969, in response to protests from the Soviet Union after a group of citizens had attempted to forward a petition through the center in Moscow, the Secretary General directed the fifty-one Information Centers throughout the world to discontinue the practice. Regret over the Secretary General's action was expressed by a number of governments, and many NGOs protested.[20]

Education and Promotion

Least controversial have been the UN's promotional and educational activities, intended to contribute to greater sensitivity and community of values in human rights. The Advisory Services program, instituted by the General Assembly in 1953, includes expert services, which are little used, and fellowships and seminars, which are very active.[21] Regional as well as world-wide seminars, attended by governmental nominees serving in personal capacities as well as by nongovernmental observers, have been held at the invitation of host governments in many countries in all regions. They have dealt with women's rights, apartheid, multinational societies, protection of human rights in criminal procedure, and remedies for abuse of administrative authority. Some of the seminars have produced proposals subsequently pursued by the UN bodies, as on the right of arrested persons to communicate with those necessary for their defense and on measures to combat apartheid in South Africa. However, at the 1971 seminar (in Nice, with the French government as host) on the dangers of "intolerance in all its forms and the search for ways of preventing and combating it," the Soviet-Arab bloc injected the anti-Zionist motif so vehemently that it proved impossible to conclude with the consensus customary in the final report.

The UN also publishes a *Yearbook on Human Rights*, and there are human rights publications by the Office of Public Information. Most important are studies of special problems, many serving as a basis for the formulation of conventions and recommendations, e.g., the Human Rights Commission's study on the right to be free from

---

[20] R. B. Lillich, "The UN and Human Rights Complaints: U Thant as Strict Constructionist," *American Journal of International Law*, Vol. 63, No. 3 (July 1970), pp. 610–14.

[21] United Nations Program of Advisory Services in the Field of Human Rights, OPI/403–08074–May 1971–10M, January 20, 1967.

arbitrary arrest, detention, and exile and the right of arrested persons to communicate, and the Subcommission on Discrimination studies on discrimination in education (in cooperation with UNESCO) and employment (in cooperation with ILO), and on political rights, religious rights and practices, the right of emigration and travel, slavery, children born out of wedlock, administration of justice, and its recent comprehensive study of racial discrimination in political, economic, social, and cultural matters. In August 1971 the Subcommission decided to undertake studies of minorities and genocide.

While some studies are less balanced and incisive than others, and some are more daring than others in citing specific situations in named countries, overall they reveal an impressive degree of consensus on fundamental principle, and despite the difficult task of reconciling ideological and political differences, they represent important contributions to the clarification and advancement of human rights. One of them, the study on the right of emigration, has served as virtual scripture for supporters of the right of Soviet Jews to emigrate. Other studies, surveys, and publications on human rights problems, with heavy emphasis on racial issues, have been sponsored by UNESCO, ILO, and UNITAR (UN Training and Research Institute).

Another UN educational activity has been human rights "observance," such as the major one held during the International Year for Human Rights (1968). 1971 was the International Year for Action to Combat Racism and Racial Discrimination, with states, UN bodies, specialized agencies, regional organizations, and national and international NGOs invited to participate. Activities recommended included appeals, evaluative studies, seminars, publications, displays, ratification of conventions, revision of school curricula, cultural exchanges, establishment of national committees, and mass media programs.

The Nongovernmental Organizations at the United Nations [22]

The UN Charter's provision for a consultative relationship between the Economic and Social Council and nongovernmental organizations has produced a great deal of value for human rights.

---

[22] See note 17.

(NGOs also maintain consultative and cooperating relationships with UNESCO, ILO, and other specialized agencies, and with the regional organizations, especially the Council of Europe.)

NGOs have proposed UN conventions or declarations, suggested wording for such instruments, labored for their adoption and ratification, disseminated information about them, proposed studies and supplied ideas and information for them, and participated in UN educational activities. They have met frequently in cooperating committees, occasionally agreeing on joint statements for presentation to UN bodies, e.g., statements endorsing the proposal for a High Commissioner of Human Rights, protesting the Secretary General's ruling proscribing the transmittal of petitions by UN Information Centers, condemning aerial hijacking and hostage taking and proposing remedial measures, and affirming the right of emigration. Generally, there has been among most NGOs considerable sympathy for the concerns of Jews, though some, especially those with a pro-Communist or pro-Arab political leaning, have been disinterested or even actively hostile.

Inevitably, the activities of NGOs have sometimes impinged on the interests or politics of member states and incurred their resentment, especially when an NGO gave information or expressed opinions critical of a particular government. The United States and other Western governments have generally reacted mildly to criticism; the Soviet Union and the Arab countries, and certain other Afro-Asian states, have reacted sharply and have attacked the accusers and the NGO system as being politically motivated.

Until recently, ECOSOC and its NGO Committee, which establishes standards and passes on applications for NGO status, was Western-dominated: in 1955 the only non-Western member of the Committee was the USSR; by 1969 the West was a minority. In 1967, with Soviet-Arab encouragement, ECOSOC launched a review of the NGO system, ostensibly to investigate charges of infiltration by the Central Intelligence Agency; but the fundamental motivation of some members was hostility to the NGO concept itself and a desire to cripple the NGOs' right to criticize governments. In this review the critical spotlight was constantly focused on organizations specializing in human rights and on religious organizations, mainly Jewish and Catholic. Jewish organizations were charged with having divided loyalties and operating as "professional lobbyists" for Israel; collaborating with South Africa; poisoning the UN atmosphere by their charges that Jewish rights are violated in the Soviet Union; impeding the anticolonial struggle; seeking to destroy cultural relations between the United States and Arab nations; attacking black militants for their sympathy with Arab causes; considering Jews a superior race; and being interested only in promoting Jewish interests and therefore not qualifying under the NGO rules which require concern for the human rights of all people.

Behind the attacks on the Jewish organizations was resentment of their efforts to draw attention to anti-Jewish discrimination and other human rights violations in the Soviet Union, of their support of Israel, and of their publicizing the persecution of Jewish minorities in Arab countries. The Soviet-Arab bloc sought to establish that support of Israel should disqualify an NGO from the UN system.

African criticism against many NGOs was based on their failure to undertake more forceful programs against South Africa's racial policies, and, in general, several African and Asian states shared the Communist view that the NGO system is a Western institution in which they have no stake.

In 1969–70 Jewish NGOs faced efforts to expel them from the NGO system and have since been discouraged from intervening as often or as vigorously as in the past on behalf of specific Jewish concerns. While general human rights organizations have been less vulnerable to attack, following the ECOSOC review they too have exhibited timidity in the use of the formal procedures to comment critically on the policies of specific countries. The International Commission of Jurists, however, was heard by the Subcommission on Discrimination without interruption when its spokesman charged genocide in East Pakistan, and the World Muslim Congress and the Communist World Federation of Trade Unions have been permitted to attack Israeli practices in the occupied territories.

Despite the harassment of the NGOs specializing in human rights, none had its accreditation revoked and the system has remained intact. (Soviet-Arab efforts to delete references to the role of "NGOs in consultative status" in UN resolutions have usually failed, though recently it has become customary to add qualifying words intended to communicate a warning—namely, [NGOs] "which have acted in good faith without political motivation." [23]) Moreover, they are included in the new ECOSOC complaint system as an acceptable source of information concerning human rights violations. UN resolutions continue to call on NGOs for help in achieving human rights objectives; the Secretariat circulates their statements and reports their activities; and delegates, including non-Western ones, frequently commend their role and affirm their importance.

Jews, Israel, and Zionism

Jewish Rights in United Nations Human Rights Forums

Jewish rights in the Arab countries and in the Soviet Union have never appeared formally on UN agendas but have often been discussed under general items. The United States, joined by Costa Rica and several other Latin American countries and by West European and Commonwealth nations, has frequently criticized the harassment of Soviet Jews, especially those applying for permission to emigrate. Israel has led a vigorous attack on the Soviet policy of persecution and compulsory assimilation of Jews and has also exposed the tragic situation of Jews remaining in Iraq, Libya, the UAR, and Syria.

These charges provoked vehement rebuttals and counterattacks by the Soviet Union and other Communist states as well as by Arab delegates. The Soviet-Arab bloc charged that Israel raised the issue of Jewish emigration from the USSR as part of a Zionist campaign against socialist states and to obscure its aggressive policies in the Middle East, and get Soviet workers for its economy. They charged that Israel (and Zionist leaders) exploited Jews by wrongly claiming "that a Jewish nation existed which united Jews throughout the world" and in fact tried to instigate anti-Semitism. The Soviet representatives denied that there has been any anti-Semitism in the USSR since the 1917 revolution and insisted that the diminution of Jewish culture was due only to lack of interest by the Jews themselves. While some Jews might wish to emigrate to Israel and would

---

[23] A/8542, December 2, 1971, Report of the Third Committee of the General Assembly, pp. 7, 54.

be permitted to do so in the future, it was not now feasible because of the state of war in the Middle East.[24]

To the challenge to their right to speak for the Jews of other countries, Israel's representatives have responded that they do not claim to represent Jews everywhere but speak only on behalf of the "Jews of silence." They contend that the UN Charter's human rights provisions entitle them to do so, and even impose the responsibility, since no other government can be expected to speak with sufficient knowledge and vigor on Jewish questions and since there is no UN machinery for dealing impartially with human rights denials in all countries.

With the Soviet-Jewish question partly in mind, Western countries sponsored a resolution at the 1970 General Assembly affirming the need for "full respect for the national and cultural identity of peoples or distinct ethnic groups" and condemning all forms of racial discrimination "wherever they may occur." Though formulated in general terms, this resolution was adopted by a relatively narrow margin, the principal opposition coming from the Soviet-Arab bloc, which contended—as these states often did in opposing human rights measures of general applicability—that it diluted the emphasis on southern Africa. The supporting vote included, in addition to the West, most of Latin America and a large group of Afro-Asian states.[25] (Ironically, earlier, in the drafting of the Universal Declaration and the Genocide Convention, it was the Soviet Union which had argued forcefully for provisions safeguarding minority cultures and the Western nations which had opposed them.)

Largely as a result of Israel's initiative, and notwithstanding the unfavorable balance of forces and the generally unfriendly climate in the UN organization, the Jewish situation in the Soviet Union and Arab countries has received more attention than most other human rights situations except anti-black discrimination in southern Africa and alleged violations of Arab rights by Israel—more, for example, than political repression in Greece, anti-Moslem violence in India, massacres of Bengalis in East Pakistan, and mass killing of Ibos in Nigeria, of southern blacks by northern Arabs in the Sudan, and of Chinese by Moslems in Indonesia.

---

[24] Report of the 27th Session of the Commission of Human Rights, February 22–March 26, 1971, Geneva (E/4949; E/CN 4/1069).

[25] Resolutions of the General Assembly at its 25th Regular Session, 1970 (GA/4355).

Israel in United Nations Human Rights Forums

During the UN's first two decades Arab-Israeli issues were dealt with mainly in the General Assembly and the Security Council, as political questions. Following the June 1967 war, Arab grievances against Israel were injected into many other spheres of UN activity, especially those concerned with human rights (apparently as part of a strategy launched at the International Conference on Human Rights in Teheran [26] in the spring of 1968). The Arab attacks have extended to Israel's friends and supporters, especially the United States, and to Zionist and other Jewish organizations. The Arabs have had the backing of the Communists and many Afro-Asian states; Israel had occasional help from the United States and several West European, Latin American, and black African nations, though many preferred to avoid unpleasantness by staying on the sidelines and abstaining rather than voting negatively on Arab-sponsored resolutions.

The Soviet-Arab strategy has utilized all opportunities to attack not only particular laws and policies of Israel—its immigration and nationality laws, religion-state laws, treatments of Arabs, occupation policies—but its very legitimacy as a state. It has linked Israel with South Africa and with colonialism, and depicted it as hostile to the aspirations of the colored races and to liberation movements. Thus the 1970 General Assembly approved by a substantial vote an Arab resolution condemning "Governments that deny the right of self-determination of peoples recognized as being entitled to it, especially the peoples of Southern Africa and Palestine," and affirming the legitimacy of the struggle of peoples under colonial domination "to restore to themselves that right by any means at their disposal." (The reference to "Palestine" was retained on a special vote in which the combined "nays" and abstentions exceeded by thirteen the forty-seven "yeas"; almost all the Western and Latin American states and most of the black African nations either voted against that reference or abstained.[27])

The Soviet-Arab axis also sought to insert into general resolutions

---

[26] Final Act of the International Conference on Human Rights, Teheran, April 22–May 13, 1968, A/Conf. 32/41, *American Journal of International Law*, Vol. 62, No. 3 (July 1969), pp. 508–26.

[27] See note 25.

or conventions wording designed to encompass alleged Israeli practices: for example, the Nuremberg definition of "crimes against humanity" (in the Convention on the Non-Applicability of Statutory Limitations to War Crimes and Crimes Against Humanity) was amended by adding the words, "eviction by armed attack or occupation" (after the phrase "inhuman acts resulting from the policy of apartheid" suggested by the Africans).

In general, it has been nearly impossible recently for anyone in any UN body to comment on a matter pertaining to Jews, even if unrelated to the Middle East, without Arab intrusion to divert the discussion to Israeli and Zionist wrongs.

Israel's occupation of Arab territories has been an especially attractive target. A few days after the June 1967 war the Security Council adopted a resolution recommending that the governments concerned respect the humanitarian principles of the 1949 Geneva Conventions governing the treatment of prisoners of war and "the protection of civilian persons in time of war." On the authority of this resolution the Secretary General appointed a special representative with instructions to inquire into the condition of Arabs in Israeli-occupied territories as well as of Jewish minorities in Arab countries. Although Syria at first cooperated informally with the special representative, it soon joined the UAR in denying that the resolution applied to the Jewish minorities. In September 1968 the Security Council formally restricted the special representative's mandate to the "Arab territories under military occupation by Israel." [28]

The Arab states then began systematically to extend their anti-Israel maneuvers into the UN human rights bodies in emulation of what the Africans had done earlier in relation to South Africa. The spring 1968 Teheran Conference had requested the General Assembly to appoint a special committee to investigate human rights violations in the occupied territories, and the Human Rights Commission "to keep the matter under constant review." [29] From this initiative stemmed two special investigations, under the auspices of the General Assembly and the Human Rights Commission respectively. Israel refused to cooperate with either of them on the grounds that they were biased in purpose, improperly initiated, and

[28] Nigel S. Rodley, "The United Nations and Human Rights in the Middle East," *Social Research*, Vol. 38, No. 2 (Summer 1971), pp. 217–40.

[29] Teheran proclamation and resolutions; see note 26.

prejudicially conducted and that they failed to inquire also into the situation of Jews in Arab countries.

The Assembly's special committee to investigate Israeli practices in the occupied territories was narrowly authorized in 1968 by one vote more than the combined "nays" and abstentions, indeed (in view of some absences) by a minority of the membership. To this committee were elected, in a disputed procedure, Yugoslavia and Somalia with Ceylon as chairman, none of which had diplomatic relations with Israel. After delays the committee moved rapidly in the spring of 1970 and prepared a report based on oral testimony taken at hearings in Europe, the Middle East, and New York and on written submissions mainly from Arab sources. The report concluded that Israel was violating the human rights of the Arab population in the occupied territories, as well as the Fourth Geneva Convention, and recommended that it unilaterally withdraw from the territories, since human rights were violated by the very fact of the occupation. The Assembly (again by minority action, the combined "nays" and abstentions exceeding the "yeas") endorsed the committee's conclusions and recommendations and called on it to continue its investigation.[30]

Due to the delay in the activation of the Assembly's investigation, Israel's occupation policies were also examined by a working group of experts appointed by the Human Rights Commission in the spring of 1969 (by 13 to 1 [Israel], with 16 abstentions). The membership of the working group was identical with that previously assigned the task of investigating maltreatment of prisoners and infringement of trade union rights in South Africa. Its first report, based mainly on Arab sources, concluded that though most of the complaints received related to the period immediately following the June 1967 hostilities, and though evidence for the subsequent period was inconclusive, it was the "opinion" that Geneva Convention violations had occurred, especially in Israeli security measures.

At the Commission's 1970 session the Arabs amplified their charges, rejecting various qualifications included in the report and proposing a resolution which cited as findings what the report had characterized as "allegations." The adoption of the resolution (again, a minority action) was based exclusively on the affirmative

---

[30] See note 25.

votes of the Arab and other Moslem states and the Communist states, plus India; the majority, including all the black African, Latin American, and even some Asian states, abstained or declined to participate. But, though the vote was a "moral" defeat for the Arabs, the resolution was approved because the majority did not dare vote against it, and thus added to the UN record of condemnations of Israel, this time in a human rights context.[31]

While member nations differ as to whether ad hoc investigative bodies should function as quasi-judicial entities or only as fact finders, few were unaware of the political character of both bodies investigating Israel's occupation policies. Observers have criticized them as faulty on many grounds: that their members consisted of representatives of states having unfriendly relations with Israel rather than of independent experts; that they were not independent of the organs that created them; that they did not examine the admittedly one-sided evidence presented to them; that they led witnesses and failed to cross-examine them properly; that they conducted the hearings loosely, members often being absent; that the hearings were held in locations not conducive to objectivity; and that the conclusions and recommendations were not strictly related to the evidence.[32]

But though these investigations were unfair and unpleasant to Israel, they might serve as precedents for future inquiries into other situations: for the first time compliance with the Geneva Conventions was made the subject of an investigation by an international body with human rights jurisdiction; and for virtually the first time human rights investigations were mandated without the consent of the state concerned. (The investigations by the Trusteeship Council and the Assembly's Colonialism Committee concerned non-self-governing territories which were held to be outside the exclusive

---

[31] The resolution also gave the working group a mandate to continue its investigation. A similar debate took place at the commission's 1971 session in connection with the working group's follow-up report. Reports of the 26th and 27th sessions of the Commission on Human Rights, February 24–March 27, 1970, New York (E/4816, E/CN 4/1039), and February 22–March 26, 1971, Geneva (E/4949; E/CN–4/1069).

[32] John C. Bender, Ad Hoc Committees and Human Rights Investigations: "A Comparative Case Study in the Middle East"; Rodley, *op. cit.*, pp. 241–67; Felix Ermacora, "International Inquiry Commissions in the Field of Human Rights," *Human Rights Journal* (Cassin International Institute for Human Rights, Strasbourg, France), Vol. I, No. 2 (June 1968), pp. 180–218.

jurisdiction of the metropolitan states. Even in the case of South
Africa, which refused its consent and is unquestionably a metropolitan territory, the resolutions mandating investigation of its practices were justified on the argument that the situations in that
country threatened peace, overriding the UN Charter's domestic
jurisdiction limitation.[33])

Anti-Semitism and Zionism

Arab spokesmen (and their Communist allies) in the United Nations have asserted that while they abhor Zionism, they are friendly
toward Jews. Israeli delegates respond that the distinction between
anti-Zionism and anti-Semitism is a tactic and that the former is
but a euphemism for the latter. Of course, emotional, ideological,
and material interdependence between Israel and Jews elsewhere
makes it difficult to draw subtle distinctions, even for Arabs who
might be inclined to do so (and they exist, though silenced by the
shrill mood of the Arab world).

The wide compass of Soviet-Arab hostility to Zionism, both
theme and fervor overlapping into anti-Semitism, was displayed in
their campaign to exclude a condemnation of anti-Semitism from
conventions on the elimination of racial discrimination and religious intolerance. Anti-Zionist and anti-Semitic attitudes combined
also in ECOSOC's NGO review (1967–70), in which the main
targets of the Soviet-Arab bloc were the World Jewish Congress
and the Coordinating Board of Jewish Organizations. Though
neither Israel nor Zionist organizations played a conspicuous role
in conceiving or promoting the idea of a UN High Commissioner
for Human Rights, Soviet and Arab spokesmen insinuated that it
was intended that the office would serve as an instrument of Zionism's sinister design.[34]

Toward the end of 1971 the heated exchanges between Israel and
the Soviet-Arab bloc boiled over. Angered by Israel's adamant negotiating position and by the harassment of Soviet and certain Arab
UN mission and diplomatic personnel by the Jewish Defense League,
Arabs and Communists employed invective bordering on explicit
anti-Semitism—as in their repeated use of distorted analogies be-

---

[33] Rodley, *op. cit.*
[34] Statement of Soviet delegate in A/C.3/SR1900–1901 (December
8–9, 1971).

tween the biblical "chosen people" concept and the Nazi "superior race" doctrine. The invective reached such a level that observers were asking whether the UN itself was not becoming a platform for dissemination of the very hatred which its own resolutions had condemned and which the Convention on the Elimination of Racial Discrimination expressly forbade.

Regional Human Rights Systems

It has been commonly accepted that regional systems for the protection of human rights could be more effective than a global system because their members tend to share a common heritage of political traditions as well as common ethnic, linguistic, religious, and other cultural characteristics. Such regional systems have existed for many years in Western Europe and Latin America. In 1967 the UN Human Rights Commission commended regional human rights commissions "within or outside the UN system." [35] During the debate the following year, however, the Communist states made clear their opposition to a human rights system for Eastern Europe. India opposed one for Asia, and the Philippines was the only Asia-Pacific state to support it (though it had been endorsed by a conference of lawyers from the Asia-Pacific region convened by the Ceylon section of the International Commission of Jurists).[36]

An Arab Commission on Human Rights was established several years ago by the League of Arab States, and the idea of an African system received considerable support at UN regional seminars in Dakar (1966) and Cairo (1969).[37] But the consensus at Cairo was that any African commission should have only educational functions. In the UN Commission on Human Rights, the sponsors of a resolution endorsing the conclusions of the Cairo seminar success-

---

[35] Report of 23rd Session of Commission on Human Rights, February 20–March 23, 1967, Geneva (E/4322; E/CN/4/940).

[36] Report of the 24th Session of Commission on Human Rights, February 5–March 12, 1968 (E/4475; E/CN–4/972).

[37] UN Seminar on the Establishment of Regional Commissions on Human Rights with Particular Reference to Africa, Cairo, September 2–15, 1969 (Council of Europe doc. H[69]12, Strasbourg, September 18, 1969); A. H. Robertson, "Commission on Human Rights for Africa," *Human Rights Journal* (Cassin Institute), Vol. II, No. 4 (December 1969), pp. 696–702.

fully blocked an amendment emphasizing the role of regional commissions in realizing the standards of the Universal Declaration and other UN human rights instruments.[38] The Arab Commission on Human Rights has initiated steps toward an Arab Charter of Human Rights, and the Arab League's Council has recommended that its member states establish national commissions on human rights. But at present the Arab League's educational efforts appear aimed principally against Israel, a state outside this regional system, rather than against human rights violations inside its member states.[39]

The European System [40]

The European Convention on Human Rights, adopted in 1950 and in force since 1953, guarantees twelve civil and political rights plus several others added in later protocols. A separate European Social Charter was adopted in 1961 and has been in force since 1965.

Sixteen states became parties to the European Convention: Aus-

---

[38] Report of the 26th Session of the Commission on Hunman Rights, February 24–March 27, 1970 (E/4816, E/CN–4/1039).

[39] E/CN.4/1089 (note by Secretary General containing information submitted by Arab League in response to ECOSOC resolution 1159 [XLI] on cooperation with regional intergovernmental organizations concerned with human rights).

[40] *European Convention on Human Rights:* Collected Texts, Council of Europe, Strasbourg, 1969; Thomas Buergenthal, "The Domestic Status of the European Convention: A Second Look," *Journal of International Commission of Jurists,* Summer 1966, pp. 55–96; James C. Fawcett, "Human Rights in Europe, 1968," *Patterns of Prejudice,* January–February, 1968, pp. 11–13, 17; E/CN.4/L.1117/add. 1, January 6, 1970 (containing December 19, 1969, Council of Europe communication responding to ECOSOC Resolution in 1150 [XLI] on cooperation with regional intergovernmental bodies concerned with human rights); T. Buergenthal, ed., "Human Rights: The European Convention and Its National Application," *American Journal of Comparative Law,* Ann Arbor, Michigan, Vol. 18, No. 2 (1970), pp. 233–366; A. B. McNulty (Secretary to the European Commission of Human Rights), "Stock-Taking on the European Convention on Human Rights," European Commission on Human Rights (Council of Europe), Doc. No. DH (71) 9, Strasbourg, October 1, 1971; Parliamentary Conference on Human Rights (Consultative Assembly, Council of Europe), Vienna, October 18–20, 1971, reports on "What rights should be protected?" (AS/Coll. DH [71]3) and on "How can the existing protection of human rights be strengthened?" (AS/Coll. DH [71]5), Strasbourg, 1971.

tria, Belgium, Cyprus, Denmark, Federal Republic of Germany, Greece, Iceland, Ireland, Italy, Luxembourg, Malta, Netherlands, Norway, Sweden, Turkey, and the United Kingdom. (Of the members of the Council of Europe, only France and Switzerland did not join.) Greece denounced its agreement and withdrew from the Council of Europe in December 1969. The Social Charter has been ratified by eight states: Austria, Cyprus, Denmark, Federal Republic of Germany, Italy, Norway, Sweden, and the United Kingdom.

As with the UN Economic and Social Covenant, the principal implementation of the Social Charter is a system of governmental progress reports which are examined by several Council of Europe bodies, including a committee of independent experts. By contrast, the European Convention's implementation measures are more daring by far than those in the UN Covenants or even in the UN Convention on Racial Discrimination. It provides for a mandatory right of interstate complaint and an optional right of individual petition. A Commission on Human Rights composed of members serving in personal capacities is authorized to decide on the admissibility of complaints and to conciliate between the disputants, with the obligation, if its efforts fail, to issue a report which may include an "opinion" (not a "decision") on whether the facts reveal a breach of the Convention. State parties have the option to accept the compulsory jurisdiction of the European Court of Human Rights. They (or the Commission itself, as "defender of the public interest") may appeal cases to the Court, which has the power to issue binding decisions. In cases not referred to the Court, the Committee of Ministers (consisting of one representative each from members of the Council of Europe) is empowered, by a two-thirds vote, to issue decisions and to prescribe remedial measures.

In nearly twenty years of existence the European Commission has received only eight interstate complaints, concerning only three separate situations—two being "political" in inspiration (Greece against the United Kingdom and Austria against Italy) and only one (Denmark-Netherlands-Norway-Sweden against Greece) being without any evident self-interest. These complaints were considered by the Commission, by the Committee of Ministers, and by the Consultative Assembly of the Council of Europe. While the Assembly's recommendation that Greece be expelled from the Council of Europe was under discussion by the Committee of Ministers,

Greece denounced the Convention and withdrew from the Council.

In contrast to the few interstate complaints, the European Commission has received over 5,000 individual petitions, but only a small percentage, representing even fewer separate issues or situations, was held admissible and considered by the Commission, the Committee of Ministers, or the Court of Human Rights. Many of the individual petitions concerned a government's right to suspend individual freedoms in times of emergency.

Though far-reaching in principle, and though it can demonstrate a number of successes, the European system still faces legal and practical difficulties. Some states have failed to enact implementing legislation; some have failed to exercise the options to recognize the right of individual petition and the automatic jurisdiction of the Court of Human Rights. The European Convention's protections are effectively weakened by the requirement that a petitioner exhaust domestic remedies, by the expense and other complications involved in complaining to the Commission, and by ignorance on the part of aggrieved persons and their attorneys of the Convention system.

The Council of Europe has also conducted a wide variety of educational and promotional activities, and their influence and that of the Convention as a legal and moral norm are doubtless considerable. A Council committee has even discussed, adopted resolutions, and conducted quiet diplomacy with regard to human rights problems in nonmember states. This committee recently concerned itself with Soviet Jewry.

The Latin American System [41]

The American Declaration of Rights and Duties of Man was adopted in 1948; a human rights program was launched in 1953 with the decision to create an Inter-American Commission on Human Rights and prepare a regional convention. The following

---

[41] José A. Cabranes, "The Protection of Human Rights by the Organization of American States," *American Journal of International Law,* Vol. 62, No. 4 (October 1968), pp. 889–908; Sidney Liskofsky, "Latin America Prepares Human Rights Convention," *World Federalist,* May–June 1970, pp. 3–4, 14; Neale C. Ronning, "Human Rights and Humanitarian Laws in the Western Hemisphere," *Social Research,* Vol. 38, No. 2 (Summer 1971), pp. 320–35.

year the Council of the Organization of American States (OAS) adopted a statute defining in general and seemingly innocuous terms the role and functions of the Commission: to develop awareness, make general recommendations, prepare studies and reports, supply information and give advice. By liberal and even adventurous interpretation, however, the Commission succeeded in asserting wide authority to receive and examine individual petitions, conduct on-spot investigations, and issue findings and make remedial recommendations directed to particular countries. These powers were formalized in November 1965, and the Commission was subsequently raised to the status of a principal organ of the OAS, its ultimate competence to be determined by the projected convention.

The most dramatic case handled by the Commission (1965–66) followed civil war and U.S. intervention in the Dominican Republic. On request of the OAS Secretary-General that the Commission use its good offices there, it investigated charges of human rights violations, intervened on behalf of prisoners, mediated between factions, and even supervised a presidential election. Though it subsequently considered complaints relating to other countries, including Brazil, member states have been reluctant to allow it to play a comparable role again.[42]

After several postponements the American Convention on Human Rights was adopted at a Special Inter-American Conference in San José, Costa Rica, in November 1969. Dealing mainly with civil and political rights, the Convention (considerably influenced by prior UN and Council of Europe instruments) contains wording suggesting that it is not self-executing. It also contains an article limiting the obligation of federal governments. (In contrast, the UN Covenant on Civil and Political Rights expressly excluded limitations in favor of federal as compared with unitary states, which doubtless has discouraged ratification by some federal states.)

In regard to implementation the American Convention generally resembles the European Convention, but is more advanced in an important respect: reversing the European Convention's provisions, it makes the right of individual petition mandatory and the right of state complaint optional. The American Convention provides for an expert commission with members serving in personal ca-

---

[42] Anna P. and Phillipe S. Schreiber, "The Inter-American Commission on Human Rights in the Dominican Crisis," *International Organization*, XXII (Spring 1968), pp. 508–28.

pacities and for a regional human rights court whose jurisdiction the parties have the option to accept.

At the Costa Rica conference, Chile, Colombia, Costa Rica, Ecuador, Guatemala, Uruguay, and Venezuela generally supported a strong Convention; the hemisphere's "big three"—Argentina, Brazil, and Mexico—and the Dominican Republic, Panama, and Nicaragua adopted a conservative stand on most issues. Given the volatile politics of Latin America and the apparent leftist trend, however, these postures may change. It is difficult to predict, moreover, when the eleven ratifications required to bring the Convention into force will be forthcoming. Though no one expected the United States seriously to consider ratification, at least not for a long time, it played an active role at Costa Rica, siding generally with the "liberal" members on substantive provisions, for example, on the rights of free speech, press, and assembly; and on implementation, for example, the right of individual petition, and the establishment of a court. But perhaps with a view to minimizing obstacles to its own ratification some day, it sided with the "conservative" faction as regards a non-self-executing interpretation of the Convention, safeguarding states' rights and permitting reservations.

To date neither the European nor the Latin American system has had any cases directly relating to Jewish rights, because, happily, there have not been major assaults on Jewish rights in those parts of the world.

International Human Rights in the Future

In his seminal work on the concept of an international bill of rights, written in 1943–44 at the height of Western enthusiasm for an international system to prevent repetition of Nazi-like evils, the late and eminent jurist Hersh Lauterpacht recognized that the accomplishment of this goal is fraught with difficulty. Alluding to the inherent conflict between international human rights and the valued principle that each people shall be free to determine its own system of government, he wrote: "We are not at liberty to assume that this problem will be lightly solved." The politicization of human rights has magnified the difficulties. (Lauterpacht did not fail to perceive that possible development and stressed that even international human rights law was subject to the higher natural law of justice.) [43]

The record of organized international protection for human rights to date reflects achievement and promise, frustration and setback.[44] The forces which have produced that record cast their shadow ahead, and prospects for human rights in the coming decade are also mixed. Discontent with the United Nations among Western states, and more recently in Israel, has grown, and promises no early improvement; even committed UN supporters, who earlier regretted its inability to impose its collective will on member states, now question the desirability of giving such authority to an organization dominated by blatant political majorities.

Ardent supporters—including some Jewish supporters—of international protection of human rights, decrying what they consider perversions of the spirit of human rights and of norms and institutions designed for their protection, are pessimistic, and some have greater fears than hopes for international human rights activity in the future. Others, however, see brighter prospects and, in any event, no better alternative to the UN system, for human rights as for other international problems.

Pessimist Appraisal

In general, pessimists and some who consider themselves realists foresee "more of the same" in the international system and therefore in the UN. In this heterogeneous and dangerously divided system, they assert, it is unrealistic to expect the UN to play an affirmative role in protecting human rights: with its members differing radically in ideology, institutions, culture, power, economic development, and national needs and goals, there is not sufficient community of values to enable them to collaborate meaningfully in a universal system of human rights protection. Human rights problems, moreover, are rooted in complex socioeconomic, military-political, and technological-environmental factors, and their solutions lie in long-term changes to which the UN's human rights

---

[43] Hersh Lauterpacht, *An International Bill of the Rights of Man* (New York, Columbia University Press, 1945), p. 15.

[44] Louis Henkin, "The United Nations and Human Rights," *International Organization*, Vol. XIX, No. 3 (1965), pp. 504–17.

approach can contribute little. Nationalist revolutions in progress throughout the world are minimally influenced by the UN, and there are too few national interests or constituencies to support respect for international legality and provide domestic undergirding for international human rights measures. It is hardly likely that the Communist states will give up their insistence on sovereignty over their citizens or their opposition to supranational institutions, including any international machinery exercising meaningful administrative or judicial functions.[45] Nor, though its resistance is manifested differently, is the United States likely to begin to take seriously the concept of international "protection" as compared with "promotion" of human rights.[46]

Western pessimists question even the utility of the norms in the UN's declarations and conventions, if only because they permit—as in principle they must—limiting individual rights in the collective interest. There is a world of difference between countries and between ideologies in their perspectives on individual rights and on national interest and in their responsiveness to domestic and world opinion, and it is extremely difficult to supervise the inevitable delicate balancing of individual freedom and national interest in a universal system.

To the pessimist, the UN record confirms his fears. He cites the failure to establish permanent general institutions or procedures for dealing with specific denials of human rights; international impotence in the face of massive and violent assaults on human rights in many countries; neglect of fundamental personal liberties; verbal gestures to human rights principles while their authors nullify them with self-serving interpretations; obstructing enlargement of the UN's authority while bemoaning its incapacity to deal with concrete violations; and on the other hand, ad hoc investigations and quasi-adjudications that were not impartial; politically distorted use of UN forums; debasement of the quality of discourse about hu-

---

[45] Franciszek Prtzetacznik, "The Socialist Concept of Protection of Human Rights," *Social Research*, Vol. 38, No. 2 (Summer 1971), pp. 337–61.

[46] John R. Schmidhauser and Larry L. Berg, "The American Bar Association and the Human Rights Conventions: The Political Significance of Private Professional Associations," *Social Research*, Vol. 38, No. 2 (Summer 1971), pp. 362–410; Philip E. Jacob, "The Political Ethos and Human Rights: An International Perspective," *Social Research*, *op. cit.*, pp. 199–216.

man rights issues; double standards in relating to human rights policies of friends and foes; abuse of human rights forums to attack the State of Israel; harassment of the NGOs, especially the Jewish ones, because their concerns are at variance with Communist-Arab objectives; and general impeding of NGO efforts to draw attention to concrete human rights violations.

Even the UN's achievements are deprecated. Ultimately, the UN's contributions depend on the incorporation of convention norms into domestic law, but how many states will ratify the significant conventions, and will those where they are most needed? Will, for example, South Africa ratify the Convention on Racial Discrimination, or the Soviet Union the Covenant on Civil and Political Rights? Which conventions will the United States ratify? [47] How many states will accept the optional but crucial right of individual petition? How many will ratify frivolously, cynically, as a propaganda gesture? And how many, having ratified, will effectively translate the norms into domestic law for enforcement by executives and courts?

Nor is the pessimist impressed with the implementation machinery in UN conventions. The right of individual petition, believed to be the key to effective implementation, is optional in both the Civil and Political Rights Covenant and the Race Discrimination Convention, and is even unlikely to be accepted by enough states to put it into effect for a long time to come. Even the right of state-to-state complaint is optional in the Civil and Political Rights Covenant, and in any event, is unlikely to be used because states are loath to complain against one another regarding internal conditions lest they disturb "friendly relations" and provoke retaliation. The International Court of Justice has little part in human rights enforcement, is wholly eliminated from both Covenants, and is optional (on Communist insistence) in certain conventions (e.g., consent to marriage); in other conventions (e.g., genocide, slavery, political rights of women) the Communist states in ratifying them have entered reservations to the Court's compulsory jurisdiction. The only procedure that appears to have general ac-

---

[47] Hearings before Subcommittee of the Committee on Foreign Relations, U.S. Senate, 90th Congress (on Conventions on Political Rights of Women, Abolition of Forced Labor and Slavery), February 23–March 8, 1967, and 91st Congress (on Genocide Convention), April 24, 27, and May 22, 1970.

ceptance, and is actually in operation under the Convention on Racial Discrimination, is the requirement of governmental reporting, but such reports tend to be evasive or self-serving—and the initial experience with this procedure has not been promising.

The pessimist's questions bite even deeper. How adequate is the level of UN discussion about human rights, and how much is actually known about the extent, variety, and causes of their violations? How valid are some of the normative formulations that have emerged from the opportunistic and even fortuitous ways in which UN instruments are made? Is not the prevailing emphasis on economic and social rights, which require for their realization an interventionist government, likely to blunt the libertarian thrust of the human rights instruments? Conceding the need to evolve additional norms to meet technological and social change, is there not the danger of so expanding the list of rights as to blur any order of importance? Have not the various methods of implementation used internationally, from moralizing to sanctions, proved ineffective? If the ultimate tool available to the UN is world opinion, do its resolutions in fact represent world opinion? What indeed is world opinion, whom does it influence and how? [48]

The pessimist, then, remains dubious as to whether the UN can be of more than peripheral value, if that, in advancing the worldwide cause of human rights. That Israel and its supporters should be sparing in their enthusiasm over the UN's human rights achievements, and over its prospective role, is understandable. As a relatively new state, Israel shares with other new states, and for that matter, with older ones, aversion to external criticism and to international inquiry into its internal policies. This attitude is perhaps more understandable in Israel's case, in that the Hitlerian horrors are still vivid in the memories of a large part of its population, which holds that rather than being a subject of constant criticism and even challenges to its right to exist, the survival and security of a Jewish state should be a central concern of the UN. In Israel's view, it has been under unceasing political and military attack by its Arab neighbors since it gained statehood nearly twenty-five years ago and only its own self-reliant courage and daring saved it from possible extinction in 1967.

---

[48] Richard Bilder, "Rethinking International Human Rights: Some Basic Questions," *Human Rights Journal*, Vol. II, No. 4 (December 1969), pp. 557–607.

Given more than little warrant by the UN's political arithmetic and the resulting intemperate harassment of Israel in the UN human rights bodies, many Diaspora Jews share Israel's disappointment, creating tension with the traditional Jewish commitment to international protection of human rights to which a history of persecution has predisposed them.

The "realist" is less dubious, but also less than confident, about prospects for regional systems of human rights protection. For example, how will the Inter-American human rights system fare if Latin America moves increasingly to the left? Chile, like Cuba, has already declared its hostility to the OAS, describing it as an instrument of American imperialism. Notwithstanding the profusion of human rights resolutions, declarations, and conventions adopted by the Latin American nations over decades, there is a vast gulf between the rhetoric in these documents and the reality in almost all countries. Political and civil rights give every appearance of attenuating further as revolutionary terrorism seeking fundamental change is matched by intensified governmental countermeasures.[49]

An Optimistic Perspective

As in regard to the UN generally, whether one's attitude toward its human rights achievements, past and prospective, is negative or affirmative depends on perspective, which (temperament aside) depends on national, ideological, and political identifications and sympathies. It depends too on how past expectations were met, on whether one emphasizes achievements or failures, on what alternatives one perceives. One can accept the pessimist's criticisms yet draw different conclusions, if one applies a different time perspective and has confidence that necessity (i.e., the imperative of humanity's survival with a measure of dignity) will be the parent of invention and evoke the rationality for man to adapt his vested interests and cherished values to his vision.

The optimist recognizes that at this juncture in history the fate of human rights in particular countries must depend ultimately on the alertness and vigor of their own peoples in defense of their

---

[49] Neale C. Ronning, *op. cit.*

rights. It is now obvious that the world's human rights problems are too many, too varied, too changing, and too elusive to be embraced within an all-encompassing, smoothly operating universal system (as some early proponents of an International Bill of Rights believed), and many methods and programs—international, regional, and national, governmental and nongovernmental—will be required. What can be done to solve or alleviate human rights problems through the UN is complementary and interstitial, and in immediate impact probably less would be achieved than through recourse to the specialized agencies, regional organizations, bilateral governmental intercessions, nongovernmental organizations, or the mass media—the other elements in today's "international system."

But if the UN's contribution has been limited, it is far from insignificant. While the UN's human rights system lacks an adequate base in shared values and common national goals, it has made a crucial and enduring contribution by establishing that human rights are a proper subject of international concern and governed by "general principles of law recognized by civilized nations" (one of the sources of international law specified in the statute of the International Court of Justice). The UN system is embryonic and imperfect, but its consensuses (declarations, conventions, and resolutions) have contributed importantly to authentic value-sharing and have had legitimating effects and political impact.

The United Nations will continue to inspire a vast range of activity by the regional intergovernmental organizations (the Council of Europe, Organization of American States, Organization of African Unity, Arab League) and by international and national nongovernmental organizations. Indeed, the very unhappiness with the state of human rights reflects the heightened awareness and the awakened conscience which the UN has achieved. The vision of a universal human rights system, for which the UN Charter has provided the constitutional basis, had led to a code of human rights law and moral injunction covering the gamut of human relationships. Despite generality of formulation, escape clauses, and inadequate implementation, the Charter will continue to have a profound influence on the mores, laws, and policies of nations.

The provisions of the Universal Declaration, the draft covenants and the various conventions, will be increasingly reflected in national constitutions and statutes and in judicial holdings. Especially if it is used even more imaginatively and dynamically than now, these documents, as the embodiment of the international conscience, can be the inspiration and basis for research, teaching, publications, mass media programs, seminars and conferences, and other forms of community action.

The influences of international human rights activity are constantly felt in the open societies of the West: for example, following the September 1971 Attica prison tragedy advocates of penal reform invoked the Standard Minimum Rules for the Treatment of Offenders adopted by the UN in 1955. But in the closed society of the Soviet Union, too, courageous dissenting intellectuals and Jews pleading for permission to emigrate have supported their case with references to the Universal Declaration and other international human rights instruments. Even more remarkable and encouraging was the establishment in November 1970 by several leading Soviet scientists and literary personalities of a Committee on Human Rights, perhaps the first authentic nongovernmental group in the country since the early twenties, with the stated purpose of disseminating human rights documents of "international and Soviet law" in its "theoretical and constructive criticism of the present state of the Soviet system of legal safeguards for individual freedom." Unprecedented in Soviet history was this statement in the Committee's preliminary report on its intended program: [50]

> Mankind through its struggle for rights, has come to understand that certain rights are inalienable, and that the sovereignty of the state must be limited in matters that might reduce the scope of such rights regardless of the political goals of the social system. . . . Just such rights are proclaimed in the Universal Declaration of Human Rights; just such goals are guaranteed by the Covenant on Civil and Political Rights.

The report further stated:

> While emphasizing the doctrinal differences between Soviet and Western law and without repudiating the earlier Communist theory of the withering away of the state and of law, Soviet jurists are working together with their Western colleagues to draft UN instruments on human rights. . . . It is unimportant that some consider this collaboration a propaganda move. . . . It is

[50] Social Problems, bimonthly journal of Soviet Committee on Human Rights (disseminated in samizdat form), Moscow, Issue No. 8, November–December, 1970.

important that representatives of opposing legal systems have been able to overcome their doctrinal differences and to strive for cooperation and mutual understanding in [this] most consequential field of law. It is important that Soviet legislators and jurists recognize the general significance of fundamental human rights.

Intellectual, Ethical, and Ideological Currents

Some observers see hope in that, as perhaps never before in history, people in all countries, regardless of ideology, politics, and state of development, are questioning fundamental values and institutions, asserting claims and expectations, and harboring a sense of imminent change.

> . . . There is a slow change of political sentiment, among ordinary men, which has been noticeable in different countries, both Communist and capitalist . . . In a phrase it might be called the return of repressed liberal values to the center of common consciousness.
>
> In the general pessimism left by the disgrace of Communist persecutions, and by the disgrace of the Vietnam war, the vindication of basic decencies takes the place of other political ambitions. In spite of the concentration of power in the hands of governments, of presidents and prime ministers, the old excuses for indecent political practices are no longer believable, and least of all by the educated young, some of whom will soon share power. Neither "raison d'état" nor the needs of a coming social revolution, the two standing excuses of right and left, seem acceptable justifications in places where they would have been accepted some years ago.[51]

Nationalist feelings are continuously affected by foreign influences carried by ever more efficient communications media. Changing military technology has radically modified concepts of national security, leading many statesmen to think of security in terms more constructive for the world-at-large—for example, by reducing instability in underdeveloped nations through more generous assistance for their economic and social development.[52] In general, there is greater understanding of the causes of disorder and crisis in the

---

[51] Stuart Hampshire, *The New York Times*, December 8, 1971, p. 37.
[52] Robert McNamara, address before the American Society of Newspaper Editors, *The New York Times*, May 19, 166, p. 11.

human condition and of the need for international cooperation in dealing with them. These developments are bound to encourage renewed receptivity to clarifying the norms, new and old, required for man's survival on the planet in conditions of freedom and dignity and to developing international machinery for implementing these norms.

Also significant is the growing dialogue among theologians, physical and social scientists, physicians, lawyers, and other professionals, in the United States and elsewhere, in regard to the moral, social, and legal implications of developments in science, e.g., computerized record-keeping, electronic surveillance, birth control, genetic engineering, organ transplants, use of drugs to alter intelligence, emotions, and behavior. The UN studies emanating from the regrettably politicized Teheran Conference will prove one of the more lasting contributions of that conference and may yet produce new norms to protect fundamental human rights.

Human Rights—A New Intellectual Discipline

An encouraging development is the founding of the René Cassin International Institute of Human Rights in Strasbourg, France,[53] and the Jacob Blaustein Institute for the Advancement of Human Rights in New York, and the founding or projection of analogous institutes in other countries. Parallel with (and partly as a result of) that development is the rise of interest in international human rights in colleges and universities, particularly law schools. At the 1971 session of the UN Commission on Human Rights, UNESCO was requested to query its member states on how human rights are taught in universities and to give the Commission its views on developing an independent scientific discipline of human rights, taking into account the principal legal systems of the world, with a view to facilitating the study of human rights at the university level and subsequently at other levels of education.[54] Academic and intellectual leaders have been debating whether the range of subjects dealt with under the human rights umbrella is sufficient to warrant

---

[53] *Human Rights Journal* (Cassin Institute), Vol. II, No. 1 (January–March 1969), pp. 5–19.

[54] Report of the 27th Session of the Commission of Human Rights, February 22–March 26, 1971, Geneva (E/4949; E/CN-4/1069).

classification as a distinct academic discipline, what its elements would be, what its relationship would be to established legal and other disciplines, and how it would be taught at various levels of education.[55]

In time states will come to accept meaningful international implementation. Though the two omnibus Covenants provide meager implementation, the far-reaching Convention on the Elimination of Racial Discrimination, already in operation, includes a potentially strong implementation system, and the ILO has a long-established system of considerable effectiveness. Various proposals for implementation under the authority of the UN Charter, e.g., an office of UN High Commissioner for Human Rights or other means of investigating recurrent patterns of gross human rights violations, remain on the UN agenda and have behind them significant governmental support. Despite their shortcomings, the General Assembly's Committees on Apartheid and Colonialism and the Human Rights Commission's expert groups investigating human rights conditions in southern Africa and Israeli-occupied territory have established important precedents for receiving private petitions, hearing private witnesses, dispatching field missions, and for quasi-adjudication and remedial recommendations. There will be deterrent and educational value even in the occasional trading of accusations in regard to human rights situations in particular countries.

Goals and Prospects for the 1970s [56]

Some see the future of human rights in far-reaching supranational institutions, with legislative, judicial (e.g., a world court of human rights, world habeas corpus and international penal jurisdiction), and even enforcement powers. For the more cautious optimist, shorter-range and less visionary goals (which may also take a long time to achieve) include persuading governments to ratify the

---

[55] *Proceedings*, American Society of International Law, 1971, pp. 240–60.

[56] *The United Nations: The Next Twenty-five Years*, 20th Report of the Commission to Study the Organization of Peace (Louis B. Sohn, chairman) (New York, November 1969), 70 pp.; Louis Kutner, *World Habeas Corpus* (New York, 1962), 295 pp.; *Montreal Statement of the Assembly for Human Rights*, March 22–27, 1968, Montreal; *For All Humanity*, Report of the Committee on Human Rights of the National Citizens' Commission (published by the American Jewish Committee and the United Nations Association–U.S.A.), May 1966.

prepared conventions; completing other conventions or declarations on subjects on which work was stalled (e.g., freedom of information, arbitrary arrest, religious rights, the right of emigration); and initiating or resuming the norm-setting process on other important old and new subjects (e.g., human rights in armed conflict, the impact of science and technology, the administration of justice, the right of national, ethnic, and religious minorities to preserve their cultural identity).

These goals call for greater recognition of the right of individual petition; the establishment of genuinely independent committees of experts (permanent as well as ad hoc) to receive and investigate complaints, private as well as governmental; the creation of an office of UN High Commissioner for Human Rights; the upgrading of the UN bodies concerned with human rights, with the right of aggrieved parties to appear before them in person (as they have been permitted to do before the Committees on Colonialism and Apartheid). (Other proposals—which some human rights advocates consider dubious—seek the establishment of a UN grand jury to indict perpetrators of crimes against humanity, e.g., in South-West Africa, and a UN register to keep dossiers on such criminals.) Also important—at least more realistic than contentious procedures in the present sharply divided international society—is expansion of the UN's educational and promotional activity in human rights.

The prospects for regional activity obviously differ radically with the degree of regional cohesion and institutional development and the political dynamics of the region. They vary from Eastern Europe, where there is express governmental opposition to a human rights system; Asia, where there is hardly a glimmer of movement; the Middle East and Africa, where there are small beginnings; to the modest Latin American and the advanced West European systems. Hopefully the experience and precedents of the latter systems will be reflected in developments in the other regions.

Nongovernmental organizations will remain indispensable to human rights progress on the international and national levels. NGOs have greater freedom than official bodies to initiate ideas and activities and, as the UN system recognizes, are a necessary instrument for carrying out programs recommended by official bodies. In many countries they are able to prod the government to fulfill existing obligations and to undertake new ones.

NGOs have suffered setbacks in the UN system, but sympathetic states and their own efforts will help them regain their effectiveness. There is much they can contribute even within prevailing limitations. With ingenuity and discretion, they can still call attention to violations, for example, by citing texts of objectionable national laws while avoiding invidious characterizations. The procedure adopted in 1971 for dealing with "communications" offers an opportunity to bring to the UN's attention "gross and reliably attested violations." Though NGOs have no part in the supervisory machinery of the UN Convention on the Elimination of Racial Discrimination, they can communicate information informally to members of the implementing committee; they can also request friendly delegates to comment on a particular situation in the course of discussions on pertinent subjects. At the least, they can address appeals to the Secretary General or to the UN ambassador of the country concerned—with appropriate publicity when helpful. If they have the resources, they can prepare and publicize their own commentaries on UN studies of particular issues or can undertake independent studies.

NGOs are obviously not limited to working within the restrictive, formal UN procedures. Indeed, many view as one of their cardinal functions the rendering of services that official bodies are unwilling or unable to provide effectively—principally, to help aggrieved individuals or private groups bring their human rights problems to the world's attention through the mass media. They can also advance international norm-setting by helping to clarify (through research and conferences) tentative formulations which have bogged down in official bodies due to ideological or political impediments—e.g., the stalled efforts to deal with freedom of information, freedom from arbitrary arrest, the right of emigration, religious rights, and minority cultural rights—and thereby prod official bodies to act on them.

No one can say with confidence whether the pessimistic or optimistic perspective will prove more realistic, whether the hopeful or discouraging tendencies in the international system will dominate, whether even modest, short-term goals will be realized. Anticipated changes in the UN system, notably the arrival of the People's Republic of China, make prognostication even more hazardous.

At the May 1968 Teheran Conference, called in commemoration of the twentieth anniversary of the Universal Declaration for the purpose of assessing the UN's accomplishment and projecting future directions, there was general agreement that while the world organization's norm-setting achievement had been substantial, progress in implementation had lagged. The Australian delegate expressed the view that "if the last twenty years may be called the stage of definition, the next twenty may prove to be the stage of implementation." Doubtless he was expressing a hope more than an expectation.

Overall, despite the increasing interdependence of nations and the proliferation of transnational influences during the past quarter century, nations will doubtless remain as sensitive as ever about their "sovereignty," especially in regard to the human rights of their inhabitants, and loath to open their societies to serious scrutiny and supervision, much less to third-party decision making. Still, international scrutiny has begun and it will not be easy to deny its precedents; rudimentary international machinery has been created and it will not be easy to leave it idle. The prospect is favorable for the modest machinery mandated to receive and investigate complaints, to issue reports and recommendations, and to conciliate—in effect, for an improved process of bringing to bear on human rights violations and below-par conditions the therapeutic force of world opinion. And despite the melancholy history of human rights violations in many lands, world opinion does influence the conduct of governments, though they will rarely admit it. Governments are sensitive to it because it affects national prestige, which is not unrelated to national power. There is increasing recognition that:

[. . . to provide a relentless, continuing, impartial contemptuous] publicity for the indecencies of policies and of police action that occur every day in South Africa, Czechoslovakia, Greece, Portuguese Africa, the jails of the U.S.A. and South Vietnam, Pakistan, the Soviet Union, and many other places, seems now rational politics. No other rationality has a hold.

To give publicity to every violation of human rights all the time, with all necessary disloyalty, seems to me the simple requirement of a rational political morality now. Corresponding to the combination across frontiers at the pinnacles of power, publicity and protest do cross frontiers, and do sometimes shake authority and do sometimes change policies.[57]

---

[57] Hampshire, *op. cit.*

At the same time, there is no reason to expect that politics and the double standard will disappear from the UN's implementing activity, though their manifestations are likely to change with new political issues and alignments. The Communist states, with the collaboration of Africans and Asians, will continue to impose their emphasis on racial discrimination, self-determination, and, in general, on collective as against individual rights; [58] these emphases will become even stronger with the entry of Communist China. With a population more than two-thirds that of the member nations of the three regional organizations—being itself, in a sense, a regional system, and a tightly knit one—China is not likely to view with enthusiasm international scrutiny of its internal practices. Soviet-Chinese competition in the UN will complicate human rights as it will other UN activities, and may induce many members to avoid alignment with either by supporting bona fide, impartial implementation of international standards.

But there are glimmers of liberalization in regard to human rights in the USSR and China themselves. Some new nations too, having savored the fruits of independence and attained some measure of national cohesion, economic viability if not plenty, and external and internal security, may begin to acquire a taste for "Western" liberties and show fuller recognition of the fact that, while the issue of racial discrimination is of overriding importance, other forms of discrimination—ethnic, religious, political—also warrant international attention and that the race issue itself is not limited to situations of black-white confrontation.

There is yet much progress to be made in the Western nations, including America. They must learn how to guarantee their peoples' economic and social rights—to jobs, education, medical care, housing, social security—which occupy equal status with the civil and political freedoms in the Universal Declaration. They must cooperate more conscientiously with international efforts to solve the economic problems of the poorer nations and with efforts to end the clinging colonialism in southern Africa and eradicate the white racism in that region and everywhere in the world.

Probably the happiest development for human rights would be

---

[58] Edward T. Rowe, "Human Rights Issues in the UN General Assembly, 1944–46," *Journal of Conflict Resolution*, Vol. XIV, No. 4, pp. 425–37.

the settlement or alleviation of some of the festering conflicts which plague various regions, notably Southeast Asia and the Middle East. Some form of political settlement in the Middle East, in particular, would not only improve the lot of Jews in Arab and Communist lands and end human rights issues in the territories occupied by Israel, but presumably would also close the unhappy chapter in which the Soviet-Arab alliance has dominated and sabotaged UN human rights forums with its anti-Israel and anti-Semitic preoccupations. It might modify the Soviet-Arab axis on human rights issues generally and moderate its opposition to new institutions and procedures.

So long as tension in the Middle East and other areas persists, the "politicization" of UN human rights activities, the perversion of human rights principles, and the misappropriation of international human rights machinery will continue to discredit the organization's human rights activities. But there are built-in limits to such abuses. Afro-Asian states may tire of anti-Israel attacks and other Arab preoccupations that distract from bona fide issues that concern many nations much more. The limited value of minority decisions, even of majorities achieved over substantial dissent, may also encourage restraint. Some "abused" states have withdrawn from particular bodies (the United States and Great Britain from the General Assembly's Committee on Colonialism) or have refused to recognize them (Israel, the bodies investigating its occupation policies). Some have refrained from joining new conventions and the institutions they established.

The friends of human rights can and must do better. In the UN's role as formulator of values, promoter and educator, conciliator, and universal marketplace (however noisy) for argument about values and issues, it is not inevitable that the more numerous or the loudest will always win out. The voice of reason, courageously raised, can also be heard and will often prevail. In the recent past, Western states have been less than effective in arguing their own versions of truth and justice against those of the Communist, Arab, and other extremist voices of both left and right. They have reacted too passively to torrents of false information about themselves and to prejudice, vituperation, and slander against others, and they have failed adequately to focus attention on violations of personal freedom or minority rights in the lands of their accusers. More forceful leadership on their part, especially by the United

States, could signal to other nations that the UN's human rights activities are to be taken seriously.

In sum, the events of our era have confirmed the critical need for international human rights institutions to scrutinize, admonish, exhort, and educate, and thereby to influence national laws and attitudes. No government or people is immune from impulses and pressures to discriminate against minorities, persecute the dissident and the deviant, oppress the poor, or otherwise short-circuit the demands of justice. When internal opposition is silenced or impotent, there can be no protection against national violations except in international protection. The beginning of such a system exists and is not likely to be reversed; the question is whether it will be strengthened and what will be its forms and scope, its emphases, its responses to prevailing ideological and political currents, its specific applications.

In the introduction to his Annual Report for 1971, UN Secretary General U Thant observed:

> Theoretically, the United Nations has little standing [concerning the violations of human rights within the frontiers of a state] and they are all too common. Legally, the membership of the United Nations has done an admirable job on human rights. The necessary texts exist. But, practically, where does an individual or group of individuals find recourse against oppression within his own country? The time has surely come when governments in the United Nations must make a determined effort to give justice a worldwide dimension.[59]

His appraisal of the overall organization applies as well to its human rights role:

> The United Nations and the concept of internationalism as embodied in the Charter are sometimes viewed with less than enthusiasm, and even on occasion with resentment by governments . . . it is a dangerous illusion to believe in the present state of the world, that life can be safe without that concept and without a world organization that embodies it. Much of the usefulness of the United Nations is unknown and indeed intangible. But, however faulty, it represents an aspiration and a method of trying to realize a great ideal. Nations and peoples will turn their backs on this great endeavor at their greatest peril.

---

[59] Introduction to the Report of the Secretary General on the Work of the Organization, September 17, 1971 (A/8401/Add. 1).

Conclusion

Implications for the American Jewish Community

Louis Henkin

American Jews will respond to the turbulence of the 1970s much like other concerned American citizens, but the condition of the State of Israel and of Jews elsewhere in the world will confront them with special dilemmas.

In the extended and arduous pursuit of peace, American Jews will continue to be particularly sensitive and sympathetic to Israel's needs and views; American Jewish spokesmen will continue to help the American and Israeli governments to understand each other and to reduce whatever differences cannot be eliminated, mindful that the relation of American Jews to each is different in character and justification—to the United States, that of citizens; to Israel, the more delicate one of friends. The American Jewish community will help educate the American public, including the young and the New Left, and gain sympathy for Israel around the world. The American Jewish community will also help to educate the Israeli public to fuller awareness of the views and expectations of the rest of the world.

In peace, in war, or in the tense non-peace that may prevail through the decade, Israel will need assistance and friendship. It will depend heavily on U.S. aid, including liberal terms for buying arms and other defense needs. The American Jewish community itself has known how to give economic aid and will no doubt develop new imaginative programs of aid, trade, and joint enterprise.

American Jews, as individuals or collectively, cannot solve Israel's internal problems; indeed, their criticism and even advice will not be heartily welcomed. It is vital to Israel, however, that it deal effectively with these problems, and how well it does will affect not only its cause but will concern other Jewish communities as well.

American Jews will also have to help interpret Israel to their youth and the young American Jew to Israel, and bridge the gap between American Jewish youth and their Israeli peers, particularly in Israeli universities.

The American Jewish community's tasks in regard to Jews in the rest of the world will be no less difficult, in some respects just as delicate. As the strongest Jewish community in the Diaspora, the responsibility of leadership has been thrust upon it. American Jewry will have to cooperate with Israel and the Western European and Latin American Jewish communities in their battle against revived anti-Semitism, in their approach to Christianity, Christian Churches, Christian neighbors, and in aiding the Jews in Eastern Europe. It will have to cooperate with Jews in Western Europe and Latin America to support Israel, and to find contemporary meaning for Jewish identity and community and how to communicate it to their young. It will have to cooperate with Israel to help maintain Jewish communal life in Western Europe, Latin America, and, marginally, also in Eastern Europe.

The fate of Jews in Eastern Europe will require especially difficult decisions. Jews who want to emigrate, whether to Israel or elsewhere, must be helped to do so without aggravating the isolation of Jews who remain or hastening the demise of communities. Even vestigial communities whose future is too bleak to warrant long-term investment must have support for their communal life and links to the stronger communities in Western Europe.

Organized American Jewry must be constantly vigilant as to what happens to Soviet Jews. While rejecting violence, it will have to decide when to shout in protest and when suppressing the cry may facilitate intercession or other, more effective influences. American Jews must influence governments and international bodies to insist on Jewish rights. They must press the Soviet Union to permit emigration to the West and to Israel in accordance with its international commitments and official pronouncements and promises, and to give equal cultural rights to the many who will stay.

The international protection of human rights, finally, will pose for American Jews special tasks and dilemmas. Jewish organizations have been in the forefront of organized efforts to improve international recognition, promotion, and protection of human rights. Recently, they have shown signs of discouragement and doubt about their effort, especially when the Arabs and the Soviet Union have abused international forums by attacks against Israel and American Jewish organizations.

No one can prove, or assert with confidence, that international activities have been effective to undo or deter repression. The liberal's confidence in them may be only an article of faith. But it is a faith worth acting on, and American Jews cannot afford to leave these avenues untried and abandon them to forces hostile to human rights in general and Jewish rights in particular. Despite failures, inadequacies, abuse, "radicalization," and perversion, the UN and regional human-rights organizations provide a forum for airing accusations of violation, some means for investigating them, some pressure for redress and remedy, and some deterrence for the future. They make it possible and proper for governments of goodwill to challenge violations by others and for nongovernmental organizations and news media to press for governmental action and to obtain other nongovernmental support and cooperation. These activities must be maintained, government and group participation must be expanded. Enemies of human rights must not be allowed to weaken or frustrate them.

Today, societies, institutions, and individuals are being "radicalized" or confused by some who promise ends that are unattainable, some of them undesirable, by means that are abhorrent, cannot succeed, can tear down what has been achieved only to replace it with something worse, perhaps by chaos. If there were any doubt about the validity of human rights and democratic doctrine in principle, concern for the welfare of Israel, of Jews abroad, of Jews in the United States, would require American Jews to stand firm on the values enshrined in the American Bill of Rights, the Universal Declaration of the United Nations, and other national and international charters of liberties.

American Jewry must rededicate itself to the cause of genuine democracy, of universal human rights and welfare. In the end, Jews can be effectively protected only as particulars within a universal program of respect and progress for all. The human rights of all must be defended against violation by anyone, anywhere.

Index